Contents

Prologue		v
Acknowledgements		ix
Preface		xi
1	DRV Strategy	1
2	PAVN Tactics	18
3	Kham Duc	34
4	Ngok Tavak	59
5	Reinforcements	87
6	Mother's Day	108
7	Aftermath	163
8	Analysis	184
9	Conclusion	194
Appendix		198
Glossary		217
Sources		222
Index		243

James D. McLeroy dedicates this book
to the memory of
Special Forces Master Sergeant M. C. Windley,
SOG One-Zero, dedicated Bac Si, fearless warrior
and
Dr. Mary Lou Sherbon,
loving sister of a Vietnam warrior
and special friend of many others.

Gregory W. Sanders dedicates this book
to the memory of
Army First Lieutenant Dale Reising,
Advisory Team 92, MACV,
who gave his life for his country
in Go Cong Province, South Vietnam,
on May 29, 1970,
and
Professor Gordon Bakken,
California State University, Fullerton,
whose legacy lives on in his students.

Prologue

The only visible remains of Kham Duc Special Forces camp were the battered concrete base and jagged steel stump of the flagpole. Knee-high grass hid the half-buried foundations of its buildings, and the only traces of its once-long airstrip were scattered patches of asphalt in a broad field of weeds. Standing on the flagpole base, I stared at the low hills on the northeast and southwest ends of the airstrip, then west at the tall, jungle-covered hill looming over the valley. My gaze drifted eastward past the new town where a little village used to be, past the overgrown airstrip, past the hidden camp site, past the heavily vegetated river gulch behind it to the taller hills overlooking the valley on the other side of the river.

The last time I saw that valley, it looked like a war movie. Once I lived and nearly died there, and for me it is a valley of ghosts. They are the ghosts of the many hundreds of North Vietnamese Army (NVA) soldiers we killed there and the ghosts of almost two hundred Vietnamese civilians—women, children, and old men of the village—killed by those NVA soldiers. As I surveyed the peaceful scene in June 1998, memories of the way it looked thirty years before in May 1968 slowly drifted back in a lurid collage of sights, sounds, and sensations:

— a desperate voice in the night, shouting on the radio over the noise of firing, begging for air support for his indigenous company, about to be overrun by an NVA battalion
— flashes of firing and explosions in the darkness, where small squads on isolated hilltop outposts were being overrun and killed by NVA shock troops
— helicopters crashing and burning; planes crashing and burning
— the throbbing whine of a piston-engine attack plane, trailing smoke, straining to climb high enough for the pilot to bail out before it burned up and plunged to earth

- the shrieking howl of jet fighter-bombers streaking by so low and close that I could glimpse the pilots' helmets
- the shattering blasts of high-explosive bombs; the crackling ripple of cluster bombs; the rasping growl of automatic aircraft cannons and multi-barreled aircraft machine guns
- enemy bodies hurled through the air like rag dolls from a bomb hit on an anti-aircraft gun
- the pitiful face of a doomed North Vietnamese Army soldier, wide-eyed and ashen with terror, stumbling toward me like an obedient robot through a maelstrom of bullets and shrapnel, as his comrades were falling all around him, knowing his wretched life was measured in seconds
- the chilling sound of Special Forces commandos, determined to fight to the death against the onrushing horde of NVA soldiers, saying terse farewells to each other
- the thunderous boom and roiling mushroom cloud of the camp's exploding ammunition dump; the roar of huge black rubber fuel bladders along the airstrip erupting in red fireballs
- the greasy feel and acrid smell of my damp, salt-encrusted fatigues under a heavy flak jacket, sweat-soaked, dirt-smeared, and re-soaked in three days of heat, humidity, and tension
- flashes of sheet lightning inside a dark, towering monsoon cloud moving toward the valley, threatening to envelope it and cancel our close air support, the only thing keeping us alive

I thought then that I would never return to that haunted valley. When I finally did thirty years later, it was with a U.S. military casualty recovery team searching for the scattered remains of long-abandoned American soldiers and Marines. More U.S. missing-in-action cases resulted from the battle of Kham Duc Special Forces camp and a temporary camp site south of it called Ngok Tavak than from any other battle in seven years of major U.S. combat in the Vietnam War.

As soon as I returned to Kham Duc, I began to sense a deep, vague awareness that some important part of me had never fully left that morbid killing ground—and probably never will.

James D. McLeroy

I first saw Kham Duc in July 1970, when it was reoccupied for six weeks in a joint operation by a battalion of the Americal (23rd) Division and a South-Vietnamese battalion. The brief 1970 operation, in which I played a very minor role, was a "walk in the sun," as the grunts used to call an easy patrol, compared to the battle there two years before. I returned to Kham Duc in 2006, searching for answers to lingering questions about those who fought there in May 1968.

As we entered the Kham Duc valley, the air seemed heavy with the specter of the missing American soldiers abandoned there and at Ngok Tavak five miles to the south. Most of the men who were at Kham Duc in 1970 had no knowledge of those missing-in-action from the 1968 battle. I did. Before flying to Kham Duc from the Americal Division base camp at Chu Lai on July 12, 1970, I learned of the abandoned bodies of those poor souls. Privately, I believed the Army had betrayed not only those men, but their families as well, leaving them to grieve with a lifetime of unanswered questions about their fate.

Decades later, retired Major General (MG) A. E. Milloy, the Americal Division commander when Kham Duc was reoccupied, told me that nearly all those men who were missing-in-action from the 1968 battle didn't stand a chance. In an unusual departure from his normal gentlemanly manner, he spared no unkind words for the officers he felt were responsible for their deaths, including General William Westmoreland.

Such a harsh condemnation from General Milloy was unexpected, because I knew his reputation. He was as aggressive a senior commander as ever served in South Vietnam, but he did not tolerate recklessness, especially with the lives of those he commanded. He was an up-from-the-ranks soldier's general, who knew from his own battlefield experiences in World War II and Korea the kind of missions that unnecessarily waste the lives of American soldiers. His comments gave me a new perspective on the Kham Duc missing-in-action cases. Reconciling what happened there in May 1968 was ultimately a question of accountability.

As we drove through the north end of the valley onto the remains of the old airstrip, my mind was filled with thoughts of those abandoned men. I thought, too, of the many hundreds of enemy soldiers, many of them boys fresh from North Vietnam, who were wasted in a battle over an innocuous little camp. I wept for all of them, friend and foe alike. I resolved then and there to learn how and why such a large, yet little-known battle of the Vietnam War occurred, and who was responsible for its outcome. I owed it to them all, I thought.

Gregory W. Sanders

Acknowledgements

The co-authors are most grateful to Dr. Lewis Sorley, eminent military historian, for recommending this book to the Association of the United States Army (AUSA); and to Joseph Craig, AUSA book editor, for recommending it to Casemate.

James McLeroy is especially grateful to Sharon Louise Cox for her expert assistance in interviewing several Kham Duc battle veterans and editing numerous drafts of the manuscript over a mutually turbulent twenty-year period. Also appreciated for their exceptionally valuable contributions are (in alphabetical order): Lew Alton, Bob Henderson, Jack Kull, Bill Laurie, Nancy McKarney, Merle Pribbenow, Don Richardson, Bill and Ann Schneider, George Sever, Hugh Shelton, and Steve Sherman.

Additionally appreciated for valuable contributions are (in alphabetical order): Bill Bell, David Blomgren, Barry Booth, Pat Brady, Tim Brown, Don Buchwald, John Burtt, David Carr, Adam Carter, Kathleen Carter, Myra Christopher, Michael Crawford, Jack Deleshaw, Bob Destatte, Dovan Do, Dianne Etheredge, Elliott Etheredge, Rhett Flater, Max Friedman, Bert Fuller, Jim Garlitz, Dwight Gradin, Phil Hall, Les Hines, Johnny Jacks, Marty Keef, Ruth Keef, Ky Ba Phan, Lan Thanh Le, Lee Lanning, Tim Lee, Wayne Long, George Marlin, Robert Mascharka, Larry Nguyen, Harley Patrick, Chris Pelkey, Charles Pfeifer, Homer Pickens, John Plaster, Joe Rimar, Mike Rollinson, William Rosson, Gordon Rottman, Paul Schmehl, Carl Schneider, Bill Schrope, Jack Schulimson, Mike Shepherd, Barry Spink, John Stewart, Uynh Dang, Greg Voral, Chuck Whittle, John Wilson, Mac Woodard, Jim Zumwalt, the Kham Duc and Ngok Tavak battle veterans who shared their experiences, the non-participants who shared their special knowledge, and the research staffs of National Archives II in College Park, MD and the LBJ Library in Austin, TX.

Gregory Sanders would like to especially acknowledge and thank the following people for their contributions to the research, writing, and documentation of this book: Teri Sanders, dear wife and best friend, whose encouragement and support over the years made the journey that led to the completion of the book a joy; our children Sarah, Andrew, and Michael; and my father-in-law and mother-in-law, Don and Edith Harrington, whose prodding was essential to the success of the effort.

A special thanks is also extended to close friend Gregory Winterbottom, a Vietnam-era veteran whose triumph over disabilities serves as a model of grit and determination; to Art Hansen for his support and perspectives; and to Professors Ron Rietveld and the late Carmen Hardy, California State University Fullerton, who ignited my passion for history.

Appreciation is also extended to: Bill Deeter, MIA Researcher, Embassy of the United States of America, Hanoi, Vietnam, for his assistance in navigating through the MIA search and recovery process; Pat Brady, Army MG (Ret.) and Medal of Honor recipient, for looking after me when I became ill at a Vietnam War symposium and responding to numerous email inquiries about the Ngok Tavak battle; the late Albert E. Milloy, Army MG (Ret.), who provided unique perspectives on the Vietnam War and the Kham Duc battle; my comrades at American Legion Post 432, Cambria, California, especially (in alphabetical order) Glenn Donaldson, John Ehlers, Terry Farrell, Brian Griffen, Bill Knoop, Mel McColloch, and Ron Waltman for constantly reminding me of their desire to see the book published before they expire; Nancy McKarney for creating the illustrations so important to an understanding of the battle; and to the scores of Vietnam citizens who went out of their way to assist me in two trips to the battlegrounds that led to a fuller understanding of the events recounted in this book.

Preface

"… their [U.S.] Dien Bien Phu is still to come, and it will come …"

PAVN SENIOR GENERAL VO NGUYEN GIAP[1]

Of all the large battles in the U.S. Phase (1965–72) of the Second Indochina War (1957–75) in the former Republic of Viet Nam, the least known and most misunderstood is the battle of Kham Duc-Ngok Tavak from May 10–12, 1968. Kham Duc, a U.S. Army Special Forces (SF) camp near the Laotian border of Quang Tin Province in I Corps, and Ngok Tavak, a temporary patrol base five miles south of it, were attacked by two full regiments (3,000–4,000 troops) of the North Vietnamese Army's (NVA) 2nd Division. Like the still-misunderstood war itself, it is a prime example of the difference between superficial appearance and factual reality.

This is the only history of the dual battle published by authors with in-depth knowledge of it and personal combat experience in it. One lived at Kham Duc and led an elite group of U.S. and indigenous Special Forces troops in the battle. The other witnessed a detailed analysis of the battle at the Americal Division headquarters prior to a six-week, two-battalion, joint operation at and around Kham Duc in 1970. Both are former Army officers with masters degrees in history.

We independently researched this battle for more than ten years in all the primary and secondary sources, including the few Vietnamese sources. We independently revisited Kham Duc, interviewed many direct and indirect battle veterans, and read the interview transcripts and statements of other battle participants, including former NVA officers.

Our unique combination of personal experience in the battle and in-depth research into all aspects of it is the justification for our correction of the factual omissions and our contradiction of the nonfactual statements and/or factual misinterpretations in all the other published accounts of it.[2] The facts that we personally experienced and/or learned from many other primary sources are directly contrary to all the uninformed and misinformed orthodox versions of the battle.

Kham Duc did not "fall" and was not "overrun." It was also not "an American defeat,"[3] "an embarrassing defeat,"[4] "a major defeat for the U.S. military,"[5] "one of the most serious [U.S.] defeats,"[6] "a [U.S.] battle debacle,"[7] "an unequivocal [U.S.] debacle,"[8] a [U.S.] "disaster,"[9] "a decisive North Vietnamese and Viet Cong victory,"[10] "a total North Vietnamese victory,"[11] "a Khe Sanh in reverse,"[12] "the high point for Hanoi" in 1968,[13] "one of the great [US] disasters of the war,"[14] or evidence of a combat "stalemate" between the U.S. and NVA/VC (Viet Cong) forces.[15]

All those negative evaluations of the battle are based on the erroneous assumption that it was an unsuccessful attempt to defend the place.[16] In fact, it was a successful effort to inflict mass attrition on a major NVA force with minimum U.S. and allied losses by voluntarily abandoning an anachronistic little trip-wire border camp serving as passive bait for the attack.

We realize that the use of the term "bait" to describe Kham Duc's role in the battle is controversial and requires clarification. In Westmoreland's book he called Khe Sanh a place to "lure" NVA troops to their death.[17] As both a noun and a verb "bait" is just a synonym for "lure," but its neutral definition is very different from its emotional connotation. For most Americans the use of U.S. troops as live bait to attract a larger enemy force is outrageous.

As a verb, "to bait" implies a deliberate action by an actor with a motive for the action. That is NOT the meaning of the word as applied to U.S. actions at Kham Duc. In 1968, the use of U.S. troops as bait in the *active* sense of baiting a trap with them was not an *acknowledged* tactic;[18] the term "bait" was not used in any *formal* military planning;[19] and no military unit or installation was ever *officially* designated as bait.[20] But as a noun, bait is as bait does.[21] Anything can serve as *passive* bait, even if that was neither its original nor its primary function.[22]

In Vietnam there were many NVA and VC attacks on isolated SF camps. Westmoreland did NOT *actively* plan to use those camps as bait for such attacks, but in his "strategy-of-tactics" such attacks were not entirely unwelcome, because they concentrated the normally elusive VC and NVA troops for mass attrition by U.S. firepower.[23] The role of SF border camps as *passive* bait for Westmoreland's defensive attrition tactics was merely the result of their prior location in conspicuously vulnerable places for different reasons.

Kham Duc, like Khe Sanh, was a dramatic example of Westmoreland's "lure and destroy" defensive attrition tactics that complemented his "search and destroy" offensive attrition tactics. It was another major (although strategically meaningless) tactical victory for his operational strategy of mass enemy attrition and a major tactical defeat for the two NVA regiments because of a universal military fact: massed airborne firepower attacking in ideal conditions is always tactically superior to massed infantry repeatedly exposed to such attacks with inadequate anti-aircraft defenses.

A hastily improvised air counterattack involving some 350 sorties of almost 150 combat aircraft in three days of ideal weather for visual flight totally ravaged the NVA attackers. The more they massed to attack in clear daylight, the more they were annihilated by concentrated air firepower. The air counterattack continued for two days after the ground attack. During those five days, B-52 strategic bombers dropped more than 15,000 bombs around Kham Duc.

The NVA casualties at Kham Duc and Ngok Tavak are not recorded or are still a state secret of the Socialist Republic of Viet Nam, but a reasonable estimate of them can be made. In 1968, two full-strength NVA infantry regiments had 5,000 troops: 3,600 combat troops and 1,400 combat support and logistics troops.[24] Troop losses of 50 percent or more were common in all the NVA and VC human-wave infantry attacks.[25]

Even if only half of the NVA troops at or near Kham Duc and Ngok Tavak were killed or mortally wounded from three days of air attacks and ground fire, plus two days of unrestricted carpet bombing, the two NVA regiments probably lost between 1,500 and 2,000 troops. Total U.S. Army, Air Force, and Marine fatalities at, near, or as a direct result of Kham Duc and Ngok Tavak were forty-six men.[26]

Many of the 112 wounded U.S. soldiers and Marines did not require hospitalization, and some of those who did soon recovered and returned to their units. Almost all seriously wounded U.S. troops were quickly evacuated to modern hospitals and almost all of them survived. Most seriously wounded NVA troops in that and all their other battles against U.S. combined-arms forces did not survive.[27]

The battle began on the night of May 9/10, 1968, with a mortar and rocket barrage on the Kham Duc SF camp. Simultaneously, the SF and Marine temporary patrol base at Ngok Tavak was attacked by an NVA battalion that penetrated it, but did not overrun it. That afternoon, the surviving defenders of Ngok Tavak abandoned it, escaped, and were rescued by Marine helicopters. The bombardment of the Kham Duc SF camp continued sporadically on May 10 and 11, while a reinforced U.S. Army infantry battalion arrived and deployed around its airstrip.

In the early morning darkness of May 12, NVA troops overran four of the camp's hilltop outposts. Later that morning, battalion-size units of the two NVA regiments launched two mass attacks against U.S. troop positions around the airstrip. Both attacks were shattered by an almost unprecedented concentration of air firepower. A third battalion-size attack was destroyed just as it was about to begin. That afternoon, the last mass ground attack was a multi-company assault on the SF camp's most vulnerable perimeter. As the last U.S. reinforcements were being evacuated by air, the suicidal attack was annihilated by a napalm strike dangerously close to the SF trench.

Twelve aircraft were shot down during the three-day battle, including a C-130 transport plane carrying 183 refugees from the nearby village. It exploded and burned, killing all aboard. More than 1,000 people—military and civilian, U.S. and Vietnamese—were evacuated by air, but thirty-seven Americans, living and dead, were left behind at Kham Duc and Ngok Tavak. Only four survived. Three of them were rescued a few days later, but the fourth endured five hellish years as a prisoner of his sadistic VC and NVA captors.

Despite the appalling numbers of NVA casualties, their attack on Kham Duc was both a tactical failure and a strategic failure for seven reasons: 1) it failed to penetrate the camp or airstrip while U.S. troops were there; 2) it failed to lure any large U.S. military unit from a populated area; 3) it failed to attract major media attention; 4) it failed to kill or capture enough U.S. or allied troops for a propaganda film; 5) it failed to capture any source of food or civilian labor; 6) it failed to enable the NVA to occupy the site, as long as U.S. combat forces were active in I Corps; and 7) it failed to enable the NVA to use the road south of the camp any more or any differently than they did before the battle, as long as U.S. combat forces were active in I Corps.[28]

The Kham Duc SF camp had only two functions: basic training for indigenous militia recruits and occasional launches of top-secret SOG (Studies and Observations Group) reconnaissance-commando teams into Laos. After the camp was abandoned, both functions were replaced elsewhere with no major tactical loss.[29] In 1970, a reinforced U.S. Army battalion and an Army of the Republic of Viet Nam (ARVN) battalion reoccupied the Kham Duc valley and patrolled around it for six weeks, partly to prove that they could always do so at will.[30]

On May 12, 1968, Kham Duc was potentially as strategically important for the North Vietnamese Army forces as Dien Bien Phu was for the Viet Minh forces on May 7, 1954. On that date the Communist-led Viet Minh forces captured a large French base near the Laotian border of North Vietnam. With massive technical, logistics, and artillery support from his Communist Chinese allies, General Vo Nguyen Giap, the Viet Minh commander, timed the final assault on the French defensive positions for the day before the start of the Geneva Conference to negotiate the end of the First Indochina War (1946–54).[31]

The capture of Dien Bien Phu did not tactically defeat all the French forces in Indochina, but it strategically defeated the French government in France. By critically demoralizing the war-weary French public, the filmed fall of Dien Bien Phu caused the Socialist French government to immediately withdraw its forces from Tonkin (northern Vietnam) and eventually from the rest of Indochina: Annam (central Vietnam), Cochin China (southern Vietnam), Cambodia, and Laos.

We do NOT claim that the North Vietnamese Politburo attempted to make Kham Duc a U.S. Dien Bien Phu, because we found no documentary or testamentary evidence of that intent. The official history of the People's Army of Vietnam (PAVN) 2nd Division strongly suggests it, however. Among its many other nonfactual distortions and fantasies, its fictional account of Kham Duc's defenses is clearly based on the French defenses at Dien Bien Phu, and its fictional account of the NVA attack on Kham Duc is a virtual copy of the Viet Minh attack on Dien Bien Phu.[32]

We also do NOT compare Kham Duc to Dien Bien Phu or Khe Sanh in terms of its size or strategic effect. We only argue that the NVA capture of Kham Duc on May 12, 1968, could have had a strategic impact on President Lyndon Johnson in that critical month and year of the war. His awareness of its strategic potential is evidenced by the fact that GEN Westmoreland personally sent a warning telex about the ongoing battle to GEN Wheeler, Chairman of the Joint Chiefs of Staff, on May 12, 1968. Wheeler sent it immediately to the National Security Council, and the National Security Advisor, Dr. Walt Rostow, sent it immediately to Johnson at his Texas ranch. Years later, Johnson considered it important enough to include in his memoirs.[33]

If more than 1,000 U.S. and allied troops had been killed or captured at Kham Duc, a humiliating propaganda film of their capture and death would have been made by the NVA film crew sent from North Vietnam for that purpose.[34] The film would have been given to all the television news journalists among the 1,300 reporters from thirty-nine nations then in Paris to cover the start of negotiations for ending the U.S. role in the war. It would have been repeatedly and sensationally broadcast on both U.S. and international television channels.

The emotional impact of such a film on most Americans likely would have been similar in strength, but opposite in effect, to that of the filmed capture of Dien Bien Phu on most of the French population. It could also have had a catalytic effect on LBJ's hyper-macho personality and militant anti-Communist ideology at the bitter end of his long political career.[35]

We realize that comprehensive knowledge of any large and complex battle is impossible, and that many veterans of this battle know certain personal facts about it that we cannot know. For the same reason, most battle veterans do not fully understand everything that did and did not happen there before, during, and after it. Some insist on believing things about it or their role in it that are nonfactual. Others refuse to believe things about it or their role in it that are factual.[36]

We also acknowledge that perfect objectivity in our narrative and analysis of this battle is impossible, despite our firm commitment to objectivity as an ideal. Some degree of unintentional subjectivity is inevitable in the narrative and analysis of any event in which the author was an active participant. Nevertheless, pending future revisions of this book with new data or new interpretations of our data, we believe this is the most factually accurate narrative and most comprehensive analysis of the dual battle of Kham Duc–Ngok Tavak currently possible.

N.B.—Most numbers referring to dimensions and time and most numbers ending in zero should be read as if preceded by "approximately, roughly, about, around, some, estimated," *etc.* to avoid excessive repetition of such numerical qualifiers.

Notes

1   Giap's answer to a question by an admiring foreign journalist on whether the American war would end with the defeat of U.S. forces in another large, decisive battle like Dien Bien Phu. Fallaci, Oriana. *Interview With History* (Boaston, MA: Houghton Mifflin, 1976), p. 85.

2   All the published accounts of the Kham Duc battle contain material omissions, factual errors, and/or factual misinterpretations. In 1971, an eight-page article on Ngok Tavak was published by an Australian officer (White) commanding the SF and Marine troops there. In 1976, an 87-page monograph on Kham Duc was published by a U.S. Air Force officer (Gropman). A 1983 book on tactical airlift in Vietnam (Bowers) has five pages on Kham Duc. A 1984 book on Australian forces in Vietnam (McNeill) has eight pages on Ngok Tavak. Another 1984 book on the U.S. Air Force in SE Asia (Berger) has two pages on Kham Duc. A 1985 book on the U.S. Army Special Forces in Vietnam (Stanton) has four pages on Kham Duc. A 1989 book on tactical air support in Vietnam (Mrozek) has two pages on Kham Duc. A 1990 book on the Vietnam War (Morrison) has five pages on Kham Duc. A 1993 book on the Vietnam War in 1968 (Spector) has ten pages on Kham Duc. A 1994 book on Air Commandos (Chinnery) has five pages on Kham Duc. A 1995 historical atlas of the Vietnam War (Summers) has a one-page summary of Kham Duc and a good map of it. A 1997 book on Marines in Vietnam (Shulimson) has three pages on Kham Duc and Ngok Tavak. A 1999 book on the Ho Chi Minh Trail (Prados) has five pages on Kham Duc. A 2000 book on U.S. air power in the Vietnam War (Nalty) has eight pages on Kham Duc. A 2000 encyclopedia of the Vietnam War (Tucker) has one page on Kham Duc. A 2008 book on Ngok Tavak (Davies) is a partly fictionalized account. A 2011 book on SOG (Gillespie)

has two pages on Kham Duc. A 2011 autobiography (Warner) has five pages on Kham Duc. A 2017 book (Kolb) has seven pages on Kham Duc. There are also several superficial magazine articles and a grossly nonfactual Wikipedia article on it.

3   Spector, Ronald. *After Tet* (New York: The Free Press, NY, 1993), p. 175.

4   Davies, Bruce. *Ngok Tavak* (Crows Nest, NSW, Australia: Allen & Unwin, 2008), p. 118.

5   en.wikipedia.org/wiki/Battle_of_Kham_Duc, accessed on May 12, 2015.

6   Gillespie, Robert. *Black Ops, Vietnam* (Annapolis, MD: Naval Institute Press, 2011), p. 149.

7   Davies, *op. cit.*, p. xvii.

8   Spector, *op. cit.*, p. 176.

9   Stanton, Shelby. *Green Berets At War* (Novato, CA: Presidio Press, 1985), p. 161.

10 Wikipedia article, *op. cit.*

11 Stanton, *op. cit.*, p. 165. Chinnery, Philip. *Air Commandos* (NY: St Martin, 1994), p. 211.

12 Spector, *op. cit.*, pp. 166, 175.

13 Prados, John. *The Blood Road* (NY: John Wiley, 1999), p. 281.

14 Nolan, Keith. *House To House* (St Paul, MN: Zenith Press, 2006), p. 22.

15 Spector, *op. cit.*, p. x. From mid-1965 to mid-1972, the war was a political stalemate, but it was never a combat stalemate, because the U.S. and NVA/VC forces were never tactically equal. That misperception is due to the ambiguous use of the word "stalemate." During those critical seven years, President Johnson prohibited U.S. ground forces from attacking NVA forces in Laos, Cambodia, and North Vietnam and prohibited the U.S. air forces from conducting a truly strategic air campaign in North Vietnam. In 1968, however, most of the VC combat forces were killed or defected, and in 1972, most of the NVA forces in South Vietnam were killed by South Vietnamese forces supported by U.S. airpower. The NVA survivors retreated to the sparsely inhabited western border regions of the country, and for the next two years the internal war was effectively won. The NVA were not able to resume their invasion of South Vietnam until 1975, two years after all U.S. forces were withdrawn and one year after Congress prohibited essential logistics and combat air support for the South Vietnamese forces. The modern, conventional, Soviet-equipped North Vietnamese Army then invaded South Vietnam again and conquered it.

16 Mrozek, Donald. *Air Power and the Ground War In Vietnam* (McLean, VA: Pergamon-Brassey's, 1989), p. 85: "At Kham Duc ... the position was ... not held."

17 Westmoreland, William. *A Soldier Reports* (Garden City, NY: Doubleday, 1976), p. 348.

18 "... the [base] was ... bait for the enemy—a lure to attract [them] to a seemingly easy target. Then all available combat power was brought to bear ...." *1969 MACV Command History*, Annex G: "The Defense of Fire Support Base Crook."

19 In answer to a question by President Johnson, Secretary of State Dean Rusk stated: "... in that sense Khe Sanh is bait." Barrett, David. *Uncertain Warriors* (Lawrence, KS: University of Kansas Press, 1993), p. 599.

20 In the 1967 battle of Ap Gu near the Cambodian border of III Corps a battalion CO, LTC (later General) Alexander Haig, said of his battalion's role: "We were put in as bait …." Appy, Christian (ed.). *Patriots* (NY: Viking Penguin, 2003), p. 399.

21 "… we were … used as bait to see what was there." Brennan, Matthew. *Brennan's War* (Novato, CA: Presidio Press, 1985), p. 51. His chapter 4 is titled "BAIT."

22 In July 1966 two Troops of the 1st Squadron, 4th Cavalry were used as bait for an ambush by a Viet Cong main force regiment. Stanton, Shelby. *The Rise & [sic] Fall of an American Army* (Novato, CA: Presidio Press, 1985), pp. 105–06.

23 An SF veteran of the 1970 battle of Dak Pek SF camp believed the SF camps were "… bait to… concentrate [the enemy]… so we could hit him with overwhelming firepower." Wade, Leigh. *Assault On Dak Pek* (NY: Ivy Books, 1998), p. 102.

24 Rottman, Gordon. *North Vietnamese Army Soldier, 1958–75* (Oxord, UK: Osprey Publishing, 2009), p. 11.

25 *Ibid.*, p. 54.

26 See Chapter VII, Aftermath, note 19 for their names.

27 A former CG of the 2nd NVA Division stated that they had no organic hospital and few medically qualified doctors. PAVN LTG Nguyen Huy Chuong in *Su Doan 2, Tap 1* [Second Division, Volume 1] (Da Nang, Socialist Republic of Viet Nam: Dang Uy va Chu Huy Su Doan 2 [2nd Division Party Committee and Division Headquarters], Da Nang Publishing House, 1989), p. 89; translated by Merle Pribbenow. Wounded troops had to be carried through jungle-covered mountains to crowded, unsanitary field hospitals, many of them underground, where medical equipment, supplies, and doctors were always scarce and often inadequate. In or on the way to such hospitals, most severely wounded men died from hypovolemic shock, septic shock, or disease. Dr. Le Cao Dai in Appy, Christian. *Patriots* (NY: Viking, 2003), pp. 13–140. Dr Le also stated: "The most severely wounded people died at the front before they could be evacuated." Zumwalt, James. *Bare Feet, Iron Will* (Jacksonville, FL: Fortis Publishing, 2020), p. 40. PAVN LTG Nguyen Xuan Hoang stated: "… our logistics forces, who were farther from the Americans, took greater losses than the combat units [due to B-52 carpet bombing]." Curry, Cecil. *Victory At Any Cost* (Washington, D.C., Brassey's 1997), p. 257.

28 In June 1998 McLeroy saw a large billboard at the northwest entrance of Kham Duc town with a Soviet-style painting proclaiming it the site of a great victory of the heroic People's Army. On May 12, 2013 Sanders saw a large, concrete monument on a hillside near the northwest entrance to the town marking the 45th anniversary of the glorious PAVN victory at Kham Duc.

29 After the evacuation of Kham Duc, SOG established a new launch site in I Corps, first at Mai Loc then at Quang Tri. It also increased the use of its launch sites at the Dak Pek SF camp in northern II Corps and the Nakhon Phanom (NKP) air base in Thailand. At those sites the weather for visual flight was more reliable than at Kham Duc. From NKP, Air Force HH-53E helicopters could reach any place in SOG's authorized operating area in Laos. The basic training program for CIDG recruits in I Corps was continued at Ha Thanh SF camp in Quang Ngai Province.

30 "After Action Report Elk Canyon I," Headquarters, 2nd Battalion, 1st Infantry, 196th Brigade (undated); attached maps and charts dated September 19, 1970.

31 Chen, King C. *Vietnam and China, 1938–1954* Princeton, NJ: Princeton University Press, 1968), p. 305.

32 It claims that Kham Duc had ten fortified "strongpoints" and the NVA attack "peeled away" the five outer ones first, then destroyed the five inner ones with artillery fire. In fact, Kham Duc had no strongpoints, and the NVA had no artillery there. It claims the 2nd NVA Division defeated the 196th Light Infantry Brigade at Kham Duc. In fact, two-thirds of the 196th LIB was not there, and one-third of the 2nd NVA Division was not there. It claims the survivors of Kham Duc fled on foot toward Thuong Duc. In fact, only four U.S. soldiers fled on foot, and three of them were later rescued. All the other troops and civilians were evacuated by aircraft, and none of them went to Thuong Duc. *Su Doan 2, op. cit.*, pp. 110–16.

33 Telex message from Westmoreland to ADM Sharp in Hawaii, GEN Wheeler in Washington, and LTG Goodpaster in Paris; May 12, 1968. Westmoreland Papers, MAC 6210 and 6222, U.S. Army Center for Military History, Fort Lesley J. McNair, Washington, D.C. Telex message from Bromley Smith, NSC, to Walt Rostow, NSC, forwarded to LBJ ranch, May 12, 1968: "Reports from Saigon re Estimate of Enemy Intentions in Kham Duc Area". LBJ Library, Austin, TX; National Security Files (NSF); Vietnam Country File, box 67, folder 2A (5), I Corps and DMZ, 5/68–11/68, documents 110 and 111. Johnson, Lyndon. *The Vantage Point* (NY: Holt, Rinehart, and Winston, 1971), p. 508.

34 The leader of the PAVN film team at Kham Duc was Nguyen Van Huu, and his cameramen were Le Viet The and Le Kim Nguyen. Message from CDR JTF-FA Honolulu, HI, J2 to SECDEF Washington, D.C., SUBJ/Research and Investigation Team (RIT) Report of Interview of Mr Nguyen Van Huu, 30 June, 1995.

35 Hershman, Jablow. *Power Beyond Reason* (Fort Lee, NJ: Barricade Books, 2002), pp. 12–20.

36 Some believe they were on the last plane out of Kham Duc. In fact, the last C-123 had only three passengers, and the last C-130 carried only Vietnamese civilians and SOG troops. Some believe they saw an NVA flag on one of the hilltops. In fact, there were no flags there. Some believe they saw a U.S. soldier hanging naked upside down in a tree on a hilltop outpost. In fact, none of the aircraft crews flying over and around the hilltops saw anyone in a tree. Some claim to have performed impossible feats of valor (assuming they were even there). One man thinks he saw Westmoreland there on May 12. In fact, no U.S. general was there on May 12, although two Army major generals were briefly there on May 10.

DRV Strategy

"Orthodox armies are the ... principal power ..."

At different times and places, the Second Indochina War (1957–75) in South Vietnam had some of the characteristics of a revolution, an insurgency, a guerrilla war, and a civil war. Primarily, however, it was always an incremental invasion of South Vietnam by the North Vietnamese Army, initially supported by their indigenous Viet Cong subordinates.

At first, the NVA invasion was covert and indirect, but in 1968 it became increasingly overt and direct.[2] Both the NVA and the VC were always controlled by the Political Bureau (Politburo) of the ruling Lao Dong [Workers] Party in Hanoi, the capital of the totalitarian police state euphemistically named the Democratic Republic of Viet Nam (DRV).

By 1967, Ho Chi Minh, the President of the DRV, was an aged and ailing figurehead, whose only power was the prestige of his name as the founding father of the nation in 1945. The *de facto* leader and chief strategist of the DRV was Le Duan, First Secretary of the ruling Lao Dong Party, from 1960 until his death in 1986. Le Duan was not a charismatic dictator. He was a Machiavellian manipulator, who ruled collectively through the DRV's multilayered committee system.

The most important one during the long war was the five-man Subcommittee for Military Affairs (SMA) of the Politburo's Central Military Party Commission. The DRV's grand strategy in its eighteen-year quest to conquer the Republic of Viet Nam and establish NVA hegemony in Cambodia and Laos was always controlled by the five key men of that subcommittee, all of whom were indirectly controlled by the militant zeal and dominant persuasiveness of Le Duan.[3]

Chinese influence in the First Indochina War (1946–54) caused the Politburo to initially adopt Mao Tse-tung's (aka Mao Zedong) rural-based, three-stage, protracted attrition model of Communist revolutionary warfare in the Second Indochina War.[4] The long-term goal of the Maoist model, and thus the DRV model, was the third stage: a decisive military victory by large, conventional Communist forces over large, conventional anti-Communist forces.[5]

The first stage of the DRV model from 1957 to 1962 was terrorism and guerrilla warfare by local VC squads (six to twelve troops) and platoons (eighteen to thirty troops). The second stage from 1962 to 1967 was short-term attacks on vulnerable targets by semi-conventional, mobile companies (fifty to 100 VC/NVA troops) and battalions (150–300 VC/NVA troops). From 1969 to 1972, those tactics continued with mostly NVA troops. The third stage from 1972 to 1975 was conventional, positional warfare by regular NVA regiments (1,000–3,000 troops) and divisions (6,000–10,000 troops).

When the Geneva Conference of 1954 officially recognized North and South Vietnam, some 90,000 Communist South Vietnamese moved north to the DRV. About 80,000 of those "regroupees" were Viet Minh veterans of the First Indochina War. Between 5,000 and 10,000 others were ordered to bury their weapons, live quietly in South Vietnam, and await future orders.[6]

Many South Vietnamese Communists who moved to the DRV became regular soldiers in two NVA divisions composed exclusively of them. Some 4,500 others were trained as covert military and political cadre. Their mission was to organize Communist Viet Minh veterans in South Vietnam in guerrilla squads, platoons, and companies.

Other regroupees were trained as armed agitation-propaganda (agitprop) teams. The agitprop mission was to recruit disaffected South Vietnamese civilians to serve as local auxiliaries of the main VC guerrilla forces. Agitprop teams indoctrinated them in revolutionary ideology and organized them in covert intelligence and logistics networks.

In 1957, the Central Office for South Vietnam (COSVN), an extension of the Hanoi Politburo, ordered the Communist Viet Minh veterans in South Vietnam to initiate a series of rural terror campaigns against local governments and organize shadow Communist governments. To enforce Communist control in the villages they threatened, intimidated, kidnapped, tortured, and assassinated an estimated 36,000 village leaders, influential civilians, and their families.[7]

In May 1959 the NVA's Transportation Group 559 began work on the Truong Son Strategic Supply Route, later known as the Ho Chi Minh Trail, through the mountains and jungles of eastern Laos. With the protection of more than 12,000 NVA troops in Laos, the construction workers completed the first stage of the route in October 1959. By the end of 1960, 3,500 regroupee cadres had used it to infiltrate back into South Vietnam.[8]

In May 1961, 500 senior and mid-level NVA regroupee officers left for South Vietnam on the Ho Chi Minh Trail network. The next month, they were followed by 400 junior NVA regroupee officers and senior NCOs. By October 1961, covert NVA cadres had recruited and organized two VC battalions. After all the regroupee cadres were sent back to South Vietnam, regular NVA troop units began to infiltrate it in increasingly large increments.

In the Spring of 1963, the first regular NVA battalion consisting of 600 cadres and soldiers crossed the Demilitarized Zone (DMZ) and entered the Republic of Viet Nam. Their mission was to augment the strength of VC platoons and companies, train them, and develop them into semi-conventional VC/NVA battalions and regiments. Company-size VC forces were organized at the district level, battalion-size VC/NVA forces were organized at the province level, and regiment-size VC/NVA forces were organized at the regional level.

In November 1963, the President of the Republic of Viet Nam (RVN), Ngo Dinh Diem, was assassinated in a military coup, resulting in a critically weakened central government. The DRV Politburo decided to escalate the war from the mobile second stage of the Maoist strategy to the positional third stage. In the Spring of 1964, the entire 325th NVA Division moved into the RVN. By the end of 1964, 30,000 new

VC troops had been recruited, trained, and organized in five VC/NVA regiments. In January 1965, regular NVA units and main-force VC units fought five regiment-level battles and two battalion-level battles against the Army of the Republic of Viet Nam (ARVN) forces.

In the Spring of 1965, Hanoi sent seven more NVA regiments to South Vietnam plus sapper, artillery, and other specialty battalions. In September 1965, the 9th VC Division was formed. Later that year, two more VC regiments were organized.[9] The war then began to change from a VC insurgency covertly controlled and supported by the NVA to an increasingly overt NVA invasion supported by their VC subordinates.

In November 1965, three regular NVA regiments spearheaded a conventional invasion of the Central Highlands of South Vietnam. Their tactical objective was to cut South Vietnam in half there, deploy the rest of the NVA into the RVN, and attack Saigon simultaneously from the north and west. Their strategic objective was to conquer the RVN as quickly as possible before the expected arrival of large U.S. conventional forces.[10]

In the Ia Drang Valley battle in November 1965, the NVA learned that their attempted transition to third-stage, positional warfare was too late. Two of the three NVA regiments leading the invasion were mauled by a U.S. reinforced airmobile battalion with heavy artillery and air support.[11] For the next two years, the NVA/VC forces were forced to revert to second-stage, mobile warfare, while the U.S. conventional escalation of the war rapidly increased.

By April 1967, the five men in the DRV Politburo's SMA faced two critical situations. First, the mobile, semi-conventional, main VC forces that had been fighting the U.S. troops since late 1965 were losing the war of attrition. With their air mobility and greatly superior firepower, Westmoreland's big-unit, combined-arms "search and destroy" campaigns, although clumsy and often inefficient, were relentlessly pursuing the VC combat forces into their formerly secure base areas in South Vietnam and steadily depleting them. The survivors were being exhausted by having to constantly evade the airmobile U.S. forces on foot.[12]

By the end of the first half of 1967, VC and NVA combat, medical, and desertion losses exceeded 15,000 men per month, and the VC desertion rate was doubling every six months. NVA infiltration averaged 7,000 men a month, and VC recruitment averaged 3,500 men a month. More

VC/NVA forces were being lost by attrition than were being gained by NVA infiltrators and VC recruits.[13] The depleted VC ranks were being filled by inexperienced, minimally trained, and increasingly younger NVA troops. As their age and training decreased, their combat effectiveness also decreased.

The second critical situation for the SMA was that the U.S. bombing campaign in North Vietnam, although far more tactical than strategic and interrupted eight times by the U.S. President, was severely degrading the economic infrastructure of the DRV, much of which was too large to be moved or concealed, and was threatening to destroy what was left of it. The DRV had been converted to an importing economy and was reduced to little more than a conduit for Soviet and Chinese war supplies. Farm workers had to be used to repair the constant bomb damage, which led to food shortages, food rationing, and malnutrition.[14]

The Politburo knew that an unrestricted, sustained, truly strategic escalation of the U.S. air campaign in North Vietnam would be disastrous both for the DRV's economic infrastructure and for their ability to support their VC/NVA forces in South Vietnam. They also knew that a major U.S. land invasion of eastern Laos to permanently interdict the Ho Chi Minh Trail network and destroy their sanctuary bases in Laos and Cambodia would be equally catastrophic for their forces in South Vietnam.[15] Despite their fanatical determination to win, they feared that unless they could prevent those two worst-case possibilities, they could lose the war in both the south and the north.

Under such conditions, Le Duan abandoned Mao's protracted war strategy. In mid-1967, in a radical move to regain the strategic initiative he replaced Mao's attrition model with Lenin's *coup de main* model.[16] It required the rapid seizure of a few strategic targets in the RVN capital, Saigon, together with a simultaneous, nationwide, civilian insurrection of both rural "peasants" and urban "proletarians."

He believed that by coordinating all the VC forces with a few large NVA units in a sudden General Offensive he could incite a nationwide General Insurrection. According to his Leninist ideology, the "revolutionary masses" of South Vietnam would then spontaneously join the victorious VC and NVA forces in a popular uprising to overthrow the U.S. "neo-colonialist oppressors" and their "puppet" South Vietnamese regime.

Le Duan called it the August 1945 Strategy, assuming it would be as successful as Ho Chi Minh's virtually unopposed seizure of power in August 1945.[17] If he had compared the military context of Ho Chi Minh's 1945 success with that of his similar strategy in 1967, he would have seen that no significant points of comparison existed. Giap and his Politburo supporters, including Ho Chi Minh, recognized the fatal fallacy in Le Duan's new strategy and opposed it as militarily unrealistic and potentially disastrous.[18]

Giap agreed that they needed a decisive victory in a large battle, but he disagreed with Le Duan's assumption that dispersed VC forces could defeat the superior firepower of the U.S. and ARVN forces in simultaneous, nationwide assaults against heavily defended urban targets. Despite the increasing VC losses, he wanted to prolong second-stage mobile warfare by attacking only vulnerable U.S. and ARVN units and avoiding large battles that risked more major losses in the main VC combat forces. He urged delaying the transition to third-stage positional warfare, until U.S. political will to continue the war was clearly exhausted.[19]

Ignoring Giap's advice, Le Duan marginalized him in the Politburo and gave command of the 1968 General Offensive/General Insurrection campaign to Giap's ambitious subordinate, GEN Van Tien Dung. Giap then temporarily exiled himself in Hungary for "health reasons." Ho Chi Minh, whom Le Duan also marginalized in the Politburo for his support of Giap's opposition to Le Duan's strategy, temporarily exiled himself in China for much-needed medical treatment.[20]

The culmination of Le Duan's 1967 strategy was intended to be a decisive victory over large U.S. forces in a major, set-piece battle comparable to the 1954 battle of Dien Bien Phu. That iconic event was officially portrayed as the triumph of the heroic revolutionary masses, but Giap's name was always prominently associated with it. Le Duan was jealous of Giap's wide popularity and wanted to win a strategically decisive battle against American forces without Giap.

Le Duan apparently chose the U.S. Marine base at Khe Sanh as the target.[21] Lacking technical military knowledge, he did not understand that he could never match Giap's 1954 victory over the French forces at Dien Bien Phu with a 1968 victory over the U.S. forces at Khe Sanh for technical reasons beyond his control.

Khe Sanh had an all-weather, twenty-four-hour, radar-controlled bomb targeting system. It had virtually unlimited, first-priority air support. It had secure, external artillery support. It had acoustic, seismic, and infrared sensors that could detect all NVA troop locations and movements. With that data, the overwhelming U.S. air and artillery firepower superiority could preempt any number and size of ground attacks under any conditions.[22] Westmoreland confidently welcomed a multi-divisional NVA attack in such a remote area with no possibility of collateral damage to civilians from concentrated U.S. firepower.

The NVA isolated Khe Sanh by land, bombarded it with long-range artillery, dug deep trenches near its perimeter, and repeatedly attacked the dominant nearby high ground. The crude, World War I entrenching and bombardment tactics that were successful against the French at Dien Bien Phu in 1954 resulted in the loss of an estimated 10,000–15,000 NVA troops at Khe Sanh in 1968 without ever penetrating the perimeter of the Marine base.[23]

On the last day of January 1968, Le Duan launched his nationwide General Offensive/General Insurrection campaign. Some 84,000 VC troops simultaneously attacked five of the six major RVN cities, thirty-six of the forty-four provincial capitals, and sixty-four district capitals. As Giap predicted, they lost an estimated 58,000 troops and failed to achieve any of their main objectives. Some VC troops held out for three weeks in Hue and parts of Saigon and Cholon, but most of them were eventually killed, and the relatively few survivors retreated.[24]

Not surprisingly, there was also no General Insurrection of South Vietnamese civilians. The mass civilian atrocities of the defeated VC forces in Hue and other towns even alienated most formerly passive VC sympathizers. For the first time, widespread feelings of national patriotism and urban hostility toward Communist forces began to develop in South Vietnam.[25]

If Le Duan was surprised by the monumental failure of his 1968 Tet strategy, his surprise was likely equaled by the U.S. media's portrayal of it as the failure of Westmoreland's attrition strategy and by implication the failure of President Johnson's war in Vietnam.[26] The five key men in the Politburo's SMA must have known that the disastrous losses of their troops in the 1968 Tet battles actually validated the effectiveness of

Westmoreland's mass attrition strategy beyond his own most optimistic expectations.

The U.S. media's radically misleading reporting of those battles, their failure to report the nationwide losses of the VC/NVA forces, and their discrediting or ignoring the tactical successes of the U.S. and ARVN forces was a serendipitous gift to Le Duan. His unexpected propaganda victory in America in 1968 far outweighed all the tactical failures of his forces in South Vietnam.

Most of the U.S. media seemed to believe a simplistic cliché about the war in Vietnam: if the "counterinsurgency" forces are not consistently and visibly winning the "guerrilla" war, they must be losing it or else hopelessly stalemated.[27] That widespread fallacy was based mainly on the rumors, gossip, and superficial impressions of a few cynical American reporters in Saigon.[28] Their militarily ignorant view of the war was pseudo-authenticated by their brief, occasional visits to U.S. troops in the field for background scenes to enhance their staged war reporting.[29]

Their consistently negative view of the war was further validated by a key, deep-cover DRV agent of influence. A graduate of an American college who spoke fluent American English, he was a staff reporter for *Time* magazine in Saigon. After the NVA conquest of South Vietnam, comrade Pham Xuan An revealed his true identity as a general in the DRV intelligence service.

His unique contribution to the ultimate NVA victory was not tactical information from spying, but strategic disinformation covertly planted in his frequent conversations with credulous U.S. reporters, who passed on his disinformation messages in their reports to the U.S. public. His "poisoning the well" technique discredited the American military's war reports and convinced many reporters that, contrary to official claims, U.S. forces were losing the war to the "Viet Cong."[30]

Most U.S. news editors were not pro-Communist, but many of them seemed to be almost viscerally anti-anti-Communist. They ignored or minimized the fact, reported by a few objective journalists in Vietnam, that the VC fought the 1968 Tet battles with semi-conventional tactics, not guerrilla tactics, and that the U.S. and ARVN troops crushed the VC forces with conventional tactics, not counterinsurgency tactics.[31]

DRV STRATEGY • 9

Those news editors seemed not to understand that in the Tet battles the U.S. and ARVN forces destroyed most of the main VC combat forces, and the few surviving VC were no longer an existential threat to RVN sovereignty. Most importantly, they minimized or ignored the critical fact that the ravaged VC forces were being replaced by regular NVA troops in an accelerated and increasingly overt invasion from North Vietnam.[32]

In 1968, most Americans got their international news in capsule form from network television, and there were only three national television networks. Some TV news editors were more like editorial writers than disinterested journalists objectively reporting factually balanced news. Many were also prejudiced against the U.S. military in Vietnam. Their negative visual and semantic messages in 1968 led to the widespread belief that as long as the "VC guerrillas" could fight big battles, the U.S. forces must be either stalemated or losing the "counterinsurgency" war, regardless of the radically unequal tactical results of those battles.[33]

Many U.S. news editors, following the lead of the *New York Times*, also seemed to be prejudiced against South Vietnam's authoritarian regime. They summarily dismissed the fact that the DRV and the RVN were two nations, not one nation with two names, and despite their racial, language, and cultural similarities, the two Vietnams, like the two Koreas and the two Germanys, were officially recognized as such. They ignored the fact that all governments in all wars for national survival, including the U.S. government under Lincoln in the American Civil War, are necessarily authoritarian. They implicitly compared the authoritarian wartime government of South Vietnam to the democratic peacetime government of America, instead of to the Stalinist police state of North Vietnam.[34]

The irony of the failure of the NVA's 1968 Dien Bien Phu strategy at Khe Sanh and the failure of the VC's General Offensive/General Insurrection strategy everywhere else in South Vietnam in 1968 is that both of those moribund strategies were resuscitated by the politically adversarial U.S. media. That unexpected result evidently convinced Le Duan that a second series of such battles in May would be reported by the media as U.S. defeats, regardless of the grossly disproportionate NVA losses in those battles, merely because they were fought.

The DRV had a propensity for commemorative battles, and May was important to them for eight historic events: 1) Ho Chi Minh's birthday; 2) the 150th anniversary of Karl Marx's birth; 3) the founding of Giap's "Vietnam Liberation Army" in 1945; 4) the founding of the Lao Dong Party in 1951; 5) the Dien Bien Phu victory in 1954; 6) the beginning of the Ho Chi Minh Trail in 1959; 7) the founding of the military facade called the People's Liberation Armed Forces (PLAF) in 1959; and 8) the strategically decisive Second Geneva Conference in 1961.[35]

The NVA had no tactical need to attack Kham Duc or Ngok Tavak. The pseudo-soldiers of Kham Duc's Civilian Irregular Defense Group (CIDG) had never even attempted to interdict the constant infiltration north and south of the camp by thousands of NVA troops. Because of that fact, the use of two reinforced NVA regiments to attack a place of so little intrinsic value was tactically senseless. A far better use of those troops would have been in the attacks on more important targets in the second wave of the NVA's General Offensive in May.

Nearly thirty years later, retired NVA MG Phan Thanh Du, the operations officer of the 2nd NVA Division in the battle of Kham Duc, implied that the main NVA tactical objective of the attack was simply to lure U.S. reinforcements to that remote area and destroy them.[36] The reason given for the battle in the official history of the 2nd PAVN Division is that it was a prerequisite for repairing QL (*Quoc Lo*; National Road) 14 north and south of the Special Forces camp and extending an old French road eastward toward to the piedmont and coastal valleys.[37]

That plan was totally unrealistic as long as U.S. combat forces were active in I Corps. A constant and ultimately futile NVA engineering effort would have been required to repair the damage caused by frequent air attacks on the new road and frequent artillery attacks from American fire bases in range of QL 14 in the more open terrain east and south of Kham Duc.

Exploiting the U.S. domestic political divisions over the war was not contemplated in the Politburo's original strategy for their 1968 General Offensive, but by May of that year it might well have been another reason for launching the second wave of their offensive. The Politburo had learned that any large-scale NVA victory anywhere in South Vietnam would be publically exploited in the U.S. by the pro-Communist "anti-war" movement.

An April 8, 1968 memorandum by the Central Intelligence Agency's (CIA) Office of National Estimates (ONE) noted that a decisive stage in the war had arrived, and intensified military action would strengthen Hanoi's bargaining position against the United States in Paris.[38] A May 3, 1968 memorandum by the CIA's Directorate of Intelligence concluded that Hanoi could be planning to launch major military actions in South Vietnam just before or shortly after the opening of the Paris talks for the same purpose.[39]

A May 6, 1968 CIA memorandum on the likely North Vietnamese strategy in Paris and South Vietnam assumed that the Communist position in South Vietnam was "not at all what [the Politburo] thought it would be … when they conceived the winter-spring campaign last year." It concluded that the military initiative had passed to the U.S. in many areas, but the NVA forces would make every effort to regain it.[40]

That memorandum predicted a coordinated DRV military/diplomatic strategy in the following months of 1968. It considered the timing of the Politburo's May 3 agreement to meet the U.S. delegation in Paris and the simultaneous timing of the NVA's nationwide "Mini-Tet" May offensive in South Vietnam "no accident." It, too, predicted that future Politburo actions would be designed to enhance the DRV bargaining position in Paris.[41]

The NVA's 1968 General Offensive was predicted to culminate in a large, set-piece battle somewhere in I Corps. In allied intelligence circles it was called the "Dien Bien Phu gambit" or the "other shoe scenario."[42] U.S. military intelligence also predicted a strong NVA military initiative to influence the Paris peace talks. It was speculated that a dramatic NVA victory in a large battle with significant American losses might influence the 1968 U.S. Presidential election by swaying public opinion in favor of a radically anti-war candidate.[43]

If Le Duan's strategy for the second phase of his 1968 General Offensive did include a large, decisive battle in May just prior to the start of the Paris peace talks, the target of that battle seems to have been Kham Duc. In President Johnson's memoirs years later, he recognized the potential impact of the Kham Duc battle on the start of the Paris talks. Although unknowingly understating the size of the attacking NVA forces by half, he wrote:

> Just before dawn on May 12, the day before the full Paris talks began, a North Vietnamese regiment attacked our troops in northern I Corps near Laos [Kham Duc]. Westmoreland reinforced the units under attack, then skillfully pulled them out. Once again, the North Vietnamese had been denied a tactical victory, but we knew they would continue to try. They wanted to create the impression that they were stronger than they were and could strike at will.[44]

Le Duan's choice of Khe Sanh for his first Dien Bien Phu gambit was the result of his own ideological self-delusion and military ignorance, but his apparent selection of Kham Duc as the target of his second Dien Bien Phu ploy was realistic. Although smaller than Dien Bien Phu, its physical characteristics were eerily similar. Compared to the 6,000 Marine, SF, and ARVN defenders of Khe Sanh, who were constantly supported by virtually unlimited air and artillery firepower, Kham Duc was like ripe, low-hanging fruit.

The problem with attacking it as a strategic gambit was that capturing or killing a few more U.S. Special Forces men and their indigenous troops would not attract major American media attention, and a film of such a remote and insignificant event would have no strategic propaganda value. Unless the attack resulted in the capture or death of numerous U.S. troops, the media could not portray it as a U.S. Dien Bien Phu, as they had repeatedly tried to portray Khe Sanh.[45] Enough reinforcements had to be sent to Kham Duc to make their death or capture sensational television news in America.

The huge number of reinforcements sent to the 1967 battle of Dak To, another SF camp in II Corps, gave Le Duan reason to expect that Kham Duc would be similarly reinforced.[46] He evidently thought that the best way to attract major reinforcements to Kham Duc was to convince Westmoreland that if he did not heavily reinforce it, it would soon be overrun by a large NVA force. Apparently to convey that message, the NVA planned to first attack Ngok Tavak, a small, temporary patrol base south of Kham Duc, where an SF indigenous mercenary company and an anomalous Marine artillery platoon were encamped.

In addition to their probable strategic objective at Kham Duc, the NVA had at least two tactical objectives. First, they wanted to lure an Americal Division brigade away from its defense of the lowland population centers to increase their chance of success in their attacks on those targets. Second, they aimed to inflict prolonged attrition on the U.S. reinforcements sent to Kham Duc. Its remote location surrounded by jungle-covered mountains close to the NVA's supply lines and sanctuary bases in Laos was ideal for their large-scale ambush tactics.

Le Duan undoubtedly knew that a shocking, nationwide American media message about the fall of Kham Duc might favorably influence the pending peace talks in Paris. With the tactical odds so strongly in his favor and with so much strategic potential at that critical time, he must have considered his maximum risk of losing up to two-thirds of the 2nd NVA Division by gambling on the transitional May weather at Kham Duc a calculated risk well worth taking.

Notes

1 Griffith, Samuel (trans.). *Mao Tse-tung On Guerrilla Warfare* (NY: Praeger, 1961), p. 60. Mao repeatedly stressed that guerrilla warfare alone cannot win wars against large, determined, conventional armies. Only other large, determined, conventional armies can do so.

2 "We were invading, but we did our best to disguise ourselves as native liberators." NVA COL Huong Van Ba quoted in Chanoff, David and Van Toai, Doan. *Portrait of the Enemy* (NY: Random House, 1986), p. 153.

3 The other members of the SMA were Le Duc Tho (Le Duan's loyal deputy) and three NVA generals with overlapping offices in the Ministry of Defense: Vo Nguyen Giap (Minister of Defense and Commander of the NVA), Nguyen Chi Thanh (senior Political Commissar of the VC forces in South Vietnam), and Van Tien Dung (Giap's deputy and Le Duan's protégé). In 1967, Nguyen Chi Thanh died, and Le Duan replaced him with Pham Hung, a close friend. Lien-Hang T. Nguyen. *Hanoi's War* (Chapel Hill, NC: University of North Carolina Press, 2012), p. 25.

4 In 1966, a third VC regiment formed the 5th VC Division. That same year, two more NVA regiments arrived from the DRV, and in 1967 a third NVA regiment joined them to form the nominal 7th VC Division, which was actually another NVA division. Doyle, Edward *et al. The Vietnam Experience: The North* (Boston, MA: Boston Publishing, 1986), pp. 16–24.

5 Lien-Hang, *op. cit.*, pp. 26–27.

6 Doyle, *op. cit.*, pp. 16–17. At the same time, some 900,000 North Vietnamese moved south. Hundreds of thousands more wanted to leave, but were not allowed to do so. Fall, Bernard. *The Two Viet-Nams* (2nd ed.) (NY: Praeger, 1967), p. 129. Fall, Bernard, *Viet-Nam Witness* (NY: Praeger, 1966), p. 76.

7 Doyle, *op. cit.*, pp. 18, 20, 22, 24.

8 *Ibid.*, pp. 29, 32.

9 "Aggression From the North: The Record of North Vietnam's Campaign To Conquer South Vietnam," Department of State Publication 7839, U.S. Government Printing Office, Washington, D.C., 1965. "The North Vietnamese Army In South Vietnam," paper presented by W. Averell Harriman, Chief U.S. Delegate at the Paris meeting with North Vietnamese delegates, May 27, 1968. "Working Paper On The North Vietnamese Role In The War In Viet-Nam," May 1968—U.S. Department of State.

10 *cf.* Moore, Harold and Galloway, Joseph. *We Were Soldiers Once … And Young* (NY: Random House, 1992).

11 *Ibid.*

12 In the rainy season most VC units stayed in their camps for about a month, but in the dry season they moved every ten to fifteen days. Wilkins, Warren. *Grab Their Belts To Fight Them* (Annapolis, MD: Naval Institute Press, 2011), pp. 35–37. "… we were on the move all the time. Our health and fighting ability got worse and worse." Bui Van Tai, NVA assistant platoon leader, quoted in Chanoff, *op. cit.*, p. 171.

13 Davidson, Phillip. *Vietnam At War* (Novato, CA: Presidio Press, 1988), pp. 407, 425, 434–38, 467.

14 *Summary of the Ten Year Southeast Asia Air War, 1963–1973*, vol. 2, suppl. Doc. III-N, 21, USAF Historical Research Center, Maxwell AFB, AL. Dougan, Clark *et al. The Vietnam Experience: Nineteen Sixty-Eight* (Boston, MA: Boston Publishing, 1983), p. 56.

15 Bui Tin. *From Enemy To Friend* (Annapolis, MD: Naval Institute Press, 2002), pp. 41, 74, 88.

16 A *coup de main* is a method of gaining control of a government by a sudden, decisive seizure of a few strategic urban targets. On November 7, 1917 Leon Trotsky organized a *coup de main* in Petrograd, then the capital of Russia, that enabled Lenin's troops to seize the key control points in the city with no effective opposition. The previous government was not overthrown, because there was no government left to overthrow. The Communists gained control of the nation by political default, not by military conquest.

17 On August 19, 1945 Ho Chi Minh seized power with a *coup de main* in Hanoi. Robbins, James. *This Time We Win* (NY: Encounter Books, 2010), pp. 64–68. At that time, control of Vietnam could be easily taken by anyone bold enough to claim it. Fall, *Two Viet-Nams, op. cit.*, p. 61.

18 Lien-Hang, *op. cit.*, pp. 95, 99, 101–02. Ironically, in 1930 Mao's forces suffered huge losses by following an order by the Central Committee of the Chinese Communist Party to launch simultaneous attacks on heavily defended urban targets.

19 Lien-Hang, *op. cit.*, pp. 101–02.

20 *Ibid.*, p. 99.

21 The NVA claim that Khe Sanh was a mere "diversion" is risibly absurd. No sane commander would risk three of his best divisions to "tie down" or "isolate" the equivalent of only one enemy regiment. That claim, typical of Communist propaganda, is a reversal of the facts. It is confirmed in the memoir of one of the few NVA survivors of three attacks against the ARVN perimeter at Khe Sanh. Delezen, John. *Red Plateau* ([n.p.] Corps Productions, 2005), pp. 112–13. In reality, Khe Sanh tied down and severely attrited with massive U.S. air and artillery firepower two or three NVA divisions that could have been far more effectively used in the simultaneous and potentially strategic battle of Hue.

22 Westmoreland, William. *A Soldier Reports* (NY: Doubleday, 1976), pp. 336–40.

23 Summers, Harry. *Historical Atlas of the Vietnam War* (NY: Houghton Mifflin, 1995), pp. 58–59.

24 *Ibid.*, pp. 138–39. Dougan, *op. cit.*, p. 43. Tucker, Spencer (ed.). *The Encyclopedia of the Vietnam War* (NY: Oxford University Press, 2001), pp. 204–06, 396–99. An estimated 58,000 VC/NVA troops were killed compared to fewer than 4,000 U.S. troops, fewer than 5,000 ARVN troops, and about 14,300 civilians. Davidson, *op. cit.*, pp. 425–29, 434–38, 474–75, 546–47. Summers, *op. cit.*, pp. 130–35. Braestrup, Peter. *Big Story* (Novato, CA: Presidio Press, 1983), pp. viii–xvi. Dougan, *op. cit.*, p. 120. Robbins, *op. cit.*, pp. 195–206. Doyle, *op. cit.*, pp. 119–20.

25 Dougan, *op. cit.*, pp. 119–20.

26 An NBC news special on March 10, 1968 stated, "... the war as the Administration has defined it is being lost." Spector, Ronald. *After Tet* (NY: The Free Press, 1993), p. 5. Davidson, *op. cit.*, pp. 484–88. "... the public was experiencing the bloodshed through the new technology of television. The summaries were not believed. The projected experience was." Oberdorfer, Don *TET!* (NY: Doubleday, 1971), pp. 158–59.

27 "Much of the doomsday atmosphere generated in the United States by the Tet Offensive was caused by extremely pessimistic reporting by press and television." Lewy, Guenter. *America In Vietnam* (NY: Oxford University Press, 1978), p. 127. "Thanks to the [U.S.] media, which exaggerated the damage caused by the [Tet] offensive, the American public was bedazzled." Bui Tin. *Following Ho Chi Minh* (Honolulu, HI: University of Hawaii Press, 1995), pp. 62–63.

28 The most influential print and wire service reporters in Vietnam from 1961 to 1963 were Homer Bigart and David Halberstam of the *New York Times* (NYT), Peter Arnett of the Associated Press (AP), and Neil Sheehan of United Press International (UPI). Prochnau, William. *Once Upon A Distant War* (NY: Time Books, 1995), p. 154. "... no other part of American journalism so visibly ... takes its moral and political guidance from the *New York Times* as does network television." "[TV correspondents] left New York ... ingrained with the growing anti-Vietnam and anti-military viewpoint of *Times* editors." "TV news crews understood that any kind of propagandistic reporting was justified, as long as their editor's anti-war

message was conveyed." Kennedy, William. *The Military and the Media* (Westport, CT: Praeger, 1993), pp. 89, 101–03.

29 "U.S. forces in action … were not covered firsthand by many journalists.""Relatively few [reporters] saw any combat (i.e., at battalion level or below) prior to Tet." "… it was rare for [them] to spend the night with a U.S. company or battalion in the field … long enough to see the [combat] as the troops or their leaders saw it." Braestrup, *op. cit.*, p. 24. Most TV and print reporters centered their attention on Saigon. Hammond, William. *Reporting Vietnam* (Lawrence, KS: The University Press of Kansas, 1998), p. 110. They could leave their Saigon hotels in the morning, drive or fly to the war, drive or fly back with their film and reports, and be home the same day. Oberdorfer, *op. cit.*, p. 160. Watching the war from the comfortable roof of the Caravelle Hotel in Saigon was a nightly social event. *Ibid.*, p. 183.

30 *cf.* Berman, Larry. *The Perfect Spy* (NY: Smithsonian Books, 2008). An began as the aide of the representative of the British news agency, Reuters. "Having a good Vietnamese aide was crucial, and An was the best." "An went everywhere with the gang." *Ibid.*, p.462.

31 "… the editors back in the United States seemed to have a social agenda that romanticized the Vietnamese [Communist] freedom fighters." Tucker, *op. cit.*, p. 259. They seemed much less interested in the frequent mass atrocities of the Communist VC and NVA forces.

32 "Everywhere in South Vietnam many of the ablest and most experienced Viet Cong cadres, administrators, and combat leaders were dead or prisoners by the end of 1968." Spector, *op. cit.*, p. 282.

33 "… the editors and producers … were not always able to keep their own political agendas … out of the editing process." Tucker, *op. cit.* "… the dominant opinion of the reporters and their editors … [was] that the war was a stalemate." Oberdorfer, *op. cit.*, pp. 160– 61.

34 Pro-Communist propagandists always claimed that Vietnam was a single, artificially divided country, but during its 20-year life from 1955 to 1975 the Republic of Viet Nam was officially recognized as a sovereign nation by 88 other nations. The far-left demonstrators who promoted that claim were not actually anti-war, because they supported the VC/NVA war against South Vietnam. They were only opposed to U.S. anti-Communist participation in that war. Robbins, James. *This Time We Win* (NY: Encounter Books, 2010), p. 61. Some leftist journalists, in response to criticism of the news media by "anti-war" protestors, stopped calling the North Vietnamese Army the enemy. Gans, Herbert. *Deciding What's News* (NY: Pantheon Books, 1979), p. 201.

35 At that conference the inept diplomacy of a grossly incompetent U.S. ambassador, Averell Harriman, resulted in the arbitrary prohibition of a limited U.S. invasion of eastern Laos and Cambodia, which made those nations permanent sanctuaries for VC and NVA forces and a permanent route for the Ho Chi Minh Trail. *cf.* Summers, *op. cit.*, p. 68.

36 Phan Thanh Du quoted in Davies, Bruce. *The Battle For Ngok Tavak* (Crows Nest, NSW, Austraolia: Allen & Unwin, 2008), p. 187.

37 Chuong, Nguyen Huy. Su Doan 2, Tap 1 [2nd Division, Vol. 1] (Danang, Socialist Republic of Vietnam: Second Division Party Committee and Headquarters, Danang Publishing House, 1989), pp. 100–01; excerpts translated by Merle Pribbenow.

38 "ONE Memo for DCI: Speculation on Hanoi's Motives", Memorandum for the Director, April 8, 1968, Office of National Estimates, Central Intelligence Agency, Washington, D.C.

39 "Hanoi's Paris Initiative and the Possibility of a New Communist Military Offensive", Memorandum SC No. 08360/68, May 3, 1968, Directorate of Intelligence, Central Intelligence Agency, Washington, D.C.

40 "Hanoi's Negotiating Position and Concept of Negotiations", IM 0587/68, May 6, 1968, Central Intelligence Agency, Washington, D. C.

41 *Ibid.*

42 Pike, Douglas. *War, Peace, and the Viet Cong* (Cambridge, MA: The M.I.T. Press, 1969), p. 128.

43 In 1972, George McGovern won the Democratic Party Presidential nomination on a pledge to unilaterally and immediately end all U.S. participation in the Vietnam War. Tucker, *op. cit.*, p. 255. Davidson, *op. cit.*, p. 338.

44 Johnson, Lyndon Baines. *The Vantage Point* (NY: Holt, Rinehart, and Winston, 1971), p. 508. LBJ was aware of Harriman's desire to capitulate to the DRV demands to withdraw U.S. troops from South Vietnam. He ordered GEN Andrew Goodpaster, his personal representative on the U.S. negotiating team, to immediately inform him directly, if Harriman ever indicated any intention of doing so. Email of Goodpaster to McLeroy, April 12, 1998.

45 Tucker, *op. cit.*, pp. 90–91. Davidson, *op. cit.*, pp. 223–83.

46 Summers, *op. cit.*, pp. 128–29.

2

PAVN Tactics

"Quality [of forces] can be replaced by quantity and morale."

MAO TSE–TUNG[1]

The North Vietnamese Army, officially named the People's Army of Vietnam,[2] was known for the exceptionally determined and resilient fighting spirit of its long-suffering soldiers. The three sources of that spirit were their traditional cultural values, the national legend of their 2,000-year martial heritage, and the ruthless thought and behavior control of their totalitarian Communist government.

Eighty-five percent of the population of North Vietnam lived in rural areas. Most NVA soldiers were from small villages and farms, where the main characteristics of social life were group identification and solidarity. Individual will was always subordinate to the collective will of the extended family and immediate social community. Parents were strict with their children and demanded unquestioning obedience. Respectfulness, patience, and emotional restraint were considered essential virtues for both children and adults.[3]

The Buddhist values of most rural families were reinforced by the equally traditional values of Confucian ethics and ancestor worship. Confucianism is based on the acceptance of one's divinely ordained place in a balanced, autocratic social hierarchy. It requires obedient, harmonious relations with one's family elders, social elders, and official authorities. Rulers govern with the "Mandate of Heaven," a concept somewhat similar to the "Divine Right" of English kings.[4] Ancestor worship requires the same deferential and respectful attitude toward a family's deceased authority figures.

Preserving one's "face" means maintaining social acceptance by behaving in socially required ways. Losing "face" means the shameful humiliation of losing the respect of one's family and social community because of his or her unacceptable behavior. The threat of losing "face" was a powerful control mechanism for all Vietnamese.[5]

Most rural Vietnamese were accustomed to physical and material hardship and were taught from childhood to stoically and silently accept the inevitable vicissitudes of life. It was not a fatalistic stoicism, but a pragmatic one partially derived from the Confucian doctrine of the Golden Mean and the Buddhist doctrine of the Middle Path. One must accept some negative circumstances beyond one's control, but constantly try to make the most of those circumstances. Like the strong yet supple bamboo, one must always bend with the winds of adverse fortune, but never break.[6]

In 1968, the totalitarian dictatorship of the Democratic Republic of Viet Nam (DRV) in North Vietnam ruled its citizens by fear. The authority of the ruling Lao Dong [Workers] Party replaced the traditional authority of both family and village elders. Every aspect of every citizen's life was under total government control at all times, and no opposition of any kind was tolerated. Anyone suspected of any kind of disloyalty, even mental, was arbitrarily seized by the police and severely questioned. Those considered guilty for any reason quickly disappeared.[7]

All North Vietnamese citizens were required to report to the nearest authority anyone who seemed to have a "reactionary" or "defeatist" attitude. The expression of any negative thought about the government, the economy, or the war was illegal. The families of missing soldiers were not allowed to mourn them publicly, and anyone who questioned the authorities about a missing soldier received an intimidating visit from the internal security police.[8]

Military service to "liberate" South Vietnam from its U.S. "occupiers" was glorified as the second most sacred patriotic duty after the "salvation of the fatherland." All citizens were constantly bombarded with Party propaganda in every school, workplace, and public venue. To instill a militantly patriotic spirit in young people, films, lectures, songs, and slogans stressed the national legend of Vietnam's long history of heroic resistance to all foreign occupiers: Chinese, Mongol, French, Japanese, and

American. Every citizen was expected to always be willing to sacrifice his or her life for the DRV's "national unity" with (i.e., military conquest of) the Republic of Viet Nam (RVN).[9]

The first rule instilled in every NVA soldier was that the collective decisions of his political and military cadre would always be superior to his personal needs or wishes. To enforce that coercive collectivist dogma, every military unit had a military and political control structure. The most important and extensive aspect of recruit training was intensive political indoctrination, and every aspect of every recruit's life was politically controlled at all times.

The recruits' only source of information about the war was government propaganda, which never reported any negative war news. They were told that most South Vietnamese people would welcome them as liberators from the "imperialist U.S. invaders" and their "oppressive puppet" regime. Many naïve and fervently patriotic young volunteers were so motivated by their political indoctrination that they were willing to blindly sacrifice their lives for that noble cause. Some even had themselves tattooed with the slogan "Born in the North to die in the South."[10]

At their mandatory self-criticism and group criticism meetings each soldier was required to critique the behavior and attitude of himself and his comrades. Their political "brain washing" also required their repetition and memorization of simplistic ideological slogans. Anyone who dared to question a slogan was classified as untrustworthy for military service and was sent for hard labor duty in a mine, factory, construction project, or collective farm. The other recruits never knew where the bold or naive questioner was sent, but his immediate, ominous absence discouraged further questions.[11]

Although recruits were repeatedly told that they were winning the war in the south, some outwardly compliant draftees were secretly skeptical of their constant indoctrination and were unwilling to sacrifice their lives for the "liberation" of South Vietnam. It was rumored that no one who went south ever returned, and most of them were never heard from again. The skeptical recruits feared to express their secret thoughts, because they knew that many other recruits were eager to impress their political cadre by reporting any negative statement they overheard.[12]

NVA soldiers were organized in three-man "cells." Any soldier considered ideologically weak by his political cadre was put into a cell with those considered ideologically stronger. The other two were ordered to strengthen the weaker one's morale, motivation, and esprit with their example and encouragement. They were also required to keep him under observation and report to their political officer any suspicions about his patriotism, motivation, or fighting spirit.[13]

The mutual support and shared hardships of the three-man cells produced an emotional bond that was strengthened by their isolation from civilian society and the willingness of their military leaders to share their hardships and dangers. Despite their appalling battle casualties and wretched living conditions, most NVA soldiers remained faithful to their military "family" and "village." In their enforced isolation under the constant surveillance of their cell mates and their political officers, they had little alternative. Relatively few NVA soldiers deserted compared to the much more numerous Viet Cong deserters, especially after the VC's disastrous 1968 losses.[14]

Many NVA recruits received their basic training at special training sites like the main one at Xuan Mai near Hanoi. Basic infantry training lasted from one to three months and emphasized day and night cross-country marches of increasing length, speed, difficulty, and pack weight. The original objective was to condition them for the long, arduous journey on foot through the jungles and mountains of eastern Laos and Cambodia into South Vietnam. To strengthen them for that ordeal they received three or four times the food rations of soldiers in North Vietnam.[15]

After basic training some recruits were selected for special training as officers, medics, snipers, scouts, radio technicians, and sappers (demolitionist commandos). Specialist training lasted from a few months to two years.[16] The most elite infantry troops were reconnaissance scouts, who were carefully selected for political loyalty, physical stamina, and mental acuity. They had to master several technical skills in a difficult training course of eighteen to twenty-four months.

Their missions were always dangerous, but did not include combat. Their commanders did not want to risk losing them in battle, because scouts and local spies were their main sources of enemy intelligence.

Scouts were administratively grouped with sappers, but they had special privileges in camp and far more freedom of action than the sappers had.[17]

Beginning in 1968, recruits received brief, superficial basic training in North Vietnam and were sent directly to NVA units in South Vietnam for on-the-job training (OJT). In infantry units much of their OJT was learning to expertly dig and camouflage bunkers, trenches, and tunnels. They were also taught personal camouflage, night movement, night firing, assault firing, defensive firing, and firing at moving helicopters and armored vehicles.[18]

Most NVA combat veterans, who could have shared their practical experience with the new recruits, were not allowed to return to North Vietnam. Not only were they needed in South Vietnam, but the political officers feared that the accounts of their gory combat experiences and miserable jungle life would demoralize new recruits. The only ones allowed to return were those so severely and permanently wounded that they could no longer be useful in any way. They were kept in isolated areas to prevent the sight of their horrific wounds from demoralizing civilians and future recruits.[19]

Recruits would have been even more demoralized if they had known the actual medical conditions of most wounded NVA soldiers in South Vietnam. A former NVA doctor described the conditions in their underground hospitals as "nightmarish."[20] Nearly 50 percent of the NVA defectors in 1969 had been wounded, and 45 percent of them said the main reason they defected was poor medical care and/or inadequate medical supplies. Eighty-one percent of them had been seriously ill, and two-thirds of them suffered constantly from untreated malaria. Those conditions are vividly described in the autobiographical novel of an NVA combat veteran:

> "Clinic 8 consisted of a disheveled medical team, ragged and beaten to threads after months of … incessant withdrawals by men who had been continually surrounded, then bombed and shelled by artillery."
>
> "In the two months he had been there before being transferred to Hospital 214, he had lain buried in a flat-roofed trench, from which water gushed on both sides. His rotting flesh stank …."
>
> "Hospital 214 was little more than a shed."

"The wounded were ashen-faced, their bodies ... wasted from starvation and exhaustion."[21]

Some NVA surgeons were former combat nurses and surgical assistants whose medical knowledge was limited to practical, on-the-job training with the constantly increasing numbers of NVA and VC casualties. Many of their surgical instruments and much of their equipment had to be improvised from pieces of metal, rubber, and glass salvaged from downed U.S. aircraft.[22]

Sometimes their only electrical power was provided by soldiers pumping stationary bicycles attached to generators. After large battles the surgeons often had to operate almost constantly for several days in underground darkness with flashlights attached to their heads.[23] Arm and leg amputations, abdominal surgery, even brain surgery sometimes had to be performed with only local anesthesia or none.[24] Tied down, such patients could only scream in agony until they fainted from excruciating pain.

Some amputees had to lie helplessly in constant pain for months in dark, stinking, rat-infested tunnels, hearing the screams and moans of other wounded soldiers being sliced and sawed. Most severely wounded patients in those primitive hospitals died, and many more died from disease than from wounds. The most common causes of postoperative patient deaths were shock and infection. For those who survived the traumatic surgical operations, the main causes of death were malarial fever and acute diarrhea.[25]

The largest NVA hospital in the Central Highlands had a staff of 400 people and between 1,000 and 1,800 patients in 280 small, half-buried, thatched-roof bunkers spaced thirty yards apart under triple-canopy jungle. The doctors had to walk all day in difficult terrain, often in heavy rain, to get from one side of the hidden hospital complex to the other.[26]

The staffs of the field hospitals received very little food from the NVA, because the NVA barely had enough food for themselves. The hospital staff had to fish, hunt, and raise manioc (an edible starchy root) to survive.[27] Seventy percent of the patients and staff had debilitating illnesses, many of them fatal, from weakened immune systems caused by chronic malnutrition.[28]

Most NVA recruits had no prior experience in jungle living and no special training for it. In their jungle camps almost everyone suffered from chronic malnutrition, malaria, and diarrhea. Some also suffered from amoebic dysentery, pneumonia, beriberi, tuberculosis, yellow fever, dengue fever, leprosy, intestinal parasites, skin diseases, animal bites, infected tick and leech bites, and occasional outbreaks of cholera and plague.[29]

The average NVA soldier was slightly over 5 feet tall and weighed about 120lb. His tan or olive-green uniform was cotton, and his ankle-length, olive-green boots were canvas with black rubber soles. He had a cotton neck scarf and either a floppy cotton hat or a sun helmet made of compressed fiberboard covered with tan, brown, or olive-green cloth. He had a plastic rain cover for his sun helmet and a plastic net for attaching vegetation to it. On his canvas belt-and-suspender harness he carried a canteen, ammunition pouches, a hand grenade pouch, a wound dressing, a short machete, and a short shovel.[30]

In his canvas tan or olive-green backpack he carried another canteen, another wound dressing, weapon-cleaning gear, a plastic rain cape, a nylon or cotton hammock with nylon or cotton cord to hang it from trees, a mosquito net, a plastic sheet to use as a water-proof roof for a hammock or a heat-retaining blanket, first aid items, an extra uniform, a wool or cotton sweater, two pairs of underwear, a pair of rubber-tire or rubber thong sandals, a black cotton shirt, and black cotton pants.[31]

He was issued a five-day ration of partially cooked rice; some small cans of fish paste and meat paste to add to it; a metal cup, bowl, and spoon; wooden chopsticks; a plastic comb and toothbrush; a small towel; and a cigarette lighter for starting fires. He was allowed to have a few personal photos, some writing material, and some politically acceptable reading matter.[32]

In 1968, most NVA soldiers had 7.62mm AK-47 selective-fire assault rifles with curved, thirty-round magazines. Some had 7.62mm SKS carbines with ten-round magazines. Others had 7.62mm RPD light machine guns with 100 rounds in detachable drums. Those armed with 40mm RPG-7 rocket launchers wore a canvas vest with four long pouches for rockets.[33]

In South Vietnam NVA officers wore no rank insignia and were generically called cadres. In camp their status was shown by the slightly superior quality of their uniforms, a few symbolic adornments like belt buckles or small pistols, and conspicuous participation in the self-criticism sessions. In combat the NVA officers dressed exactly like their troops, with no symbols of rank.[34]

The NVA were masters of all the techniques of fortifying and camouflaging complex, large-scale ambush positions. Until 1972, however, most NVA officers were not equally skilled in planning and conducting multi-regimental attacks. Their battle planning, like their ideological indoctrination, was meticulous and thorough, but crude and inflexible.

NVA officers were valued far more for their unquestioning obedience to orders and their valiant, self-sacrificing example in combat than for their technical military knowledge. They were not allowed to change their orders in any way for any reason, and often callously wasted their lives and those of their brave troops by following all orders exactly as received, regardless of any changes in the tactical situation that made obeying those orders obvious mass suicide. Their blind obedience was valued far more than their lives.[35]

In 1968, basic NVA offensive tactics were human-wave assaults. Initial barrages of artillery, mortars, recoilless rifles, heavy machine guns, and rocket launchers were followed by sappers throwing hand grenades and satchel charges, then waves of infantry, blowing bugles and whistles, yelling loudly, racing forward together, firing automatic rifles, light machine guns, and rocket-propelled grenades. Their main tactic was to get so close to U.S. troops that the latter could not call for close air strikes or artillery fire for fear of being hit by their own ordnance.[36]

The NVA expected up to 50 percent casualties in every large battle, and for thousands of young, inexperienced, minimally trained NVA recruits their first battle was their last. In their carefully planned retreats, the surviving NVA troops dragged or carried away as many of their dead and wounded comrades as possible to keep the enemy from knowing the full extent of their huge losses.[37] Local auxiliaries later collected and buried the corpses and anatomical remains.

2ND NVA (PAVN) DIVISION

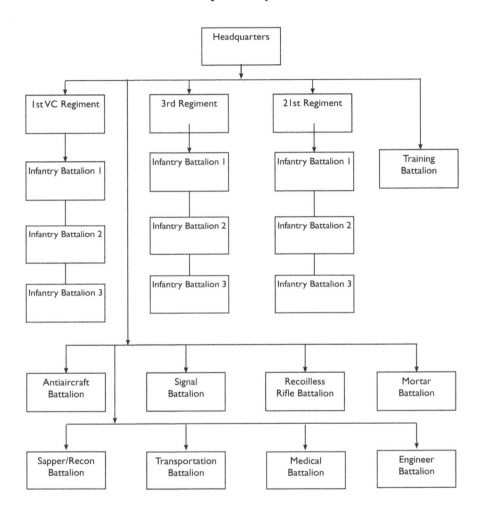

At full strength the 2nd NVA Division had 9,700 troops in three infantry regiments of 2,500 troops each, plus 2,200 troops in specialized combat support and logistics battalions. NVA/VC divisions, regiments, battalions, and companies rarely fought at full strength, except when they were preparing for a major attack against a large enemy unit. Then they tried to have at least three times as many troops as those of the enemy and preferably ten times as many, because of the enormous losses, often more than 50 percent, they expected in all their mass attacks.[38]

From January to May 1968, an estimated 80,000–90,000 new NVA troops arrived in South Vietnam on the Ho Chi Minh Trail network.[39] The NVA high command undoubtedly used some of those troops to bring at least two of the three regiments of the 2nd NVA Division to full strength for their attacks on Kham Duc and Ngok Tavak.[40]

They certainly would have done so if they thought they would need two full-strength regiments to cause major attrition in the reinforcements they anticipated at Kham Duc. Their estimate of the size of those reinforcements was likely based on the huge reinforcements sent to Dak To, an SF border camp attacked by the NVA in November 1967.[41]

On December 5, 1967, a U.S. 1st Cavalry Division aero scout platoon discovered and killed a group of NVA troops, including the commander of the PAVN 2nd Division, the 21st and 31st Regiment commanders, and 14 other key 2nd Division officers.[42] On March 14, 1968, a U.S. helicopter and artillery attack killed an estimated 100 PAVN 2nd Division troops, including some officers of the 1st VC Regiment.[43]

Those key leadership positions had to be hastily filled by senior staff officers from other headquarters, some of whom may have been selected more for their availability in time for the politically scheduled battle than for their leadership skill and combat experience in commanding multi-regimental attacks against strongly defended positions.

The 2nd Division's attack order for Kham Duc and Ngok Tavak must have been issued in early March to give their headquarters time to absorb the hundreds of new replacement troops, reconnoiter the targets, plan the attacks in detail, and rehearse them in detail before launching them in early May. For most of March and all of April, the 2nd Division absorbed replacements directly from North Vietnam.

They were very young and minimally trained for combat, but relatively healthy and totally obedient. Their weapons, uniforms, backpacks, and load-bearing harnesses were new. Lost and damaged weapons and equipment of the veteran troops were replaced by new ones from the constant flow of supplies arriving in North Vietnam from the USSR and Soviet bloc countries by ship and from China by rail.[44]

Recon scouts reconnoitered the two targets and carefully mapped the approach routes, assembly areas, withdrawal routes, and rendezvous points around the two targets for each infantry and combat support unit. From expertly hidden positions they observed both targets for several days and nights, noting and sketching in detail all U.S. and allied troop deployments, activities, and weapons.[45]

When the scouts returned to the division base, they briefed the senior staff officers in detail on the terrain, obstacles, danger areas, and check points along each section of each unit's routes to and from their objectives. The division staff then made detailed sand-table models of the targets and the key terrain around them.[46] Every squad, platoon, and company leader was meticulously briefed on his role in the attack and that of the troops on both sides of him. The unit leaders repeatedly rehearsed their assignments with their troops in day and night exercises.

The division's engineer troops, guided by the recon scouts, prepared large, hidden storage sites around the targets, where they stockpiled ammunition and other basic combat supplies. If the assault troops could not capture their targets, they wanted to have enough supplies to kill or capture as many U.S. reinforcements as possible in terrain favorable for NVA ambush tactics.[47]

In preparation for their march to Kham Duc, they disassembled their heavy weapons. They did not bring any long-range artillery, presumably because they knew they could not employ it effectively in that steep, mountainous, jungle-covered terrain or, if necessary, quickly retreat with it. The mortars, machine guns, and recoilless guns too heavy for one man to carry were slung on poles and carried by two or more men. Massive amounts of ammunition for those weapons were carried by conscripted civilian porters. Most of them had no allegiance to the NVA, but were forced to work for them under the threat of death for refusal or attempts to escape.

The camouflaged NVA troops walked slowly in single file on hidden trails to dispersed rendezvous points. Recon scouts walked 250 yards in front of battalions spaced two hours apart. The companies of each battalion walked 150 yards apart, and the platoons of each company walked 50 yards apart. They walked between six and nine miles each night or day, depending on the terrain, weather, and enemy aircraft. During the day they changed their camouflage foliage to match the vegetation they were moving through.[48]

They tried to hide their movements by maintaining radio silence. To communicate on the march they used runners and land-line telephones whenever possible. To monitor and control the movements of two regiments through mountainous, jungle-covered terrain to different assembly areas and attack positions, however, brief encoded radio transmissions were probably necessary. They hid their transmitting antennas in remote sites connected to their radios by long wires, but any radio message, however brief, was vulnerable to American interception.

Westmoreland had a unique source of ultra-secret intelligence that few people even knew existed and still fewer had access to. The electronic intercepts (ELINT) and signal intercepts (SIGINT) of the National Security Agency (NSA) provided more data on NVA strengths and movements to the CIA and military intelligence agencies than all other sources combined, including agent reports, photographs, captured documents, and prisoner interrogations.[49]

The information from the NSA's ultra-secret SIGINT and ELINT capabilities was shared with only a few key members of the senior MACV (Military Assistance Command, Vietnam) staff and selected division commanders. It was not acted on or disseminated, unless it could be plausibly attributed to another source. A leak of any intelligence gained from such highly protected methods could cause a spy to suspect that the most "secure" NVA transmissions were being intercepted.

The NSA had listening posts with special antennas near the DMZ and the Ho Chi Minh Trail that captured all electronic transmissions. Navy ships with electronic collection equipment cruising off the coast of North Vietnam also captured electronic transmissions. U.S. Air Force (AF) unmanned drones and RC-135 planes from Kadena air base in Okinawa, flying at 35,000 feet for up to eighteen hours, collected all NVA signals communications.[50]

U-2 and SR-71 spy planes based at Kadena constantly overflew North Vietnam and the Laotian Trail network. SR-71 Blackbirds flying at 90,000 feet and three times the speed of sound for twelve hours collected electronic emissions in a wide path. Their extremely high-resolution cameras took photographs so detailed that they could reveal recently used trails. Their infrared cameras could detect fresh camouflage, and their heat sensors could detect signs of campfires under the jungle canopy.[51] The content of NVA field telephone messages could not be monitored without physical access to the ground wires, but the electronic emissions from the wires may have revealed their location to the SR-71's ultra-sensitive instruments.

Intercepted messages in clear text were sent automatically by satellite to NSA analysts and translators at MACV headquarters. All encoded messages and random electronic emissions were sent via satellite to the NSA headquarters at Ft. Meade, MD. Five acres of (then) uniquely powerful computers there could reconstitute electronic emissions and decipher encoded text at the rate of three million characters per second. The decoded contents were sent via satellite to the top-secret NSA station at MACV headquarters for immediate translation.[52]

Both Westmoreland and the NVA were baiting a mass attrition trap for each other at Kham Duc; one passively, the other actively. Each opponent was inviting the other to a set-piece battle, and both were overtly accepting the invitation. If the camp was passive bait to lure large numbers of NVA troops to an isolated killing field, the conspicuous NVA threat to attack it was active bait to lure large numbers of U.S. troops to the same killing field.

For both opponents a battle at Kham Duc in May was a gamble on the arrival of the southwest monsoon in southern Laos and its secondary weather effects on the east side of the Truong Son mountain range. For one of the adversaries, the loss of that gamble would be fatal. With clear weather for close visual air support, Kham Duc could not be taken. Without it the camp was doomed. Both the weather odds and the numerical odds greatly favored the NVA.

Notes

1   Pike, Douglas *Viet Cong* (Cambridge, MA: M.I.T. Press, 1966), p. 35.

2   "People" is a Leninist euphemism for coercive central government collectivism. We use the descriptive term, North Vietnamese Army (NVA), for three reasons: 1) the Army of the Republic of Viet Nam (ARVN) was also composed of people;

2) all national armies belong to relatively small political regimes, not to the entire population; and 3) all national armies are a percentage of the national population, not the entire population. For the first reason the U.S. ambassador to the Republic of Viet Nam in 1964 and the U.S. ambassador to the Paris Peace Talks in 1968 insisted on using the descriptive term, North Vietnamese Army. Email of GEN Andrew Goodpaster (ret.) to McLeroy, May 3, 1996. Westmoreland, William. *A Soldier Reports* (Garden City, NY: Doubleday, 1976), p. 43.

3   Smith, Harvey *et al. Area Handbook for North Vietnam* (Washington, D.C.: U.S. Government Printing Office, 1967), pp. 93–106, 109–14, 221–51. Lanning, Michael Lee and Cragg, Dan: *Inside the VC and the NVA* (NY: Fawcett, 1992), pp. 29–33. Pike, Douglas. *PAVN* (NY: Da Capo, 1986), pp. 281–84.

4   Smith, *op. cit.*, pp. 137–52. Lanning, *ibid.* Pike, *PAVN, ibid.*

5   Smith, *op. cit.*, pp. 375–94.

6   *Ibid.*, pp. 93–106, 109–14. Pike, *PAVN, op. cit.*

7   Smith, *op. cit.*, pp. 376–79.

8   Chanoff, David and Van Toai, Doan. *Vietnam: A Portrait of its People at War* (NY: I. B. Tauris, 1996), pp. 44–45, 62–64.

9   Smith, *op. cit.*, pp. 221–40, 397–99, 407–08. Lanning, *op. cit.*, pp. 41–42, 64, 71–72. Smith, *op. cit.*, pp. 397–99, 407–08. Pike, *PAVN, op. cit.*, pp. 9–35.

10 Westmoreland, *op. cit.*, p. 252. Chanoff, *op. cit.*, p. 63.

11 Chanoff, *op. cit.*, p. 64. Rottman, Gordon. *North Vietnamese Army Soldier, 1958–75* (Oxford, UK: Osprey Publishing, 2009), p. 16.

12 Lanning, *op. cit.*, p. 72.

13 *Ibid.*, pp. 88–89.

14 *Ibid.*, pp. 45–50, Rottman, *op.cit.*, p. 42.

15 Lanning, *op. cit.*, 41–45. Rottman, *op. cit.*, pp. 17–20. Chanoff, *op. cit.*, p. 33.

16 Lanning, *ibid.*

17 Zumwalt, James. *Bare Feet Iron Will* (Jacksonville, FL: Fortis Publishing, 2010), p. 61.

18 *Ibid.*

19 *Ibid.*

20 *Ibid.*

21 Bao Ninh. *The Sorrow of War* (NY: Riverhead Books, 1993), pp. 140–41.

22 Zumwalt, *op. cit.*, pp. 24–25.

23 *Ibid.*, pp. 27, 57.

24 *Ibid.*, pp. 58–59.

25 *Ibid.*, pp. 38, 40. Doleman, Edgar *et al. The Vietnam Experience: Tools of War* (Boston, MA: Boston Publishing, 1984), p. 86.

26 Zumwald, *op. cit.*, p. 22.

27 *Ibid.*, pp. 28–31. Lanning, *op. cit.*, p. 114. A. Sweetland, "Rallying Potential Among the North Vietnamese Armed Forces," RAND RM-6375–1, Dec 1970, p. x.

28 Rottman, *op. cit.*, pp. 36–37. Lanning, *op. cit.*, pp. 101–05.

29 Rottman, *op. cit.*, pp. 33–36. Lanning, *op. cit.*, pp. 102–05.

30 Rottman, *op. cit.*, pp. 25–33, 48. Lanning, *op. cit.*, pp. 105–11. Doleman, *op. cit.*, pp. 92–95.

31 Rottman, *op. cit.*, pp. 21–25. *cf.* Emering, Edward. *Weapons and Field Gear of the North Vietnamese Army and Viet Cong* (Atglen, PA: Schiffer Publishing, 1998).

32 Rottman, *op. cit.*, pp. 34–36. Lanning, *op. cit.*, pp. 102–05.

33 Lanning, *op. cit.*, p. 102. Rottman, *op. cit.*, pp. 25, 30. Danner, *op. cit.*, p. 199.

34 Pike, *PAVN*, *op. cit.*, pp. 193, 196, 206. Rottman, *op. cit.*, p. 45.

35 Lanning, *op. cit.*, pp. 169–82. Rottman, *op. cit.*, pp. 47–59.

36 *cf.* Wilkins, Warren. *Grab Their Belts To Fight Them* (Annapolis, MD: Naval Institute Press, 2011), pp. 7–40.

37 "Casualties of 50 percent or higher were common." Rottman, *op. cit.*, pp. 54, 59. Doleman, *op. cit.*, pp. 92–95. Lanning, *op. cit.*, pp. 83–91, 261–62.

38 Lanning, *op. cit.*, p. 182. Humphries, James. *Through the Valley* (Boulder, CO: Lynne Rienner, 1999), p. 287. Rottman, *op. cit.*, p. 54.

39 Davidson, Phillip. *Vietnam At War* (Novato, CA: Presidio Press, 1988), p. 542. In 1966, the trip could be made in less than two weeks due to improvements to the Trail in 1965. Prados, John. *The Blood Road* (NY: John Wiley, 1999), p. 157. By 1968, it could be made in eleven days. Pike, Douglas. *War, Peace, and the Viet Cong* (Cambridge, MA: The M.I.T. Press, 1969), pp. 123, 139. Doyle, Edward *et al. The Vietnam Experience: The North* (Boston, MA: Boston Publishing, 1986), p. 120.

40 Humphries, *op. cit.*, p. 217. Sources differ on the organization of the 3rd Regiment and the 31st Regiment. Four sources state that the 3rd Regiment was part of the 2nd NVA Division, and the 31st Regiment was a separate, independent unit that was sometimes temporarily attached to the 2nd NVA Division: 1) the SRV history of the NVA; 2) the order of battle of the III MAF PERINTREP for 14–20 July 1968; 3) the 5th Special Forces Group Intelligence Estimate of 18 March 1968; and 4) the 1967 order of battle of the Americal Division. Two other sources claim the 31st Regiment was part of the 2nd NVA Division, and the 3rd Regiment was another name for the 31st Regiment: 1) the SRV history of the 2nd NVA Division; and 2) the U.S. Combined Intelligence Center Vietnam Order of Battle—1 May to 31 May 1968.

41 Westmoreland, *op. cit.*, pp. 236–39. Summers, Harry. *Historical Atlas of the Vietnam War, op. cit.*, pp. 128–29.

42 Chuong, Nguyen Huy; *Su Doan 2, Tap 1* (Danang, Socialist Republic of Vietnam; Second Division Party Committee and Headquarters; Danang Publishing House; 1989); p. 85 [translated by Merle Pribbenow].

43 *United States Military Assistance Command Vietnam Quarterly Evaluation, Jan–Mar 1968;* p. 8.

44 Danner, *op. cit.*, pp. 199–200. Lanning, *op. cit.*, pp. 173–75, 178–82. The NVA recruit captured by the Kham Duc patrol one day before the NVA attack had recently arrived in good health with a new haircut, new uniform, new pack and equipment, and a new AK-47 assault rifle.

45 Lanning, *op. cit.*, pp. 179–82. Danner, *op. cit.*, pp. 199–200.

46 Lanning, *op. cit.*, p. 181. The planning and preparation for the attacks on Kham Duc and Ngok Tavak necessarily would have been similar to the NVA procedures described in Danner and Lanning in notes 43 and 44.

47 Carpet bombing around Kham Duc for two days after the attack revealed 130 ammunition caches that produced a series of secondary explosions three to ten times larger than the bomb blasts. Gropman, Alan. *Airpower and the Airlift Evacuation of Kham Duc*, USAF Southeast Asia Monograph 7, Vol. V, Air War College, Maxwell AFB, AL (1979), p. 29.

48 Lanning, *op. cit.*, pp. 174–75.

49 Bamford, James. *Body of Secrets: Anatomy of the Ultra-Secret National Security Agency* (NY: AnchorBooks, 2002), pp. 337.

50 *Ibid.*, pp. 313–16, 323–25.

51 "By January 1968 NSA had placed Vietnam under a massive electronic microscope." "Hardly a signal could escape capture by one of the agency's antennas." *Ibid.*, p. 330.

52 *Ibid.*, pp. 317–37.

3

Kham Duc

"… never in the history of warfare have weather decisions played such an important role … [as at] Khe Sanh, the A Shau Valley, and Kham Duc …."

GEN CREIGHTON ABRAMS[1]

Kham Duc lies in a small valley in the long mountain range separating Vietnam from southern Laos. The Vietnamese call those peaks and high plateaus the Truong Son.[2] The U.S. military called their eastern side in Vietnam the Central Highlands. From high in the air the vast rainforest covering much of it looks like an undulating carpet of blue-green velvet. Beneath the overlapping crowns of trees, a maze of steep peaks and serrated ridges channel the frequent rains into rushing streams and tumbling waterfalls.

Faint shafts of pale sunlight filtered through the double and triple tree canopies dimly illuminate the green-black curtains of lush tropical foliage below. Myriad plant species, many of them gigantic, constantly struggle upward toward the hazy light. Cable-size liana vines coil tightly up massive teak, banyan, and mahogany trees, some more than 150 feet tall. Loops of flowering creeper vines interlace their towering trunks, and multicolored lichen balls decorate their massive branches. Air plants (epiphytes) living on the branches dangle their rope-like roots almost to the ground. Dark-green moss and light-green ferns adorn the trees' huge surface roots.

The pulsating cacophony of chirping, whirring insects is punctuated by squawking, whistling birds, hooting apes, and shrieking monkeys. Huge rats, scorpions, centipedes, roaches, and ants scurry in and under the soggy ground cover of fetid plant and animal refuse. Pythons and cobras slither through the shadowy undergrowth. Elephants browse in the dappled gloom, where tigers, leopards, and bears stalk deer, boar, water buffalo, and giant wild oxen (gaur).

The steamy air under the jungle canopy is debilitating. Sweat flows constantly and profusely, dehydrating body cells and leaching minerals from muscles. Malarial mosquitoes, biting gnats, and blood-sucking flies swarm in fiendish, humming clouds. Millions of thin, black leeches and grey ticks on the ground and bushes sense any warm-blooded animal nearby and drop or crawl frantically onto it. Wiggling through the smallest openings in clothing, they attach themselves imperceptibly to the skin, suck blood until grotesquely swollen, and often burst, smearing the host with its own blood.

In open areas direct sunlight and frequent rain produce fields of knife-edged grass over 10 feet tall, tree-size groves of bamboo, and nearly impenetrable thickets of thorny bushes. Solar radiation in the giant grass fields is even more stifling than under the jungle canopy, yet soon after sunset the dank mountain air becomes shivering cold. In the ominous darkness the fungus on fallen tree trunks, branches, and leaves glows with ghostly, blue-green bioluminescence.[3]

The weather in the Truong Son range is controlled by two annual monsoon seasons. For four or five months from April to November, the northeast monsoon winds blow east to west over the Gulf of Tonkin, accumulating water vapor. When the moisture-laden clouds reach northern Laos and north and central Vietnam, they rise, condense, and release torrential rain every afternoon and into the night. When it finally stops, everything drips until the next afternoon, when the daily deluge resumes.

The southwest monsoon is even more powerful. For four or five months between May and October, the winds blow west to east over the Gulf of Thailand. When the water-saturated clouds reach southern Laos and the delta of South Vietnam, they rise, condense, and release hammering sheets of rain every afternoon and often all night, flooding the Mekong Delta. Many mountain valleys experience the secondary weather effects of both annual monsoons.

Monsoon clouds often drift over parts of the Truong Son range and descend on the Vietnam side as dense, snow-white fog. It rolls down the jungle slopes like a slow-motion avalanche of whipped cream, burying the valleys in eerie whiteouts. In addition to descending clouds, the Truong Son range produces ground fog twice a day.

The harder, flatter, more open surfaces in the valleys absorb and release solar radiation faster than the steep, thickly vegetated hills do, and the morning sun heats the air in the valleys before that on the shaded slopes. When the warm, moist air in the valleys meets the cool, moist air on the slopes, it condenses into fog. As the air temperature on the slopes increases to that in the valleys, the fog gradually dissipates.

After sunset the flat valley surfaces release their accumulated solar radiation faster than the higher slopes do, and again ground fog forms. At night the fog dissipates, as the temperature on the slopes cools. In narrow valleys and ravines, where direct sunlight is blocked by hills or thick vegetation, the fog stays on the ground much longer.

Ground fog combined with descending clouds can produce overcasts 10,000 feet high. Such "zero-zero" weather (no cloud ceiling and no distance visibility) causes vertigo in pilots flying visually and makes it impossible to distinguish the air from the ground. Even in the dry season, at lower elevations misty, drizzling rain; persistent, low overcasts; and occasional, brief thundershowers are common in the Truong Son valleys, sometimes negating visual flight for weeks on end.[4] Some small valleys also have their own unpredictable micro-climates.

Kham Duc was in such a valley. In May 1968 it was the most remote and isolated U.S. outpost in I Corps.[5] Forty-five air miles west of Chu Lai on the coast, 15 air miles east of the invisible border with Laos, and 12 air miles north of the invisible border with II Corps, it lay in an oval valley 2 miles long by 1.5 miles wide at 1,100 feet elevation and was surrounded by jungle-covered hills 3,000–5,000 feet high. A tall ridge to the west and a taller hill to the east overlooked the little valley, and lower ridgelines overlooked its northeast and southwest ends.

Its location was the unplanned result of incremental evolution around an airstrip built years before for different purposes (see Appendix). The camp was lightly fortified, but was not built for a sustained defense against any modern military force. It was beyond the range of U.S. artillery and could only be supplied and defended by air, but its air support was dependent on its undependable weather.

Unlike any other SF camp in I Corps, Kham Duc had a 6,200-foot, asphalt-paved airstrip with an intermittent white stripe down the center. Lying northeast to southwest, it was 300 feet wide with cleared areas 300 feet and 500 feet beyond each end. The ridge at the northeast end had a wide notch cut into it by a bulldozer to facilitate the takeoffs and landings of large planes. A ramp at the mid-point on the western side of the airstrip led to an aircraft parking area (tarmac) of 40 yards by 50 yards.

The main SF camp was on the northeast side of the airstrip 200 feet east of its mid-point. The camp's inner perimeter was 450 feet by 900 feet, and its outer perimeter extended another 60 feet on each side. Beyond the outer perimeter, the vegetation on each side was cleared for between 60 and 200 feet. About 100 yards beyond the camp's eastern perimeter the terrain dropped off steeply into the heavily wooded ravine of the shallow Dak Se River (see graphics in photo section).

The camp's outer defenses were four wire barriers. The first was a double-apron barbed wire fence; the second was three coils of concertina wire; the third was foot-high sections of tangle-foot wire mounted on metal stakes; and the fourth was a single coil of concertina wire with a series of claymore mines spaced inside the coils.[6]

In 1968, all the buildings looked old and shabby. Their wooden frames were built on concrete slabs with tin roofs and walls of tin, plywood, or rattan on cinder block bases. Tin-covered wooden frames suspended over the screened windows could be lowered to keep out the rain. A dirt road ran through the middle of the camp from the front gate to the fenced-off rear third of it.

On the north side of the road were the sleeping quarters, eating quarters, medical bunker, latrine, and underground Tactical Operations Center (TOC) of the SF team and their ten Nung bodyguards (See Appendix). Also on that side of the road were the sleeping quarters, eating quarters, and latrine of the CIDG recon platoon and one of the CIDG companies. On the south side of the road were the sleeping quarters, eating quarters, and latrine of the other two CIDG companies and the sleeping quarters, eating quarters, underground TOC, medical bunker, and latrine of the LLDB (Vietnamese Special Forces) team.

The inner defenses of the camp began with zig-zag perimeter trenches about 4 feet deep around the camp. Their earthen walls were fortified with corrugated tin sheets held in place by steel engineer stakes laced together with wire and topped with sandbags. Bunkers with reinforced overhead cover and firing ports for .30 caliber machine guns were spaced along all the trenches.

A .50 caliber machine gun, 106mm recoilless rifle, 4.2inch mortar, and two 81mm mortars covered the western, northern, and southern perimeter trenches. The eastern perimeter trench had a center bunker with a .50 caliber machine gun and a 60mm mortar, and each end bunker had a .30 caliber machine gun.

Across a steep, thickly wooded gully south of the SF camp was a smaller camp about a quarter the size of the SF camp for CIDG trainees. In May 1968 it was temporarily occupied by sixty trainees of the 12th Mobile Strike Force (Mike Force) Company in Danang commanded by SF First Lieutenant (1LT) Paul Portinho. North of the SF camp on the same side of the runway was a large cleared area used as a firing range and hand-grenade range.

A small shack between the firing range and the SF camp housed an MRN-5 FM radio homing beacon connected to a 20-foot wire antenna stretched between two poles. It was maintained by three Air Force technicians, who lived in the SF camp. It helped pilots locate the little valley in the surrounding jungle, but did not enable them to land in zero-visibility conditions.[7]

Across the airstrip from the main SF camp and north of the tarmac was a third camp unofficially named Camp Conroy.[8] In May 1968 a 122-man Army engineer company was temporarily quartered in it. Next to it were a motor pool and a fuel storage area for the camp's generators, where two jeeps and a three-quarter ton truck were parked.

Five observation posts (OPs) numbered 1, 3, 5, 6, and 7 were occupied by CIDG squads of six to eight men. Those formerly numbered 2 and 4 were no longer occupied. Four of them were on hilltops west, southwest, north, and northwest of the airstrip. The fifth was on the edge of the river gulch east of the SF camp overlooking the shallow Dak Se River.

According to SF numbering, OP1 was on a high ridge due west of the airstrip and 400 yards above it; OP 3 was on a hill 200 yards southwest of the south end of the airstrip and 120 yards above it; OP 5 was on a hill 800 yards northwest of the airstrip and 100 yards above the village; OP 6 was 150 yards southwest of the SF camp on the edge of the river gulch; and OP 7 was on a hill 200 yards northwest of the north end of the airstrip and 100 yards above it.

The rotating CIDG squads on the OPs had PRC-25 FM radios to communicate with the LLDB team in the camp, but they were not expected to defend the OPs in the event of an attack. Kham Duc had never been seriously threatened before, and the CIDG troops did not consider their leisurely OP duty even unpleasant, much less dangerous.

In May 1968 the Kham Duc CIDG battalion had 266 troops: ninety-four in one company, ninety-one in a second, and eighty-one in a third. They were all ethnic lowland Vietnamese, not Montagnards, and were sent there under guard from jails in Danang, Hue, and Nha Trang.[9] They were not real soldiers, did not consider themselves soldiers, and had no loyalty to anyone. In an attack the best that could be expected of them was that they would not shoot at the SF team, the team's ten Nung bodyguards, or the twenty presumably loyal CIDG troops in the recon platoon, while attempting to desert.[10]

Northwest of the airstrip was a squalid little village with 272 Vietnamese civilians in thirty to forty crude wooden buildings. Most of them were the extended families of the CIDG troops in the SF camp. A few small merchants and tradesmen also lived there with their families. The SF team members occasionally ate at a little restaurant in the village, and a few villagers worked part-time in the camp as cooks and maids. The A-team (SF Operational Detachment A) knew that some of the villagers might be VC agents, but the SF medics treated the minor medical problems of all of them, and the relations between the villagers and the SF team were friendly.[11]

On May 1, 1968, the CO of the A-team, Captain (CPT) Robert Henderson III, completed his assignment at Kham Duc and was replaced by CPT Christopher Silva. The new executive officer, 1LT Eugene Bernhardt, and the new operations NCO, Master Sergeant (MSG) James Duncan, had also recently arrived.

The other members of the SF A-team were: Sergeant First Class (SFC) Richard Gill, the intelligence NCO; SFC John Lumpkin, the heavy weapons NCO; SFC Melvin Dodge, the senior medic; SFC Sidney Sheeler, the senior communications NCO; Staff Sergeant (SSG) Houston (Mac) Woodard, the light weapons NCO; and Sergeant (SGT) Robert Aycock, the junior communications NCO. There was no junior medic, but Woodard had enough medical training to serve as an assistant medic, if needed.[12]

There was no permanently assigned civic action officer or engineer NCO. With so few civilians in the village and no permanent Montagnard villages in the Kham Duc Tactical Area of Responsibility (TAOR), there was no need for either specialist.[13] The ten Nung bodyguards for the A-team doubled as instructors for the CIDG trainees.

In the fenced-off rear third of the camp was the covert SOG launch site (see Appendix). It had an underground TOC (Tactical Operations Center), sleeping quarters, eating quarters, and a latrine for the U.S. troops and separate sleeping quarters, eating quarters, and a latrine for the indigenous troops.

The entrance to the SOG TOC was down a short stairway in a tunnel to a steel door. Behind it were two CONEX containers[14] welded together to form two rooms. In the front room were ten folding metal chairs for the briefings of the helicopter pilots and the three Americans on each recon team prior to each insertion. Behind a black curtain that covered the entire wall was a highly detailed map of the Laotian Panhandle west of Kham Duc. In the back room were several kinds of radios, two folding metal chairs, and two metal cots.

In May 1968 only seven resident SOG men were stationed at Kham Duc. The OIC (officer-in-charge) of the launch site was SF 1LT James McLeroy. The operations NCO and medic was SF SSG M. C. Windley. The two SF communication NCOs were SF SSG L. B. Jones and SF SGT Talmadge Alphin. Three other SF NCOs were assigned there temporarily for maintenance and logistics chores.

At that time ninety-one SOG troops—nineteen American and seventy-two indigenous—were in training or preparing for cross-border missions. SOG's elite indigenous recon-commando troops were not CIDG and had no contact with the camp's CIDG troops, whom the SOG troops despised as a cowardly, treacherous rabble.

Kham Duc's only strategic potential was its role in one of Westmoreland's top-secret plans to win the war. He wanted to destroy the Ho Chi Minh Trail bases and the thousands of NVA troops in Laos with a multi-divisional, airmobile invasion of the Laotian Panhandle from the five northern provinces of I Corps. His plan to accomplish that strategic objective was code-named Operation *El Paso*, and its first phase was codenamed Operation *York*.[15]

In 1967 he secretly ordered the improvement of several remote airstrips near the Laotian border of I Corps as staging and logistics bases for the many aircraft required for Operation *York*. In Quang Tin Province the obvious base was Kham Duc, but its old airstrip needed extensive renovation. It also needed concrete platforms and protective revetments for two AF vans with sophisticated navigation equipment to enable all-weather, twenty-four-hour air operations. The project was codenamed *Santa Barbara* and assigned to the 70th Combat Engineer Battalion at Pleiku.[16]

The engineer battalion delegated it to their A Company, and scheduled it to begin in January 1968. It had to be postponed until April, however, because the C-130 transport planes needed to bring all the troops, equipment, and construction materials to Kham Duc were then supporting Khe Sanh, which had priority over all other U.S. air activities in Vietnam.

The A Company headquarters group arrived at Kham Duc on April 9, and the rest of the company arrived over the next seven days. Five more days were needed to bring in their heavy machines and construction materials. For eight consecutive days near the end of April no planes could land at Kham Duc due to constant low overcasts.[17] Such weather occurred often there and was especially likely in May, a transitional month for the southwest monsoon rains in Laos.

The A Company troops were officially designated combat engineers. They were excellent military engineer troops, but most of them had little or no combat training beyond introductory rifle marksmanship in their two-month basic course. Each man was issued a 7.62mm M-14 rifle, and each of their four platoons received a 7.62mm M-60 machine gun and a 40mm M-79 grenade launcher.

For their Kham Duc mission they obtained three .50 caliber machine guns, an 81mm mortar, and ammunition for them from one of the infantry units in Pleiku. The company First Sergeant, a World War II infantry veteran, taught some of the engineer troops how to fire the .50 caliber machine guns and taught a few others the basic rudiments of firing the 81mm mortar.[18]

Their main tasks at Kham Duc were to fill the holes in the airstrip with soil cement, seal the airstrip surface with asphalt, and resurface the taxiway and tarmac with asphalt. Their other tasks were to build a 100-foot by 72-foot concrete pad and protective revetment for an Air Force GCA (Ground Control Approach) radar module; a 50-foot by 36-foot concrete pad and protective revetment for an AF TACAN (Tactical Air Control and Navigation) radar module; and an aircraft parking area (tarmac) at the northeast end of the airstrip large enough for three C-130 transport planes.[19]

They began work on April 15 to upgrade the bunkers and trenches around Camp Conroy, replace its rundown buildings, and build new latrines and showers. By May 10, they had repaired most of the airstrip, built half of the new tarmac and taxiway on its north end, dug new drainage ditches on the west side around the old tarmac, and built concrete pads and protective revetments for the AF vans with GCA and TACAN equipment.[20]

Kham Duc was chosen as the first launch site for SOG's clandestine, cross-border reconnaissance and commando operations in 1965 mainly because of its long, paved airstrip and its proximity to the Laotian border. The original SOG planners knew that their ground operations would depend on helicopters, which require visual flying conditions, yet the only weather they seem to have considered in selecting Kham Duc was the rainfall pattern in the area. They apparently did not realize that the critical weather factor for visual flight is not rain, but visibility.

They evidently assumed that the nominal "dry" season in the mountains was similar to the actual dry season in the lowlands. They apparently failed to understand that fog, haze, and low clouds do not always produce rain, but they always make visual flight in mountainous terrain potentially fatal.

On the first SOG mission from Kham Duc in October 1965, weather alone cost the lives of three U.S. officers and three South Vietnamese air crewmen. A CH-34 Sikorsky helicopter with an SF captain and a Vietnamese crew and a Cessna 0–1 FAC plane with an AF major and a Marine captain disappeared into clouds that were too low to fly under and too high to fly over. The triple-canopy jungle was so thick that no one could see where the two aircraft fell into it.[21]

In July 1966, SOG finally realized that Kham Duc's weather would rarely have the visual flight conditions necessary to reliably launch and recover recon teams with helicopters. A new launch site was established at Dak To SF camp south of Kham Duc in northern II Corps, but Kham Duc was still used occasionally as a launch site in the few months when its weather was relatively stable. SOG occasionally conducted a two-week course in clandestine jungle patrolling at Kham Duc for new recon team leaders. The course was later formalized, increased to three weeks, and moved to SOG's main training base at camp Long Thanh northeast of Saigon.[22]

SOG's lack of institutional memory resulted in Kham Duc's selection again in January 1968 as the launch site for SOG's new FOB (Forward Operating Base) 4. In addition to Kham Duc's weather disadvantages, FOB 4 did not have an aircraft unit permanently attached to it and did not command the aircraft temporarily assigned to it. Most pilots and crews did not want to stay overnight at Kham Duc. The isolation under its grey, drizzling skies was depressing, and the dank quarters, dull food, and lack of entertainment beyond an occasional film were substandard compared to their much more comfortable bases on or near the coast.

If the weather at Kham Duc was bad, the helicopters could not land. Even if it was good, the time required for them to fly from the coast to Kham Duc and refuel there before flying into Laos to extract a recon team reduced the survival chances of that team. The turn-around time for the helicopters was unnecessarily lengthened by the lack of a high-speed, electric fuel pump. Kham Duc had only one slow, mechanical pump.

Another negative aspect of the weather was its effect on teams forced to wait indefinitely to begin one of the most dangerous ground missions of the war. Just before their launch, their minds and bodies were pumped with adrenaline. When their launch was indefinitely delayed day after day because of constantly unfavorable weather for visual flight, their emotional readiness for their extremely high-risk missions inevitably began to erode.[23]

Being forced to wait in that gloomy, mildewed place with nothing to do but sit, talk, and drink beer (in many, but not all, cases) caused some of them to brood on the extreme danger of their pending mission. They knew that the same weather delays that prevented the helicopters from inserting them could prevent those helicopters from extracting them, when surrounded by NVA troops or running for their lives.[24] They also knew that a life-or-death tactical emergency was a realistic possibility on every cross-border mission.

The original purpose of the Op 35 (SOG Operation 35) missions was clandestine point or area reconnaissance to collect intelligence data on the Trail network and interdict it in various ways. In May 1968, however, it seemed from the perspective of the Kham Duc launch officer that the purpose of those missions had gradually changed. He had begun to suspect that their unstated but actual function had become attracting and concentrating NVA forces for mass attrition by air firepower.

The use of cross-border recon teams as, in effect, bait for mass NVA attrition was never even mentioned, much less acknowledged, by anyone in SOG. Nevertheless, the veteran recon NCOs knew that something had unquestionably changed for the worse in Op 35.[25] It seemed to be the result of two circumstances largely beyond the control of the FOB commanders.

The first was the constantly increasing NVA activity on the Trail in eastern Laos and Cambodia. The virtual annihilation of most of the VC combat units in the Tet battles of 1968 had forced the NVA to escalate their use of the Trail network to send more North Vietnamese troops to replace their VC losses. The second was increasing pressure from higher headquarters to cause maximum attrition in the NVA forces in Laos with maximum use of air power and minimum use of U.S. troops. Ground teams were necessary to draw large numbers of NVA troops out of their expertly camouflaged locations and concentrate them for mass destruction with air firepower.

The higher headquarters seemed not to know or care about three operational problems for the SOG teams created by that strategy. First, the original standard operating procedures (SOPs) for deploying SOG cross-border teams were not indefinitely scalable. The more their missions increased, the less the original SOPs for carefully training, briefing, inserting, and supporting the teams could be followed. By 1968, SOG was taking SF men with no combat experience and minimum recon training and inserting them into extremely dangerous areas.[26]

Second, often not enough aircraft were available to support several teams in simultaneous emergencies. Teams urgently requesting extraction often had to be told that no helicopters were available, because they were all trying to extract other teams in similar or worse emergencies.[27] Third, by 1968 the NVA had learned everything they needed to know about SOG recon teams.

Using that knowledge, they trained elite NVA counter-recon teams to aggressively hunt the SOG teams, often with tracker dogs.[28] It was also suspected and later confirmed that a "mole" in the headquarters of SOG's South Vietnamese counterpart unit in Saigon was passing on to covert NVA agents all the information they received from their briefings at SOG headquarters.[29]

Increasingly, many cross-border recon missions were doomed before they were launched. In some areas the helicopters inserting the teams were destroyed by NVA anti-aircraft artillery before they could land. Immediately after leaving their insertion helicopter, many teams were ambushed or stalked by large NVA troop units, who seemed to be waiting for them there. Yet Op 35 kept sending the same teams back into the same areas, not to discover where large numbers of NVA troops were, but knowing where they were from recent insertion or extraction attempts.[30]

The FOB operations officers knew that putting teams back into those areas was highly unlikely to produce any new intelligence, because the only thing most of them could do was run, hide, and fight for their lives until they were rescued, if possible. If they survived that mission, they would often be sent back to the same place to run the same lethal gauntlet again a few days later.[31] In their desperate attempts to escape they would direct devastating air strikes on large numbers of pursuing or surrounding NVA troops.[32] As passive bait for mass NVA attrition, they usually accomplished their unstated mission, whether they survived it or not.

Responsibility for the defense of the SF/CIDG camps in I Corps was originally assigned to the III MAF (Marine Amphibious Force), but in late 1967 responsibility for the seven SF camps south of Danang was transferred to the 23rd Infantry Division (American)[33] at Chu Lai on the coast. The American's contingency plan for the reinforcement and defense of those camps was codenamed Operation *Golden Valley*.

The concept of the operation was based on two unexamined and unrealistic assumptions: first, that the attacking force would not be larger than about two NVA battalions; and second, that enough American troops would be available at any time to defend any camp from a force that size. For an isolated camp under attack by two reinforced NVA regiments in adverse weather for close air support, neither assumption was realistic. They were even less realistic for evacuating under fire all the troops and civilians in and around such a remote camp.

The American Division assigned the defense of the SF camps in southern I Corps to the 198th LIB (Light Infantry Brigade), which delegated it to the 1st Battalion of their 46th [Regiment]. On March 31, the CO of the 1/46/198 visited Kham Duc to discuss the reinforcement plan with the SF team. He then briefed the Assistant CG (Commanding General) of the American Division on the plan and met with the general's staff to discuss ways to more realistically revise it.[34]

On April 1, he made a reconnaissance flight of the area with the battalion's assistant S-3 (operations officer), S-2 (intelligence officer), Artillery Liaison Officer, and A Company CO. After inspecting Kham Duc's defenses, he revised the reinforcement plan for Operation *Golden Valley*, but only superficially.[35]

After their visits to Kham Duc, the battalion operations officer, Major (MAJ) Walter Sanders, and his predecessor, Lieutenant Colonel (LTC) Elbert Fuller, concluded that no realistic defense plan for it was possible.[36] Regardless of how the Golden Valley plan was modified, a brigade-size force could not be kept available to quickly reinforce Kham Duc prior to a major NVA attack. After the attack began, it might be too late to land such reinforcements, even if they happened to be available then.

The revised Golden Valley plan that was approved by Major General (MG) Samuel Koster, the Americal Division CG, on May 4, 1968, ignored three critical facts.[37] First, an all-weather, 24-hour defense would require constant close air support often in zero-visibility conditions, which would require the prior installation of protected TACAN and GCA navigation systems near the airstrip.

Second, a sustained defense of the camp from a multi-regimental NVA attack would require three infantry battalions with attached artillery batteries supported by an external artillery and logistics base. Third, the infantry battalions and their attached artillery batteries would need to have dug-in positions on fortified high ground around the valley, camp, and airstrip before a major attack.

The main problem with the *Golden Valley* plan was not that the potential reinforcements were inadequate for the size of the potential NVA forces threatening Kham Duc, but that their use for that purpose was unrealistic. The only way an American brigade could defend Kham Duc from a major NVA attack would be to make that mission its first priority, which was impossible. Its primary mission was defending the strategic terrain in the heavily populated lowland areas. If one of the American brigades was removed from its operational area, the NVA/VC forces would quickly move back into that area.

On April 10, a Vietnamese CH–34 helicopter from FOB 4 en route to Kham Duc was shot down a mile north of the camp, killing five recon team leaders and a Vietnamese crewman.[38] The SOG and Mike Force troops continued to train in and around Kham Duc, but by the end of April the NVA forces surrounding the camp were shooting at the helicopters frequently, making it too dangerous for them to continue using it for the insertions and extractions of SOG recon teams.

On May 1, the Kham Duc launch officer, having no more launches to coordinate and supervise there, returned to FOB 4. His Vietnam assignment was scheduled to end in fifteen days, and his mind was already back in "the World."[39]

After the evening meal on May 6, the CO of FOB 4, LTC Lauren Overby, casually told him to return to Kham Duc early the next morning. McLeroy, naively assuming it would be for some brief administrative chore, asked Overby what he wanted him to do there. Overby said he wanted him to get the SOG troops ready for an imminent mass attack by the huge NVA forces surrounding the camp.

McLeroy was stunned. He knew that the transitional monsoon weather at Kham Duc in May could prevent close tactical air support, and without it, a mass NVA attack would make Kham Duc a Vietnamese Alamo. Just as he thought he was about to survive his Vietnam combat tour, he suddenly felt doomed.

He knew that if he objected to such a mission only ten days before he was due to go home, his avuncular CO might not order him to do it. He also knew that Overby did not expect him to object to the order, and he did not. He was secretly terrified by his last mission at Kham Duc, but grimly resolved to do his best to accomplish it in the forlorn hope that it would not be the last one of his life.

In the long ride from Danang to Kham Duc in a UH-1 helicopter he was the only passenger, and in the cool air of the higher altitude he stared down at the slowly evolving landscape below. As it transitioned from the emerald-green rice paddies of the coastal plain to the brown and green scrub jungle of the foothills, he began to plan his preparations for the looming NVA attack. In his Vietnam Pre-Mission course at Fort Bragg, the defense of SF camps was stressed, and he had applied those lessons for five months at CPT Shelton's SF camp the previous year.

He knew that most of the young SOG men had little or no training or experience in defending an SF camp in a major attack. Their operations in enemy territory were so hazardous that when they returned to their launch site or FOB, they tended to have a false sense of security. The attitude of most of them about having to defend it in the unlikely (to them) event of a major attack was rather lackadaisical.

Apart from the SOG troops temporarily training and rehearsing there, Kham Duc's internal defenses were negligible. The A-team's only reliable defensive force was at most 100 men: the ten SF men, their ten Nung bodyguards, the twenty presumably loyal CIDG troops in the recon platoon, and possibly the sixty Mike Force trainees. The combat performance of the engineer troops was uncertain. They were all good soldiers, but they were not trained for infantry combat against a major NVA force, and their camp was not as well armed as the SF camp was.

The defenders of the SF camp's eastern perimeter were about 100 SOG troops. Each of the four recon teams had three SF NCOs and six to eight indigenous (Montagnard, Nung, or Vietnamese) troops. The Hatchet Force platoon of forty-five Nung troops was commanded by SF Second Lieutenant (2LT) Lee Purdy and three SF NCOs. The second three-man infiltration team of NVA defectors was commanded by CPT Bud Williams and SFC Ken Greenwood.[40]

Without reinforcements the effective defensive force in the SF camp was about 200 men: thirty-four American SF troops and 160–170 indigenous troops. The SOG troops were all extremely well-armed and mentally prepared for heavy, close combat, but their only hope of surviving a sustained attack by an overwhelming NVA force was constant, close tactical air support, which required consistently clear weather for visual flight.

McLeroy was not concerned about the veteran SF NCOs with the Hatchet Force and their CO, 2LT Purdy, who was eagerly cooperative. He was also not concerned about the cooperation of CPT Bud Williams, with whom he had a cordial relationship from his previous launch officer training at FOB 2 near Kontum. Like himself, Williams was a Ranger and fully appreciated the importance of detailed preparations, repetitious rehearsals, and rigorous inspections.

McLeroy's main concern was a potential command problem with some of the young recon NCOs. Their SOG lifestyle was radically unconventional compared to that of most U.S. military units, and their operations in enemy territory were virtually autonomous. They were not accustomed to taking orders from junior officers who were not in their direct chain of command.

They had only seen McLeroy in his semi-administrative role at Kham Duc, knew nothing else about him, and had not been told by their own chain of command that he had the authority to order them to do some unpleasant things they had not had to do before and might not understand the need for. If one of them refused to obey one his orders, McLeroy might not be able to enforce it in that unusual situation, and his command presence with them would be diminished or lost.

To avoid a potential insubordination problem, he decided to issue his instructions through his veteran operations NCO, SSG M. C. Windley. McLeroy knew the young recon men would comply with any orders relayed through Windley, because he had special credibility and status with them. A short, massively built man with a perpetual smile and a mellow Virginia accent, he was a multi-year Vietnam veteran, a highly skilled and experienced medic, and an equally skilled light weapons expert.[41]

He was also a fearless warrior, who had been on several SOG cross-border missions and relished the adrenalin rush of high-risk combat. To relieve the boredom of his isolated life at Kham Duc he sometimes voluntarily replaced one of the helicopter door gunners on hazardous insertions and extractions of recon teams in Laos.

An "old soldier" with prior years in both the 82nd Airborne Division and 101st Airborne Division, Windley was familiar with the delegation relationship between an infantry company CO and his company First Sergeant. McLeroy knew he could rely on Windley to professionally accept his orders, effectively convey them to the SOG troops, and informally handle any compliance problems with the young recon men.

As the scrub jungle foothills gradually morphed into the rain forest mountains, McLeroy turned his thoughts to the specific actions needed to defend SOG's vulnerable eastern perimeter. The first time he went to Kham Duc and saw that perimeter, he intuitively knew that if the camp was ever attacked, the main assault would come from the deep, heavily vegetated river gulch a hundred yards east of the SOG section of the camp. It was a text-book example of an ideal infantry avenue of approach, offering cover, concealment, and target proximity.

The only obstacles to an attack from it on the eastern perimeter were a few wire barriers, some claymore mines, a deep trench, and three bunkers with overhead cover. The end bunkers of the trench had .30

caliber machine guns, and the center bunker had a .50 caliber machine gun with a 60mm mortar behind it. With only about a hundred reliable shooters sleeping near the eastern perimeter, it was highly vulnerable to a surprise night attack by an NVA battalion.

Charging from the river gulch before any air support could reach Kham Duc, they could quickly overrun the sleeping SOG troops and seize the eastern perimeter trench. Once they had intermingled with the defenders, U.S. planes would not fire into the camp for fear of killing any surviving American and CIDG troops. From that protected position they could provide fire support for more NVA troops charging into the camp behind them.

When the helicopter landed at Kham Duc, McLeroy went to the SOG operations bunker and asked his two communication NCOs, SSG L. B. Jones and SGT Talmadge Alphin, if either of them could draw. One of them said he had some draftsman training. McLeroy told him to go out to the eastern perimeter trench, measure it, note the location of the three bunkers, then draw an accurate diagram of the trench on some kind of large, portable surface.

The NCO returned with the measurements and a white poster board, on which he had sketched a detailed outline of the trench and its three machine-gun bunkers. McLeroy called a meeting of all the unit leaders, showed them their positions in the trench, and told them to place there all the ammunition, food, and water they would need to sleep and fight in the trench for three days.

He informed them that, if anything happened to him, SSG Windley would be his second in command. In SOG it was not unusual for a higher-ranking man to be temporarily subordinate to a lower-ranking man with special skills or more experience for a given operation. If McLeroy became unable to command the defense of that perimeter for any reason, he considered Windley the most competent man to do so. CPT Williams, 2LT Purdy, and the senior SF NCOs at the meeting understood that fact and did not object to it.

He told them the attack would begin at night, and they and their troops had to be able to get into their assigned positions in the trench quickly and efficiently in the dark. He said Windley would meet each

unit at their barracks that afternoon and walk them and their troops to
their positions in the trench on the exact routes they were to follow at
night. He told them there would be a rehearsal that night, when they
would walk their troops on the same routes to the same trench positions
in the dark and spend the night in the trench.[42]

That night, May 7, Windley checked each unit to be sure they were in
their places with all their gear. On May 8 they rested in their barracks and
reorganized their equipment. Every man had been issued a steel helmet
and a protective vest, which they normally did not wear. Windley passed
the word that there would be a full-speed, surprise drill that night. It
went smoothly, and they slept in the trench again.

McLeroy continued to sleep in the underground TOC to monitor the
radios and respond to frequent requests from FOB 4 for status reports.
He also wanted to keep a physical separation between himself and the
SOG troops until he was actually needed in the trench to avoid the idle
familiarity that tempts some subordinates to become disrespectful. He
told Windley to radio him at the first sign of a ground attack, when he
would immediately join them in the trench.

Operation *Delaware*, a large airmobile assault 50 miles north of Kham
Duc, was planned for late April. Air Force weather forecasters predicted a
short period then as the last opportunity for visual helicopter operations
before the arrival of the annual southwest monsoon in nearby Laos.[43] A
detailed weather forecast was part of Westmoreland's briefing for every
major operation,[44] and he knew that May is the transitional month for
the southwest monsoon. He was also well aware of the visibility problems
in the A Shau Valley at that time and knew that Kham Duc is subject to
the same unpredictable weather in May.

The SF men at Kham Duc wondered why there was no decision from
their headquarters to either reinforce them heavily for the imminent NVA
attack or else evacuate them with the CIDG troops and village civilians,
while there was still time to do so. They knew that if the weather ever
prevented transport planes from landing and ground-attack planes from
providing constant, close air support, they could not survive a major
NVA attack.

They assumed that whether they were to be reinforced or evacuated,
it would have to be before the attack began. It did not occur to them

that Westmoreland might not share that critical assumption and might be willing to gamble their lives on Kham Duc's unpredictable weather. Like a rigged coin toss, the implied wager seemed to be, "Heads, he wins; tails, we lose."

Notes

1 Quoted in Winters, Harold. *Battling the Elements* (Baltimore, MD: Johns Hopkins University Press, 1998), p. 72.

2 Truong Son is archaic Chinese for Long Mountains. On French-language maps it is called the Chaine Annamitique. On English-language maps it is called the Annamite Cordillera.

3 The descriptions of the geography, flora, and fauna are partly based on: Ayensu, Edward (ed.). *The Land and Wildlife of Tropical Asia* (NY: Time-Life Books, 1975), pp. 20–21, 24–25, 51–63, 76–77, 109–16, 143–55; and on Ripley, Dillon. *Jungles* (NY: Crown, 1980), pp. 8–13, 30–41, 44–51, 52–77, 122–23, 126–27, 140–43, 182–83. They are also based on the personal observations of both co-authors, including McLeroy's five months of periodic combat patrolling in the jungles of Quang Ngai Province as a member of SF team A-104 (Ha Thanh) from June to December 1967, and Sanders' occasional heliborne psychological operations near Kham Duc from April to October 1970.

4 The weather descriptions are partly based on: Winters *et al., op. cit.*, pp. 5, 45–46, 64–68, 108. They are also based on the co-authors' own observations, including McLeroy's residence at Kham Duc from March to May 1968 and Sanders' occasional heliborne psychological operations near Kham Duc from April to October 1970.

5 Latitude: 15 degrees, 25 minutes, 48 seconds North; Longitude: 107 degrees, 48 minutes, 00 seconds East.

6 Double-apron is interconnected barbed wire slanting downward from the middle of the fence at a 90-degree angle to the ground to impede access to the top of the fence. Concertina is coiled, expandable, steel wire loops with razor-like blades. Tangle-foot is barbed wire strung in a web pattern near the ground to cause anyone walking through it to stumble. Claymores are plastic, convex, directional surface mines packed with C-4 explosive and 700 steel balls. When exploded by manual or time-delay fuses, the C-4 sprays the steel balls in a lethal, fan-shaped pattern.

7 The MRN-5 locater beacon was maintained by three airmen from the 366th Tactical Fighter Wing in Danang: MSG Teddy Reiser, Airman Mel Lawhun, and Airman Bill Dean.

8 It was named in memory of SF MSG Paul Conroy, Jr, who was killed there in a 1967 training accident. Steve Sherman's archive of U.S. Army Special Forces personnel and units in SE Asia (Houston, TX: Radix Press), Sherman1@flash.net.

9   Henderson, Robert. "Monthly Operational Summary for April 1968, Camp Kham Duc", Detachment A-105, 5th Special Forces Group (Abn). Henderson interviews by McLeroy, December 21, 1995, and May 23, 1997, San Antonio, TX. Henderson interview by Sanders, September 10, 2009, in San Antonio, TX.

10 "Most of our strikers [CIDG troops at Kham Duc] were juvenile delinquents … recruited out of the Saigon jails." Morris, Jim. *War Story* (NY: Dell, 1979), p. 150. "The Vietnamese sent only their outcasts, when the Special Forces imported strike forces into … the new frontier compounds." "[The CIDG border camps] were garrisoned by dragooned city toughs from the waterfronts of Hue and Danang." Stanton, Shelby. *Green Berets At War* (Novato, CA: Presidio Press, 1985), p. 66. "The mayors of Hue and Danang … [provided] forces of teenage hoodlums … scraped off the waterfront." Simpson, Charles. *Inside the Green Berets* (Novato, CA: Presidio Press, 1983), p. 109. In June 1967 nine Mike Force troops in training went to the village, got drunk, and started a verbal altercation with some CIDG troops. The SF CO and the LLDB CO ordered them to return to the Mike Force camp, but they refused and incited two Mike Force platoons to shoot at the CIDG troops. The CIDG troops in the camp returned their fire, and when order was finally restored, four Mike Force and two CIDG troops were dead, and nine Mike Force troops and one CIDG were wounded. Form 173 from CO, Co. C, 5th SFGA Da Nang to CO, 5th SFGA Nha Trang and CG III MAF Da Nang, Attn G-3; "Subject: Incident at Kham Duc, June 13, 1967."

11 The descriptions of Kham Duc are based on McLeroy's residence there in 1968. They are also based on Henderson, Robert. "Monthly Operational Summary for April, 1968," *op. cit.*; and McLeroy's and Sanders's interviews of six former members of SF A-team A-105 (with their ranks in May 1968): CPT Robert Henderson, MSG James Duncan, SFC Richard Gill, SFC John Lumpkin, SSG Houston (Mac) Woodard, and SGT Robert Aycock.

12 *Ibid.*

13 *Ibid.* The SF team at Kham Duc coped with the gloomy boredom of their isolation by teaching some of the CIDG and LLDB troops to play softball with them. They also adopted various pets, including a little Mongrel dog they affectionately named Shithead.

14 CONEX means Container Express, an 8' × 8' × 20' steel cargo box with a steel door.

15 Westmoreland, William. *A Soldier Reports* (Garden City, NY: Doubleday, 1976), pp. 272, 314, 318.

16 Headquarters, 70th Engineer Battalion (Combat) (Army), "Operational Report of 70th Engineer Battalion (A) for Period Ending 30 April 1968," RCS CSFOR-65 (RI), April 30, 1968.

17 Webber, Paul B., 26th Military History Detachment, Combat Support After Action Interview Report, "Upgrading KHAM DUC Air Field (Operation Santa Barbara)," July 24, 1968.

18 Waldo, Daniel. "End of Tour Interview", conducted by MAJ Paul B. Webber, 26th Military History Detachment, June 18, 1968.

19   *Ibid.*

20   *Ibid.*

21   Plaster, John. *SOG* (NY: Simon & Schuster, 1997), pp. 33–37.

22   Gillespie, Robert. *Black Ops, Vietnam* (Annapolis, MD: Naval Institute Press, 2011), pp. 52, 65, 79.

23   "[For] a week, we just sat beside the airstrip, apprehensions and premonitions growing.""I grew weary and could feel the team's confidence eroding." Plaster, John. *Secret Commandos* (NY: Simon & Schuster, 1999), p. 148."Day after day we sat at the launch site ... and all day I thought about that long, dangerous valley." *Ibid.*, p. 258.

24   "[A] 'sucker hole' might open in the ... clouds, through which we'd insert, then it would close behind us, cutting us off from air strikes or extraction." *Ibid.*"[The] sky had closed and we were stuck there ... with no possibility of air support or extraction." *Ibid.*

25   "[Our] SOG teams found NVA almost every single day across the border and always in great numbers." *Ibid.*, p. 130. "[In] three months almost half our U.S. personnel [were] casualties." *Ibid.*, p. 123."[Eight] or so teams ... carried [most of the] mission load, going out again and again." "[With] no time to train since our last mission." *Ibid.*"[The] better the team, the more likely you'd be run to death." *Ibid.*"[It] felt ... like they were being run to death." *Ibid.*"[It] felt to Stubbs like they were being run to death." *Ibid.*, p. 167.

26   "Always short of teams, SOG had a horrible record of hurriedly assembling ... inexperienced men and inserting them in dangerous targets with disastrous results." *Ibid.*, pp. 240–41.

27   "With the teams so spread out, [the FAC] would seldom fly within radio range." *Ibid.*, p.175. "[They'd] tried to call repeatedly ... on ... emergency radios ... no one responded." *Ibid.*"[No] helicopters or fighters could come to our aid." "[The FAC] could not respond immediately." *Ibid.*, p. 146. "Much of the day no aircraft would be close enough to hear us, if we called on the radio." *Ibid.*, p. 157. "[The FAC] was busy ... and ... we were on our own." *Ibid.*, p. 158.

28   In 1967, the NVA selected some of their most aggressive paratroopers from their airborne brigade and gave them special training as counter-recon teams. They expertly stalked the SOG teams, often with tracker dogs, trying to capture or kill them. *Ibid.* pp. 55, 104.

29   "[The] enemy had ... advance warning." *Ibid.*, p. 120."[They] had communications that allowed them to ... alert Hanoi on short notice." Shultz, Richard. *The Secret War Against Hanoi.* (NY: HarperCollins, 1999), p. 244. SOG did not conduct rigorous security checks on the Vietnamese locals who worked in the FOBs. *Ibid.*, p. 245. Using a VC woman as bait, VC agents lured a young enlisted clerk in SOG's headquarters into passing top-secret documents to her. Gillespie, *op. cit.*, pp. 95–96.

30   "[Being] inserted over and over into the same area." Plaster. *Secret Commandos, op. cit.*, p. 12. "[We] ... had to go ... into the same ... places where they had died." *Ibid.*"[Why] put us back in the same target?" *Ibid.*

31 One recon team leader refused a night order to conduct a cross-border recon mission early the next morning with an indigenous team he had never met. That NCO, SSG Robert Howard, was later awarded the Medal of Honor. The same CO threatened to court martial another recon team leader for cowardice, because he could not find the body of a missing recon man he was sent to recover. That NCO, SFC Fred Zabitosky, was later awarded the Medal of Honor. McLeroy witnessed both incidents at FOB 2 (CCC) at Kontum in February 1968. A SOG recon team leader at the Phu Bai FOB, 2LT Mike Rollinson, gave the same CO a written list of thirteen reasons why he refused to return to an area only one day after he and his team barely escaped from it. Another SOG recon team leader at that FOB, SFC Greg Voral, who received a Silver Star for a previous recon in Laos, refused that same CO's order to return to the same area only one day after his team barely escaped from it. Statement of Voral to McLeroy in June 1968 and statement of Rollinson to McLeroy in May 2012. The CO threatened both men with a court martial for refusing his orders, but they said they would rather face a court martial than obey his orders under those conditions. They were not court martialed and were quietly reassigned to administrative jobs at another FOB. The outrageous CO was eventually relieved of his command and sent home, allegedly for mental instability.

32 On a later 1968 mission a surrounded SOG recon team (RT Alabama) was saved by the close air support of more than 100 tactical ground-attack planes over a forty-eight-hour period. Plaster, John. *SOG: A Photo History of the Secret Wars* (Boulder, CO: Paladin, 2000), p. 114.

33 American is a combination of the words "American" and "New Caledonia," the South Pacific island where the division was activated in 1942. The name was coined by PFC David Fonesca of Roxbury, Massachusetts, who served in the 26th Signal Company. He offered the name in response to a division-wide solicitation by the division's first Commanding General, MG Alexander M. Patch, Jr. The name was approved by the War Department. The Americal was the Army's second division with a name but no numerical designation. Cronin, Francis D. *Under the Southern Cross: The Saga of the Americal Division* (3rd ed.) (Washington, D.C.: Combat Saga Press, 1951), pp. 28–29. The division was deactivated at the end of World War II and reactivated in Vietnam in September 1967 as the 23rd Infantry Division (Americal). Its three Light Infantry Brigades (LIB) were the 196th, 198th, and 11th. The 196th LIB, its first and largest brigade, was the last U.S. combat brigade to leave Vietnam in 1972. Neither the 196th LIB nor the 198th LIB was involved in the notorious My Lai atrocity of March 1968. The authoritative account of that criminal act by a few members of one platoon of the 11th LIB is Peers, William. *The My Lai Inquiry* (NY: Norton, 1979). In 1971, the Americal Division was deactivated again.

34 Chung, Donald Y. B. "Summary of Operation Golden Valley", Headquarters Americal Division, May 16, 1968.

35 One 1/46 rifle company would move to Kham Duc within one hour of notification, followed by A Battery 1/14 Artillery within ninety minutes. Three more 1/46th rifle

companies would move to Kham Duc within two hours, augmented by additional rifle companies from the 1/52 and 5/46th battalions. "Change to OPLAN 1–68 GOLDEN VALLEY (Relief/Reinforcement of CIDG Camps), May 4, 1968."

36 MAJ Walter Sanders, the 1/46th S-3, thought the Operation *Golden Valley* plan was an "extremely dangerous, if not fatally flawed mission." His predecessor, LTC Elbert Fuller, also expressed grave doubts about the practical possibility of reinforcing Kham Duc. Sanders, Walter, email to McLeroy, January 17, 2000; Fuller, Bert, email to McLeroy, January 15, 2000. CPT A. C. Sanders, CO of A Battery, 1/14th artillery, thought Kham Duc should be heavily reinforced and an artillery firebase established within range of it well before an enemy attack began. Sanders, A. C., email to William Schneider, February 25, 2003.

37 That afternoon, BG George Young, the Americal Division Assistant CG, was briefed on the *Golden Valley* plan. Owens, Garland. "Operation Golden Valley Statement," undated, p. 1; Sanders, Walter M. "198th Infantry Brigade, Daily Staff Journal or Duty Officer's Log," April 1, 1968, p. 1.

38 FOB 4 officially recorded it as a weather accident, but two SF NCOs from FOB 4, SSG Pat Watkins and SGT Charles Feller, who were flying nearby in a second helicopter, saw the crash and rescued the injured Vietnamese pilot and co-pilot, who said they had been shot down. Eye witness statement and notarized affidavit of Patrick Watkins, November 21, 2012. McLeroy sent SF 1LT John Stewart, who was patrolling nearby with a Nung platoon, to secure the site. When the remains cooled enough to be collected, the launch site medic, SSG M. C. Windley, sent them to FOB 4 for a collective memorial service. The KIAs were: CPT George Deverall, SFC Aubrey Bryan, SFC Crecencio Cardosa, SFC Samuel Padgett, and SFC Charles Wilcox.

39 McLeroy voluntarily joined the Army in October 1965 with a double draft deferment for age (26) and occupation (certified, full-time high school teacher of English, German, and Spanish). He completed the enlisted basic course at Fort Gordon, GA, and the enlisted infantry course at Fort Jackson, SC. At Fort Benning, GA, he completed the Infantry Officer Candidates course, Airborne course, Jumpmaster course, and Ranger course. At Fort Bragg, NC, he completed the Special Forces Officers course and the SF Vietnam Pre-mission course. He used three weeks of his home leave to complete the Jungle Warfare course in Panama. In June 1967 he was assigned to the 5th SF Group in Vietnam as the civic action officer and later executive officer of team A-104 at Ha Thanh, Quang Ngai Province, I Corps. (The captain of that team, Hugh Shelton, later became a 4-star general and Chairman of the Joint Chiefs of Staff.) In January 1968, McLeroy volunteered for SOG, received a top-secret clearance, and was assigned to FOB 4 as the assistant operations officer. After six weeks of tutoring at FOB 2 (CCC) by their expert launch officer, 1LT Ken Etheredge, he was assigned to Kham Duc SF camp as the Officer-In-Charge (OIC) and launch officer of FOB 4's covert launch site there. After the battle he was briefly stationed at SOG's covert launch site at Nakhon Phanom, Thailand. On his return he joined an airborne National Guard unit as the brigade parachute

officer. He was awarded the Combat Infantry Badge, Bronze Star for Valor, Bronze Star for Achievement, Army Commendation for Valor, Air Medal, Special Forces tab, Ranger tab, Army Master Parachute Badge, Vietnamese SF Parachute Badge, and Thai SF Parachute Badge.

40 Hatchet Forces were SOG's indigenous platoons and companies commanded by U.S. officers and NCOs for occasional, short-term, cross-border raiding, ambushing, and blocking missions on the Ho Chi Minh Trail network. Project Thundercloud was a top-secret intelligence operation using three-man cells of former NVA soldiers wearing NVA uniforms and with a credible cover story as NVA couriers. Inserted by helicopter near NVA units, they covertly infiltrated the units, collected tactical data for a few days, deserted, and were extracted, sometimes with a prisoner. One of the two teams at Kham Duc was launched on May 9 and recovered on May 13.

41 SF medics are the most highly trained non-commissioned medical personnel in the U.S. military. Much of their intensive, year-long medical training is more extensive than that of a nurse practitioner or a physician's assistant for an emergency room doctor. They can amputate limbs, set broken bones, treat gunshot and shrapnel wounds, extract teeth, deliver babies, diagnose local diseases, prescribe common medications, and perform surgery on any part of the body except the brain and thorax.

42 Fortunately, the latrine was not far from the trench and was not hit during the attack.

43 Fuller, John. *Air Weather Services to the United States Army, Tet and the Decade After* (Scott Air Force Base, Illinois: Military Airlift Command, U.S. Air Force, 1979), pp. 26–27.

44 Westmoreland was always "strategically sensitive to weather." Davidson, *op. cit.*, p. 500. Tolson, John J. *Airmobility 1961–1971* (Washington, D.C.: Government Reprints Press 2001), pp. 191–92.

4

Ngok Tavak

"… the operation had its own name: Dangling the Bait … inviting an enemy attack …"

JAMES WEBB[1]

Five miles south of Kham Duc a partially overgrown dirt trail, the remains of QL 14, ran along the Dak Se River on the western side of a tall, jungle-covered hill named Ngok Tavak on the maps. Southwest of the hill the trail curved eastward in a horseshoe loop around a narrow ridge west of the trail. On top of the ridge and overlooking the trail to the south and north were the ruins of an old earthen fortification called Ngok Tavak because of its proximity to the tall hill of that name (see Appendix).[2]

On January 31, 1968 CPT Robert Henderson III, CO of the Kham Duc SF A-team, sat in the back seat of a little Cessna O-1 observation plane for a routine aerial reconnaissance of his TAOR. Ten miles south of Ngok Tavak he noticed road construction near the Laotian border. It looked like an eastward extension of Route 165 from Chevane, Laos. The foot trails used for years by NVA troops to clandestinely infiltrate into South Vietnam from that point on the Ho Chi Minh Trail network were being graded into a new dirt road wide enough for trucks.

He reported it to his Danang headquarters, and four days later an AF pilot confirmed it. Shortly afterwards, an SF/CIDG foot patrol from Kham Duc unexpectedly met and exchanged fire with a squad of NVA troops south of Ngok Tavak. The encounter surprised the SF men, because they had never seen enemy troops there before.

Persistent cloudy weather prevented any further observation flights until the last day of February, when Henderson flew over the new road again to photograph it. The photos showed that during February the NVA engineers had completed it from the unmarked border of Laos to intersect QL 14 between Ngok Tavak and Dak Gle (see map in photo section).

When Henderson flew over the area the next day, he received heavy ground fire. The photos showed that NVA engineers were widening and grading an overgrown old French road northeast from where the new road intersected QL 14. On March 6, a Kham Duc SF/CIDG patrol south of Ngok Tavak sighted an NVA squad on QL 14 north of the intersection of the new road.

On March 8, Henderson and SSG Mac Woodard took ten CIDG troops from the camp's recon platoon on a patrol south of Ngok Tavak in an attempt to photograph the new road at close range. Shortly after 0830 hours, they saw and exchanged fire with an NVA squad, broke contact with them, and continued moving south. Later that day they saw and exchanged fire with an NVA platoon. For the next four hours they tried unsuccessfully to break contact with them.

Realizing that he was surrounded, Henderson finally called for an emergency extraction. An AF FAC (Forward Air Controller) arrived and directed two F-4 Phantoms to bomb a hole in the jungle canopy large enough for an AF HH-3 helicopter to land. While two A-1E Skyraiders provided suppressing fire with their 20mm cannons, the AF helicopter rescued the Kham Duc troops at 1830 hours.[3]

AF planes bombed the new roads for weeks and damaged them in thirty places, but the NVA engineers quickly repaired or bypassed the damage. Henderson then decided to use Ngok Tavak as a fire base to support SF patrols farther south and monitor the road-building activity. Three members of the SF team with an LLDB NCO and a Nung mortar instructor took a CIDG platoon to Ngok Tavak, cleared most of the overgrown foliage from the upper part of the ruin, and dug two mortar pits there.

Two members of the SF A-team at Kham Duc then brought a 4.2inch (107mm) heavy mortar and an 81mm medium mortar by helicopter to establish their effective ranges from Ngok Tavak. The surrounding trees forced the mortars to fire at such a high angle that their effective ranges were significantly reduced. After firing them and calculating their reduced ranges from Ngok Tavak, the SF A-team members took the two mortars back to Kham Duc by helicopter.[4]

Danang

In late March, LTC Daniel Schungel, the CO of the overt SF troops in I Corps, decided that the NVA road-building activity south of Ngok Tavak was a potential threat to Kham Duc. The reports from sporadic local patrols and occasional, weather-dependent observation flights were not providing him enough current, detailed intelligence on the developing enemy threat.[5]

What Schungel actually needed was the special expertise of Project Delta, the long-range reconnaissance unit based at the Nha Trang headquarters of the 5th Special Forces Group. Delta specialized in clandestine reconnaissance of enemy base areas and infiltration routes,[6] but at that time it was committed to Operation *Delaware*, a large, concurrent search-and-destroy operation in the A Shau Valley north of Kham Duc. His only other source for ground intelligence was one of his indigenous Mobile Strike Force (Mike Force) companies.

A former CO of the I Corps Mike Force described Schungel's use of them as "tactically naïve."[7] It was his euphemism for Schungel's lack of understanding of the practical limitations of the indigenous companies and his frequent deployment of them without adequate enemy intelligence, adequate combat support, and even adequate equipment.

For a jungle reconnaissance-in-force mission the appropriate choice would have been the 16th Mike Force Company, a Montagnard unit.[8] As skilled trackers and hunters, Montagnards could operate in the jungle for extended periods with maximum stealth. The urban Nung troops were not nearly as qualified for that mission, yet Schungel chose the 11th Mike Force Company, a nominal Nung unit.

He gave the command of the company to CPT John White, a young Australian officer recently attached to the I Corps Mike Force. White was eager to have the career-enhancing assignment and prudently refrained from making any negative comment that might jeopardize his first opportunity for a combat command. He received no orientation briefing, and when he finally asked for one, it was too vague to have any practical value. His only briefing for his first Mike Force mission was to "reconnoiter the area south of Kham Duc along QL 14, make contact with any NVA force in that area, and try to collect some intelligence."[9]

If he had been more experienced and self-confident, he would have objected to such a vague and superficial briefing. It did not mention NVA activities in that area, explain what "making contact" did and did not include, how long he was expected to do it, what combat and logistic support he would have, what the limitations of that support would be, or what actions he was and was not authorized to take in various tactical contingencies.[10]

Two of White's platoon leaders, Don Cameron and Frank Lucas, were Australian warrant officers and former NCOs with previous combat experience in both Vietnam and Korea. The third platoon leader, SFC Willie Swicegood, was also an SF Vietnam and Korea combat veteran. Four other SF men were assigned to White's company: SGT Glenn Miller, a communication specialist; SSG Clay Aiken, a weapons specialist; SP4 (Specialist 4th Class) David Blomgren, and SP4 Kenneth Benway, medical specialists.[11]

With five Americans, two Australians, three Vietnamese Special Forces (LLDB) men, three Vietnamese interpreters, 122 Nung troops and himself, White's company totaled 136 men. A few days later, Benway and Aiken were transferred back to the Mike Force headquarters at Danang, where they were needed more than at Ngok Tavak.[12]

Because of their small stature, the Nung troops carried light, selective-fire automatic rifles, mostly 5.56mm M-16 A1s, and about twenty .30 caliber M-1 carbines.[13] They also carried 7.62mm M-60 machine guns, 40mm grenade launchers, 66mm rocket launchers, a few 60mm mortars, several bars of C-4 plastic explosive with fuses and detonating cord, dozens of claymore mines, scores of magnesium trip flares, and hundreds of hand grenades.[14]

Ngok Tavak

On Friday, March 22, White's company was flown from Danang to Kham Duc in an AF C-130 transport plane. They spent two nights there, left Kham Duc on foot early on Sunday morning, and reached Ngok Tavak by noon. They found that it consisted of two sections divided by a shallow ditch and a few trees. The northwest half was an open area of 30 by 40 yards surrounded by trenches linking earthen bunkers. Originally used for indigenous troop assemblies, it was large enough to serve as a landing zone (LZ) for Marine CH-46 transport helicopters.

The other half of the fort was a slightly higher earthen rectangle of 50 by 70 yards also surrounded by trenches linking earthen bunkers. Ten feet above the lower rectangle a smaller rectangle of 30 by 50 yards was enclosed by earthen berms 6 feet high. The ground inside the upper rectangle was irregular with several holes and large mounds of dirt. Some of the holes had been dug by the original occupants, and two others had been dug by the Kham Duc CIDG troops for the two mortars they previously brought there for test firing.

The upper rectangle of the fort was connected to the lower one by a 150-foot earthen ramp extending from a 10-foot gap in the upper rectangle wall to a 10-foot gap in the perimeter wire below. White deployed two platoons around the LZ and the third platoon around the lower fort with the gap in the perimeter wire. His command/medical/communications bunker was a large hole in one corner of the upper fort covered with logs and three layers of sandbags. Another bunker in a corner of the upper fort stored the company's explosives and ammunition.[15] (See diagrams in photo section.)

For the next two weeks the Mike Force company conducted short patrols south of Ngok Tavak without encountering any enemy troops. On April 23, a Mike Force patrol 3 miles south of Ngok Tavak sighted an NVA observation post. White realized then that the gradual northern encroachment of the NVA force made it advisable for him to move his patrol base, while he could. He informed the Mike Force headquarters of his intention to do so, but was ordered to remain there "a short while longer."[16]

Danang

Without consulting White or even informing him, Schungel requested III MAF to send two 105mm howitzers with a Marine crew to Kham Duc and two 155mm howitzers with a Marine crew to Ngok Tavak. Instead of sending two 105mm howitzers to Kham Duc, as Schungel requested, the III MAF headquarters sent none, and instead of sending two 155mm howitzers to Ngok Tavak, as he asked, they sent two 105mm howitzers.[17]

The deployment order was sent to Battery D, 2nd Battalion, 13th Regiment, 1st Marine Division at their base near Danang. The battery CO later claimed that he objected to the order as tactically unsound, because artillery should not be placed at an isolated firebase without being in range of another artillery firebase. It also should be defended by a reliable (i.e., U.S.) reinforced infantry or armored company. His battalion CO later said he endorsed those valid objections and forwarded them to III MAF headquarters, but they were ignored.[18]

The Marine staff officer who made the decision to ignore them apparently did so under one or more of four assumptions: 1) that no 155mm Marine guns were available for Kham Duc; 2) that one indigenous mercenary company could defend the artillery pieces from a major NVA attack; 3) that a 105mm artillery shell is effective against targets under triple-canopy jungle; and 4) that 105mm guns at Ngok Tavak could effectively interdict QL 14 and provide fire support for Kham Duc to the north and Mike Force patrols to the south. The first assumption may have been factual, but the other three were not.

Westmoreland, a World War II artillery officer, later asked Schungel why the two 105mm howitzers were at Ngok Tavak. Schungel said he had planned to use Ngok Tavak as a patrol base, but when he learned of the new road from Laos, he decided to use it as a firebase. He said the guns were put there to support Kham Duc to the north and the Mike Force company to the south.[19] His first statement was false, because his only reason for deploying White's company was his prior knowledge of the new NVA road intersecting QL 14 south of Ngok Tavak.

His second statement was nonfactual, because the southern limit of the Kham Duc TAOR was beyond the maximum range of a 105mm howitzer at Ngok Tavak, and the Mike Force patrols south of Ngok Tavak were inside the guns' minimum range. Never having seen Ngok Tavak or been briefed on the details of its terrain by anyone who had seen it, Schungel did not know that the tall trees surrounding it greatly reduced the range of the guns. He also did not know that the density of the multi-layered jungle canopy in that area made 105mm shells ineffective against targets underneath it.[20]

Ngok Tavak

In the last week of April an advance party of twelve Marines from an artillery platoon and their platoon NCO suddenly arrived at Ngok Tavak in a CH-53 helicopter to reconnoiter a site for their two howitzers.[21] Their unexpected arrival appalled White, because he understood his mission to be a reconnaissance-in-force, and he considered Ngok Tavak a temporary patrol base, not an artillery firebase. The difference is critical, because a patrol base can be quickly moved to avoid an attack, but the artillery at a firebase must be defended in place. The survival of his company required maximum mobility, which an artillery anchor made impossible.

The Marines also brought a .50 caliber machine gun, two 7.62mm machine guns, several spools of concertina wire, sandbags, construction tools, C rations, and a three-quarter-ton truck. They dug foxholes for the machine guns, stacked sandbags around them and the two howitzers, strung concertina wire around their perimeter, and built a fire direction bunker. To enable their guns to fire at a slightly lower angle and give them a little more range, they knocked down some of the trees around their position with C-4 plastic explosive provided by White's troops.[22]

On May 3, thirty ethnic Vietnamese claiming to be a CIDG platoon from Kham Duc suddenly arrived on foot unannounced. The Nung troops immediately distrusted them and warned their American and Australian leaders not to trust them, but White naively accepted them at face value.[23] He did not know that the only CIDG troops considered trustworthy enough to leave Kham Duc without an LLDB NCO or officer in charge were the camp's specially selected and trained recon platoon.

He also did not know that the recon platoon would never have been sent to reinforce a Mike Force company, especially one defending a static position. If he had known it, he would have realized that the alleged CIDG platoon could not have come from Kham Duc, and a radio call to the SF A-team would have confirmed it.[24] He put the alleged CIDG platoon in the lower part of the fort with the Mike Force platoon.

Those "CIDG" troops could only have been NVA troops wearing the CIDG's tiger stripe uniforms, which could be bought at any large market, and carrying the CIDG's World War II-surplus M-1 carbines, which also could be bought or taken from captured and dead ARVN troops. The Kham Duc CIDG troops were all ethnic South Vietnamese, whose facial features are not radically different from those of North Vietnamese. The platoon leader may have been a South Vietnamese Communist "regroupee," but if not, his North Vietnamese accent was not unusual in South Vietnam. Many North Vietnamese refugees had been living there since their mass exodus from North Vietnam in 1954 and 1955.

On May 4, the other members of the Marine platoon arrived from Kham Duc in two CH-53 helicopters with a howitzer slung beneath each of them. A few days later, an Army CH-47 helicopter arrived with a 4.2inch (107mm) heavy mortar, an 81mm medium mortar, and an ammunition supply for both mortars. The mortars were not at Ngok Tavak when White arrived: he did not bring them; the Marines did not bring them; and the alleged CIDG platoon did not bring them. The SF team would not have allowed any CIDG troops to take them out of the camp unaccompanied by SF troops.[25]

The mortars could only have come from the Danang Mike Force. Since Schungel did not tell White the Marines were sending him two howitzers and an artillery platoon, which White did not request, it was hardly surprising that Schungel also did not tell him that the Mike Force was sending him a heavy mortar, a medium mortar, and ammunition for them, which White also did not request. He put the mortars and ammunition in the two mortar pits in the upper fort.[26]

LTC Schungel had personal knowledge of the NVA's potential for using tanks against Kham Duc. On the night of February 7, he was wounded at Lang Vei, an SF border camp west of Khe Sanh, when it was attacked by eleven Soviet PT-76 light tanks and several companies of NVA infantry.[27] A March intelligence report stated that the new road from Laos could support light tanks; Kham Duc was highly vulnerable to a tank attack; and the NVA 2nd Division might be planning to attack Kham Duc with tanks.[28]

Schungel requested the 5th SF Group headquarters in Nha Trang to immediately send three 106mm recoilless rifles with 100 anti-tank rounds, three 90mm recoilless rifles with 200 anti-tank rounds, 100 light anti-tank (LAW) 66mm rockets, and 200 anti-tank mines to Kham Duc.[29] Meanwhile, the A-team NCOs improvised several anti-tank explosives called fougasse.[30]

On May 4 and 5, an AF FAC observed damaged bridges and sections of QL 14 being repaired, a new bridge being built, and NVA trucks moving north from the intersection of QL 14 with the new road from Laos.[31] On May 6, a Mike Force patrol sighted an NVA platoon only half a mile from Ngok Tavak. The same day, an SF/CIDG patrol from Kham Duc discovered an NVA observation post on a hilltop 4 miles east of the camp with a clear view of the camp and a sand table model of the valley, including the camp's hilltop OPs.[32] By then, it was obvious that a large NVA force was preparing to attack Kham Duc and Ngok Tavak soon.

White had not tried to fortify Ngok Tavak before, because he did not intend to defend it. Now he urgently requested his Danang headquarters to send him more claymore mines, hand grenades, and concertina wire. He ordered his troops to clear the vegetation from the tops of the berms and knock down some surrounding trees with explosives to expand the fields of fire and simultaneously create foot barriers around the perimeter.[33]

On the night of May 6, some trip flares on the perimeter wire were ignited, and the Nung troops detonated claymore mines in that sector. On the next two nights more trip flares were ignited on the wire, and the increasingly nervous Nung troops threw hand grenades into the ominous darkness beyond the perimeter.[34]

On the morning of May 8, an inspection of the wires connected to the claymore mines around the Ngok Tavak perimeter revealed that some of them had recently been cut. Knowing that it could only have been done by the alleged CIDG platoon, White ordered them out of the lower fort and into the open space across QL 14. He simultaneously ordered the Marines to move their two howitzers out of that exposed space and into the upper fort.

Kham Duc

During April, SF 1LT Bernhardt, the executive officer of the Kham Duc A-team, led three patrols up to 9 miles south of Kham Duc. On the first patrol he received sporadic fire from snipers; on the second he exchanged fire with an NVA squad that broke contact; on the third an aggressive NVA platoon attacked him and forced him to break contact.[35] He then told the A-team at Kham Duc to start preparing for a major NVA attack.

On May 7, the I Corps SF headquarters in Danang ordered the Kham Duc A-team to capture an NVA prisoner.[36] The next day, Bernhardt, SSG Woodard, and twenty CIDG troops of the recon platoon left on a patrol with that objective. A short distance south of the camp a CIDG radio operator monitoring the radio traffic on an FM frequency often used by NVA troops heard them say that NVA scouts were moving up the Dak Se River gulch toward the SF camp.

Bernhardt immediately moved his troops to a concealed position near the river gulch with a view of the path along the river and good fields of fire for an ambush. Through his interpreter, he told the CIDG troops to hold their fire until he selected the target by firing first, then try to wound the NVA troops, not kill them.

Soon six NVA soldiers walked into the kill zone. Bernhardt wounded one, and the CIDG troops killed the others. Woodard ran out, grabbed the lightly wounded one, and pulled him into the dense vegetation of the ambush site. Bernhardt quickly moved his troops and the prisoner 75 yards away to a defensive position among the surface roots of a huge banyan tree. The prisoner had painful but non-lethal wounds in his leg and torso. Woodard gave him a shot of morphine and bandaged his wounds, while Bernhardt interrogated him through his interpreter.

The POW, a teenage draftee, willingly answered all the questions claiming that he admired Americans. He seemed in good health, was well fed, and had a fresh haircut. His pack, equipment harness, uniform, and AK-47 rifle were all new. He was a recent recruit and had just arrived from North Vietnam with 230 other recruits, none of whom had ever been in combat.

They had been taken by train from Hanoi to a station not far from the South Vietnam border, then taken by trucks through a mountain pass to Laos. Traveling in trucks at night, they had reached the new road into South Vietnam in eleven days. He and 130 men of his group were assigned to the 60th Battalion, 1st VC [NVA] Regiment of the 2nd PAVN Division. His squad was ordered to hide in part of the river gulch south of Kham Duc prior to his battalion's attack on the camp.[37]

Shortly before daybreak on May 9, Bernhardt moved his troops a mile farther north to a large field covered with tall elephant grass. While the CIDG troops chopped out a helicopter LZ, Bernhardt radioed the camp and requested an immediate extraction of the POW. As soon as the helicopter left with the POW, Bernhardt took his troops on the fastest route back to the SF camp along the Dak Se River gulch. Moving as quickly as possible, they noted many man-size holes dug into the river bank. The holes clearly were intended to conceal large numbers of NVA troops preparing to attack the eastern perimeter of the SF camp from the heavily vegetated river gulch.

Despite their forced march, Bernhardt's troops could not reach the SF camp before dark. The CIDG troops were terrified of being so close to the dreaded NVA troops for the first time. Hiding silently in the thick vegetation of the river gulch, they sleeplessly awaited the dawn.[38]

Ngok Tavak

On May 9, the leader of the alleged CIDG platoon insisted on occupying their former position inside the fort's perimeter. White refused, and they left Ngok Tavak, walking north on QL 14. Shortly thereafter, bursts of firing were heard from that direction, and the alleged CIDG platoon returned. They claimed to have been ambushed, but none of them was even wounded.[39] They undoubtedly met a group of NVA troops at the ambush site, told them what they had seen of the fort during the previous five days, faked the ambush, and returned with orders to initiate the attack from their new position outside the perimeter wire.

The Marines began to transfer their two howitzers, ammunition, machine guns, radios, food, supplies, and other equipment into the upper fort. Their small truck pulled the first 3,000lb, 20-foot long artillery piece up the dirt ramp, but the nightly rains made it so slick that the truck could not pull the second gun up it. The Marines labored all day and into the night with the help of some sympathetic Nung troops to haul the second gun by hand up the muddy ramp and into the inner fort.[40]

That afternoon, CPT Chris Silva, the new CO of the SF A-team, went to Ngok Tavak in a UH-1 helicopter to meet and confer with White about the developing enemy situation. Three of the Marines returned to Kham Duc on the same helicopter. The pilot planned to take them back to Ngok Tavak later that afternoon, pick up Silva there, and take him back to Kham Duc, but dense fog prevented it. On the night of May 9/10, Silva had to stay at Ngok Tavak, and the three Marines had to stay at Kham Duc.[41]

Silva was the only SF man from Kham Duc at Ngok Tavak, and having recently arrived at the A-camp, he saw nothing unusual about the alleged CIDG troops outside White's perimeter. Assuming that the LLDB CO sent them, he did not know that they would never have been sent anywhere outside the camp without an LLDB team member in command.[42] The Nung troops also saw nothing unusual about them, because they had refused to fraternize with the CIDG troops during their two days at Kham Duc. Consequently, they did not notice any difference between the alleged CIDG troops and the authentic ones.

On May 9, Ngok Tavak was defended by 175 men: three Australians, four Americans, three LLDB men, three interpreters, 122 Nung troops, and forty Marines, including a Navy medic.[43] The artillerymen had only superficial training for infantry combat and were not expecting to have to fight a close-quarters infantry battle that night.[44] By the time they finished laboriously hauling the second howitzer up into the inner fort by hand, it was very late and they were exhausted.

Until then they had been on 50 percent night alert, but in their new position in the inner fort they felt relatively safe compared to their prior location outside the perimeter wire. Because of the illusion of safety and their extreme fatigue they did not dig any foxholes that night. They posted six guards on two-hour shifts, inflated their air mattresses, wrapped themselves in their waterproof ponchos, and fell asleep on the open ground.[45]

Kham Duc

Windley advised McLeroy that some of the SF men were complaining about having to sleep in the trench a third night without knowing when or even if the NVA attack would come. McLeroy had to agree that they were as ready for the attack as they could be, and for the sake of morale let them return to their barracks to sleep. Ironically, the attack began that night.

At 0319 hours in the early morning darkness of May 10, sixty-eight mortar and recoilless rifle rounds from the hills east of the river landed in the SF camp. Some of the CIDG troops were killed, and SF 1LT Paul Portinho, the CO of the Mike Force trainees, was critically wounded.[46] Contrary to the NVA's usual tactics, however, they did not follow the barrage with a ground attack.

With no hesitation or confusion, the SOG troops grabbed their weapons, helmets, web gear, and protective vests and ran to their familiar positions in the trench on the same routes they had twice practiced in the dark. None of them was wounded, and everything they needed to fight a mass NVA ground attack for three days was already there.

The senior NCO of the Kham Duc SF A-team, MSG James Duncan, was in command of the team while Silva was at Ngok Tavak and Bernhardt was on patrol. He immediately radioed the SF headquarters in Danang, requesting emergency air support, and the SOG radio operators independently did the same. At 0420 hours, an AC-47 fixed-wing gunship with the radio name "Spooky" arrived and began to drop flares around the camp.[47]

That night one NVA battalion could have easily captured the camp, if they had wanted to. With no initial barrage to alert the defenders, they could have stormed its eastern perimeter from the river gulch and quickly overwhelmed the SOG troops with superior numbers before Spooky arrived. A battalion of NVA assault troops could have easily killed the few effective defenders and seized the camp's weapons, trenches, and bunkers. Once they intermingled with the U.S. troops, Spooky would not have fired into the camp.

Evidently, either the NVA commander was incompetent or else his objective was not the camp, but its defenders. He seemed to want to announce his presence there more than he wanted to capture the camp. He appeared to be waiting for something to happen before launching his main attack: either for more reinforcements to arrive or for the seasonal cloud cover to return and cancel close air support.

Ngok Tavak

Shortly after 0300 hours, the 40th Battalion, 1st Regiment, 2nd NVA Division assaulted Ngok Tavak, but the accounts of how it began differ widely. Several Marines and the Mike Force SF medic, SP4 David Blomgren, insisted that contrary to the statements of CPT White and 1LT Adams, they were not told to expect an attack that night and were all sleeping when it began.[48] CPL Henry Schunck, a Marine guard on duty that night, also said they were not warned of the imminent attack, and all the Marines except himself and the other five guards were sleeping.[49]

The attack began with the alleged CIDG troops approaching the Nung guards at the gap in the perimeter wire, repeatedly yelling, "Don't shoot! Friendly!"[50] They said it in English, apparently to prevent the Marine guards from shooting them. Their critical task was to cause the Nung guards to hold their fire long enough for the NVA assault troops to kill them.

Contrary to what some of the Marines believed, it is highly unlikely that the alleged CIDG troops led the main assault. No competent commander would choose the CIDG's M-1 carbines over the NVA's AK-47 assault rifles for an infantry charge. The carbines were inferior to the AK-47s both in the power of their rounds and the number of rounds in their sound of their firing was likely mistaken by some of the M-1 carbines,[51] and the sound of their firing was likely mistaken by some of the Marines for the sound of the carbines of the alleged CIDG troops.

NVA assault troops wearing tan uniforms and tan pith helmets ran up the ramp, firing AK-47s and throwing hand grenades and satchel charges.[52] One of the first three NVA soldiers to reach the upper fort carried a flame thrower and fired it at the first Marine he saw, Lance Corporal (LCPL) Jim Garlitz. Despite receiving second-degree burns, Garlitz shot them with his M-60 machine gun, then ran with the gun behind a nearby earthen berm, where other Marines had taken cover.[53]

More NVA troops ran through the gap, killing two Marines on the .50 caliber machine gun, but for some reason they did not use the powerful weapon against the Marines. One of the assault troops threw a hand grenade into the first bunker on the left of the gap in the perimeter wire, where SFC Swicegood was sleeping, seriously wounding him.[54]

When the Nung troops saw their wounded SF platoon leader being carried to the medical bunker and some of their comrades lying wounded or dead, they panicked. Abandoning their positions around the lower fort, they ran to the LZ area, where the other two Nung platoons were deployed.[55] At the same time, a second NVA company assaulted the LZ area.

The two Australian warrant officers commanding the Mike Force troops stopped the assault with withering fire from their machine guns, grenade launchers, automatic rifles, claymore mines, and hand grenades. The NVA attackers were further disorganized by the explosions of an old, unmarked minefield that they had to cross to reach the LZ.[56]

Several Marines, including the platoon CO and NCO, were wounded or killed before they realized what was happening. Shocked out of an exhausted sleep by the ear-splitting blasts of the sudden attack, the surviving Marines instinctively sought shelter anywhere they could find it in the chaotic darkness, and many left their rifles where they had been sleeping.[57]

Most of them did not lack courage and had faced death before from rocket and mortar fire at their base near Danang, but with their platoon leader and platoon sergeant both wounded at the start of the assault, they were leaderless.[58] They needed a decisive, experienced infantry leader to issue forceful, practical commands and show them how to defend themselves and their position in a close-quarters night attack.

Despite the shock of the unexpected attack, some Marines, including Private First Class (PFC) Dean Parrett and CPL Gerald King, began to fight back either alone or with a few other independent warriors. King suffered a serious head wound, but continued to fire his M-60 machine gun from his foxhole near the opening in the berm, killing many of the attackers as they raced through it.[59]

CPL Richard Conklin, seeing that no one was firing one of the M-60 machine guns, got behind it and began pouring out a lethal stream of fire at the NVA troops charging through the gap. PFC Paul Swenarski in a nearby position shot some of them with his M-16 rifle. The NVA assault troops fired their rifles and rockets at Conklin and Swenarski and threw hand grenades at them, wounding both men several times. Despite their wounds, the two Marines threw some of the hand grenades back and continued firing.[60]

Another blast knocked Conklin unconscious, and he fell onto the smoking-hot barrel of the machine gun. The searing pain of the burn shocked him awake, and he resumed firing. The attackers then fired a rocket-propelled grenade at him, wounding and knocking him unconscious again. The intense machine-gun fire of Conklin and King were the main reason the attackers did not overrun the inner fort in the first moments of the attack. For his conspicuous heroism Conklin received the Navy Cross, the highest valor award of the U.S. Marine Corps.[61]

A second self-motivated warrior was LCPL Henry Schunck. Despite shrapnel wounds in his legs, he ran toward the 4.2inch mortar, intending to fire it, although he had never fired one. In the darkness he met CPT Silva, running toward the same mortar pit. Silva told Schunck to follow him, and Schunck eagerly complied. Then Silva was hit by AK-47 bullets and collapsed.

Schunck ran on to the mortar pit alone, elevated the mortar barrel almost vertically, and fired all the ammunition he found there. They were illumination rounds that did no direct damage to the attackers, but made them easier for the few Marine shooters to see. Schunck then ran back to Silva and helped him get to the medic bunker.

He was running to the 81mm mortar pit when another explosion knocked him down and left him unconscious. When he regained consciousness a few minutes later, he realized that a large piece of his scalp was hanging down the side of his head. He bandaged his bleeding head as best he could with his field dressing and ran on to the 81mm mortar pit.

LCPL David Fuentes saw him there, joined him, and began to prepare the mortar shells for minimum range by pulling off the attached powder bags. Again Schunck adjusted the mortar barrel to a nearly vertical position to hit the NVA troops close to the walls surrounding the fort. As quickly as Fuentes handed him a round, he dropped it down the tube, adjusted the mortar's aim, and reached for another round. After they fired all the 81mm mortar rounds, they began firing their rifles at the attackers.[62]

The CO of the NVA troops then sent his third company into the assault on the inner fort. More NVA troops charged up the ramp and through the gap in the eastern wall, while others climbed over the side walls. An NVA soldier with a flamethrower ignited the 105mm howitzer ammunition stacked behind the two guns. It created a towering fire that silhouetted the attackers and made them better targets for the relatively few Marines shooters.[63] It also enabled Spooky, the CH-47 gunship, to locate the little fort in the surrounding darkness.

SGT Glenn Miller, the SF communications NCO, seeing the wounded Marine platoon leader and the mortally wounded platoon NCO in the medic bunker, realized that the other Marines were leaderless and ran out to help them. He saw Schunck first and told him to pick up all the rifles on the ground and give one to every Marine who did not have one. Schunck eagerly complied, and Miller showed him where each man should be positioned to create overlapping fields of fire.

Miller moved fearlessly around the fire-swept inner fort, shooting the attackers and yelling instructions to the Marines. He continued to provide a heroic example of small-unit combat leadership, until he was shot in the head and instantly killed. Schunck thinks that Miller deserved a posthumous Medal of Honor for voluntarily sacrificing his life in heroic acts of combat leadership far above and beyond his duty as an SF communication specialist. For his own conspicuously courageous acts, Schunck also received the Navy Cross.[64]

At 0420 hours, Spooky, the AC-47 fixed-wing gunship, arrived over Ngok Tavak. It was carrying ninety-three magnesium flares and 21,000 rounds of 7.62mm ammunition for its three multi-barrel Miniguns. Every fifth round was a red tracer, firing electronically in rasping bursts of 6,000 rounds per minute. They looked like a solid stream of red neon from the plane to the ground. The flares floating down under little parachutes burned for three minutes with two-million-candlepower brightness.[65] Spooky did not fire inside the fort, but the growling roar of its firing so close to the Marines caused them to seek cover in the indentations in the walls.[66]

Half an hour after first light, several helicopter gunships arrived and made strafing runs on the attackers near the perimeter walls with their Miniguns and 2.75inch rockets. Then two tactical bombers arrived. Having expended all its ammunition, Spooky began to direct the bombs and cannon fire of the two planes on suspected NVA positions in the surrounding hills. During that morning, thirty more sorties of fixed-wing ground-attack aircraft pounded suspected NVA positions around Ngok Tavak.[67]

The fight in the inner fort gradually became a stalemate, with Marines and NVA troops sporadically firing and throwing hand grenades at each other. Finally, the NVA troops began to retreat, carrying or dragging some of their dead and wounded comrades with them. To cover their retreat, they fired tear gas at the Marines three times, but it was weak and each time the wind blew it back at them.[68]

White, Lucas, Cameron, Blomgren, a few Marines, and a few of the Nung troops then counterattacked the remaining NVA troops in the inner fort. Driven by an enraged desire for revenge, they shot every one they found, including the wounded.[69] Due to his head wound, CPL Gerald King was no longer able to distinguish friendly from enemy troops and was firing his M-60 machine gun wildly. He ignored White's shouted orders to him to stop firing. To prevent him from shooting his own men, White later stated that he ordered one of his Nung troops to throw a hand grenade at King, killing him.[70]

At 0400 hours, CPT Eugene Makowski was awakened at the SF headquarters in Danang. He was ordered to go to Kham Duc immediately, load the sixty Mike Force trainees into four Marine CH-46 helicopters that would be waiting for them there, and take them to Ngok Tavak to reinforce White's company.[71]

At 0700 hours, Makowski left Danang in a UH-1 helicopter with five NCOs: SSG Richard Campbell (an SF demolitionist); SGT Jack Matheney and SP4 Thomas Perry (SF medics); SP4 Jack Deleshaw and SP4 Larry Pound (SF radio men). They stopped briefly at Kham Duc to borrow an AN/PRC-74 radio, and Campbell and Pound stayed there to assist the A-team.[72]

Makowski hastily organized the sixty trainees of the 12th Mike Force Company, packed fifteen of them into each of four Marine CH-46 helicopters, and sent them to Ngok Tavak. The UH-1 with Makowski and the other three SF NCOs also went to Ngok Tavak and landed on the LZ. Matheney, Deleshaw, and Perry then joined White's force, while Silva and some wounded Marines and Nung troops were put into the UH-1 and taken back to Kham Duc. From there an AF C-7 Caribou transport plane flew them to the Army hospital in Chu Lai.[73]

The first and second helicopters carrying the Mike Force troops from Kham Duc landed in the LZ, offloaded thirty troops, lifted off, and circled the LZ, waiting for the other two helicopters to land. The third helicopter landed, offloaded its fifteen troops, and started to lift off, when it was hit by NVA machine-gun fire from the surrounding hills and crashed back onto the LZ. When the second CH-46 returned to the LZ to rescue the crewmen of the downed helicopter, it was hit by a rocket or recoilless rifle shell and burst into flames. The two disabled helicopters partially blocked the LZ, preventing the fourth helicopter from landing and offloading its fifteen troops.[74]

An Army UH-1H medical evacuation helicopter (radio name "Dust Off") piloted by MAJ Patrick Brady arrived and landed on the LZ between the two crashed helicopters. His crewmen loaded seventeen wounded U.S. and Nung troops, and Brady flew them to Kham Duc, where they were put on transport aircraft and taken to the Army hospital at Chu Lai.[75]

Brady returned to Ngok Tavak, but did not land on the LZ, because he saw that the NVA in the hills had it registered for their mortars, rocket launchers, and recoilless rifles. He hovered his helicopter against a nearby earthen bank, while his crewmen loaded the casualties. That day he flew back and forth between Ngok Tavak and Kham Duc six times and evacuated seventy wounded men: twenty Marines and fifty Nung troops.[76]

As he was taking off with the last group, two unwounded Nung troops and an unwounded Marine helicopter pilot grabbed onto the skids of his helicopter. It had just cleared the trees and was barely out of sight of the fort, when one of the Nung troops fell off. Marine 1LT Bill Cihak, a wounded pilot of the second downed CH-46 helicopter, was straining to reach the hand of the Marine pilot still clinging to the skid, but could not get a firm grip on it, and the man fell off. Brady landed, took the second Nung on board, and immediately took off to try to find where the two men fell into the dense jungle canopy, but could not see any sign of them. Their bodies were never recovered.[77]

At 1030 hours, Schungel's Deputy CO, Marine LTC William Smith, arrived over Ngok Tavak in a UH-1 helicopter to be a radio transmission link between White and Schungel. At 1045 hours, White asked Smith to request Schungel's permission to evacuate the fort. Smith relayed the request, but Schungel ordered White to stay there until reinforcements arrived.

White told Smith the enemy situation made it impossible for reinforcements to reach him, and his troops could not survive another assault. They were exhausted from fighting all night, almost out of water and ammunition, and still taking occasional casualties from NVA troops in the surrounding hills. Smith knew that White understood the enemy situation far better than Schungel did, but he could only repeat Schungel's insistence that reinforcements would arrive by 1100 hours.

They did not arrive by 1100 hours, or by 1200 hours. White informed Smith that if they did not arrive by 1300 hours, he would leave with or without Schungel's permission. At 1300 hours he told Smith he was moving his troops out of Ngok Tavak to try to find an extraction LZ. He ordered the Marines to fire their last artillery rounds, destroy the firing mechanisms of their howitzers with thermite grenades, and pile everything of possible value to the NVA into his bunker. They doused the pile with fuel from an NVA flame thrower, exploded a claymore mine on it, and destroyed the semi-intact helicopter on the LZ with a LAW rocket.[78]

White left twelve unburied American bodies at Ngok Tavak, and Makowski collected the ID tags from each corpse. He probably thought that his surviving troops could not escape the pursuing NVA troops while carrying bodies up and down steep, muddy, jungle-covered hills. Brady later said if he had known they were being abandoned, he would have taken half of them then and returned for the rest.[79]

White may have thought there was not enough time to load them into Brady's helicopter and wait for him to return for the others, or that it would be unconscionable to ask Brady to continue risking his life for dead men. White later said that even if the bodies had been Australians, he would have made the same decision.[80]

White knew the NVA attackers expected him to go north toward Kham Duc on QL 14, where they had an ambush waiting, so he tried to escape toward the southeast. The NVA troops in the surrounding hills, not realizing that the defenders had escaped, continued to mortar the fort for more than an hour. Meanwhile, an AF FAC directed attack aircraft in bombing and strafing runs on suspected NVA positions in the surrounding hills.[81]

The escape column consisted of 113 men: three Australians, eleven Marine artillerymen, four Marine helicopter crewmen, 45 indigenous troops of the 11th Mike Force Company, 45 indigenous reinforcement troops of the 12th Mike Force Company, and five SF men. LTC Smith continued to orbit in his UH-1 helicopter high above the column to provide a radio relay link between White and Mike Force headquarters in Danang.

After moving through dense jungle for about three hours, they paused for a brief rest break when they reached the shallow Dak Se River southeast of Ngok Tavak. A quick head count revealed that several Nung troops and SP4 Thomas Perry were missing. No one knows why Perry dropped back from the middle of the column, where he was initially walking. He or one of the men in front of him may have lost sight of the man in front of him and inadvertently walked off in another direction.

If so, by the time Perry realized he was lost, he evidently could not find the column.

White did not send anyone back to search for him, believing that it would be impossible to find him quickly in the jungle, and the troops searching for him might also get lost or killed. The NVA troops pursuing the column likely found Perry and either killed him then or captured him. If he was captured, Perry apparently died in captivity.[82]

The escapees crossed the shallow river, climbed a steep hill, found a semi-cleared area on a ridgeline, and hacked out an LZ barely large enough for one CH-46 helicopter to land. White radioed Smith with their map coordinates, and Smith had four Marine CH-46 helicopters sent to evacuate them.[83] The lift capacity of the CH-46 engines was reduced by the thin mountain air and the humid daytime heat. With the weight of its armor plates, two .50 caliber machine guns, several boxes of heavy ammunition, two gunners, and three crewmen it could only carry nine or ten U.S. troops, depending on their size and equipment.[84]

After each helicopter landed and took off, it remained in orbit near the LZ to protect the next one with its .50 caliber machine guns. One by one, the four helicopters shuttled into and out of the LZ, taking small loads of men the five miles to Kham Duc and returning for more. Finally, only thirteen men were left, including White. One pilot, 1LT Rhett Flater, returned to rescue them, but by that time the pursuing NVA troops were dangerously close to the LZ.

Flater did not land on it, but backed his helicopter onto the hillside with its rear wheels on the ground and its nose in the air. The last thirteen men crowded into a cabin only 6 feet high, 6 feet wide, and 24 feet long. Their weight was too much for the CH-46 to take off, so to lighten the load all nonessential equipment and most of the fuel had to be jettisoned there.

Helmets, protective vests, armor floor plates, radios, fire extinguishers, and boxes of .50 caliber ammunition were thrown out. The two Marine CH-46 gunners kept only the ammunition belts in their machine guns. When the CH-46 took off, NVA troops began to fire at it, and the Marine gunners fired their last rounds. The passengers knocked out the windows and fired their rifles through the openings. The CH-46 barely had enough fuel left to fly the 5 miles to Kham Duc and land there at 1830 hours.[85]

Without informing Makowski, White, Cameron, and Lucas then abandoned their Mike Force troops and returned to Danang in LTC Smith's helicopter. The survivors of the 11th Mike Force Company and the trainees of the 12th Mike Force Company spent the night of May 10–11 in the CIDG trainee camp and returned to their Danang headquarters the next day in a C-130.[86]

Of the forty-three Marines and one Navy medical corpsman sent to Ngok Tavak, thirteen were killed, twenty were wounded, and eleven returned unwounded to their base in Danang.[87] In the Mike Force headquarters that night the arguments between Schungel and the Australians about their orders and actions became increasingly heated and personal. Soon afterward, White, Lucas, and Cameron were transferred to the II Corps Mike Force at Pleiku, and no Australians were ever assigned to the 5th SF Group in I Corps again.[88]

Notes

1   Webb, James. *Fields of Fire.* (NY: Bantam Books, 1979), p. 155.

2   English translation of Ngok Tavak is Sugar Palm Hill. In the language of the Jeh tribe of Montagnards, who originally inhabited the area, ngok (ngoc) is a tall hill, and tavak (tawak) is the sugar palm tree (*Arenga pinnata*). It grows wild on rainforest slopes, and an alcoholic drink is made from its sap. Email to McLeroy from Dwight Gradin, a U.S. linguist and missionary, who lived at Dak Pek and studied the Jeh language. en.wikipedia.org//wiki/Arenga_pinnata.

3   Henderson, Robert. "Camp Kham Duc Monthly Operational Summary for January, 1968," Headquarters, Detachment A-105, 5th Special Forces Group (Airborne); Neubauer, Ronald. "Monthly Operational Summary for March, 1968," Detachment A-105, 5th Special Forces Group (Airborne), 1st Special Forces. McCain, Thomas. "Special Study Kham Duc," Detachment B, 1st Military Intelligence Battalion (ARS), March 14, 1968. Henderson, Robert, interview by McLeroy, December 21, 1995, and May 23, 1997, San Antonio, TX, and interview by Sanders, September 12, 2009, San Antonio, TX.

4   Woodard, Houston, interview by Sanders, San Antonio, TX, September 12, 2009. Henderson, "Monthly Operational Summary," *op. cit.* McCain, *op. cit.*

5   Telex message from Commanding Officer (LTC Daniel Schungel), Company C, 5th Special Forces Group to Commanding Officer, Company B, 5th Special Forces Group, March 1, 1968. "Assessment of Enemy Activity in Vicinity of Detachment

A-105 (Kham Duc)" (undated). "Intelligence Estimate Update," Headquarters, 5th Special Forces Group, 1st Special Forces, March 18, 1968. McCain, *op. cit.* Alfred G. Hutchins, "Dissemination of Threat Information on Kham Duc Special Forces Camp," May 13, 1968, AFSHRC, Maxwell AFB, AL.

6 Rottman, Gordon. *Mobile Strike Forces in Vietnam 1966–70* (Oxford, UK: Osprey Publishing, 2007), pp. 41–42. Operation *Delaware* was a 29-day sweep of the A Shau Valley.

7 Davies, Bruce. *The Battle At Ngok Tavak* (Crows Nest, NSW, Australia: Allen & Unwin, 2008), p. 17.

8 Rottman, *op. cit.*, pp. 42, 46–48, 59.

9 Davies, *op. cit.*, p. 34.

10 *Ibid.*, p. 92.

11 *Ibid.*, pp. 21–22. In Davies' book, p. 91, the man in the photograph identified as SGT Ledbetter is actually SFC Willie Swicegood. There was no SGT Ledbetter at Ngok Tavak. Blomgren, David, emails to McLeroy dated August 10, 12, 17 and September 3, 2013.

12 Blomgren, *op. cit.*

13 *Ibid.* The weapons of White's troops in May 1968 were similar to those of a typical Mike Force company in I Corps in 1968. Rottman, *op. cit.*, p. 41.

14 Davies, *op. cit.*, pp. x–xii, 37. McNeill, Ian. *The Team: Australian Advisors In Vietnam, 1962–1972* (3rd ed.) (Canberra, Australia: Australian War Memorial, 1984), pp. 330–35.

15 Davies, *op. cit.*, pp. 39–40.

16 *Ibid.*, p. 43. White, John, letter to McLeroy, November 6, 1995.

17 Davies, *op. cit.*, pp. 49–50.

18 *Ibid.*

19 *Ibid.*, p. 50. The proper deployment of artillery is briefly explained in Ott, David Ewing. *Field Artillery, 1954–1973* (Washington, D.C.: Department of the Army, 1975).

20 Davies, *op. cit.*, p. 49.

21 Interview of Bernhardt, Eugene, by McLeroy, September 13, 1995.

22 Davies, *op. cit.*, pp. 57–58.

23 *Ibid.*, pp. 54–55.

24 Henderson interviews by McLeroy, *op. cit.*

25 *Ibid.*

26 Davies, *op. cit.*, p. 61.

27 Phillips, William. *Night of the Silver Stars: The Battle of Lang Vei* (Annapolis, MD: Naval Institute Press, 1997), p. 86. Shulimson, Jack *et al.*, *U.S. Marines In Vietnam: The Defining Year, 1968* (Washington, D.C.: History and Museums Division, Headquarters, U.S. Marine Corps, 1997), pp. 273–76.

28 "Intelligence Estimate Update," Headquarters, 5th Special Forces Group, 1st Special Forces, March 18, 1968.

29 Telex from Commanding Officer (Schungel), Company C, 5th Special Forces Group, to Commanding Officer (Ladd), 5th Special Forces Group, February 1968.

Henderson interviews, *op. cit.* Fougasse is an improvised flame-throwing mine consisting of a partially buried steel barrel containing a petroleum mixture and an attached detonator that hurls the burning mixture out of the open end of the barrel.

30 "Intelligence Estimate Update," Headquarters 7th Air Force Directorate of Intelligence Sierra (DIS), Vietnam Intelligence Summary 11 through 17 May 1968, pp. 36–37.

31 Bernhardt, *op. cit.* Woodard, *op. cit.*

32 Davies, *op. cit.*, pp. 59–60.

33 *Ibid.*

34 Duncan, James, interview by Sanders, San Antonio, TX, September 12, 2009.

35 Bernhardt, *op. cit.* Woodard, *op. cit.*

36 *Ibid.*

37 Davies, *op. cit.*, p. 63.

38 *Ibid.*, p. 64.

39 *Ibid.*, p. 63.

40 *Ibid.*, p. 64.

41 *Ibid.*, p. 63. On May 4, LCPL Bruce Lindsey was accidentally killed by one of his own hand grenades, while trying to make a booby trap with it. Davies, op. cit., pp. 60–61. On May 6, CPL Tim Brown became ill, was sent back to Danang for treatment, and did not return. Brown email to McLeroy. On May 9, three Marines— PFC Whisman, LCPL Higgins, and SGT Fade—were sent to Kham Duc. Whisman needed an emergency tooth extraction by the SF medic. Fade and Higgins were trying to expedite the delivery of the howitzer ammunition left at Kham Duc. Davies, *op. cit.*, p. 58. The Marines said the Army should supply the howitzer ammunition, because the guns were on an Army base. The Army said the Marines should supply the ammunition for their troops, wherever they were. White, John, letter to McLeroy, November 16, 1995. Reports of the Marine ammunition supply at Ngok Tavak are ambiguous. The Command Chronology of the 2nd Battalion, 13th Marines states that the ammunition delivered to Kham Duc had ninety flechette (Beehive) anti-personnel rounds. Davies, *op. cit.*, p. 52. Adams, the CO of the Marine platoon, noted in his log that twenty-six flechette rounds were taken to Ngok Tavak. *Ibid.*, p. 55. If so, the Marines must have fired at least nineteen anti-personnel rounds at something other than enemy personnel before the battle, since they fired no artillery rounds during the battle and had nine rounds left after the battle.

42 Davies, *op. cit.*, pp. 76–77. Adams, the CO of the Marine platoon, thought they were not prepared for their assignment at Ngok Tavak. Adams, Robert, interview by Sanders, San Antonio, TX, September 12, 2009.

43 Statement of Schunck, Henry, a Marine guard on the night of the attack, to McLeroy.

44 Duncan, *op. cit.*

45 *Ibid.*

46 Davies, *op. cit.*, p. 67. Blomgren, *op. cit.*

47 Schunck, *op. cit.*

48 Davies, *op. cit.*, p. 70. According to the "Daily Staff Journal/Duty Officer's Log; Period Covered from 0001 Hours 10 May 68 to 2400 Hours 10 May 68", Item No. 4 and 5, Company C, 5th Special Forces Group (Airborne), 1st Special Forces, the Kham Duc attack began at 0245 hours, and the Ngok Tavak attack began at 0315 hours. The Daily Staff Journal is probably more accurate than Schungel's statement in his After Action Report.

49 Blomgren, *op. cit.*

50 Davies, *op. cit.*, pp. 77–78. Statement of Garlitz, James, to McLeroy.

51 *Ibid.*

52 Blomgren, *op. cit.*

53 Davies, *op. cit.*, p. 74.

54 *Ibid.*, p. 79.

55 Schunck, *op. cit.*

56 Davies, *op. cit.*, pp. 71–72. Adams, Robert, interview by Sanders, San Antonio, TX, September 12, 2009. Davies' version of Adams's actions is ambiguous on three points: 1) It would have been virtually impossible for him to perform his alleged actions without being seen by any member of his platoon, yet none of them has stated that he saw him perform any of those actions. It is possible, however, that some of his men saw him, but for some reason omitted that fact in their statements for the record. 2) In a letter to Davies dated May 20, 2006, Adams said when the attack started, he was hit in the head by shrapnel and momentarily lost consciousness. Davies, *op. cit.*, pp. 71–72. Blomgren, the SF medic, stated that Adams was brought to the medic bunker as soon as the battle started, apparently with a brain concussion, and remained there until he was evacuated. It is possible, however, that he somehow performed the alleged actions before being wounded. 3) In the videotape of the 1995 trip to Ngok Tavak, Adams seemed to indicate that he had no memory of the battle and did not claim to have actively participated in it. It is possible, however, that his reticence at that time was due to a temporary loss of memory, from which he later recovered. Videotape of the 1995 VVA trip to Ngok Tavak. Email statements of Tim Brown and David Blomgren to McLeroy.

57 *Ibid.*, p. 79. Schunck, *op. cit.*

58 Davies, *op. cit.*, p. 75.

59 *Ibid.*, p. 213. Shulimson, *op. cit.*, p. 543. The highest valor award of the U.S. Army is the Distinguished Service Cross. The highest valor award of the Air Force is the Air Force Cross. The highest valor award of the Navy, Marine Corps, and Coast Guard is the Navy Cross. The Medal of Honor cannot be awarded by any branch of the U.S. military. It can only be awarded by the President in the name of the Congress.

60 Davies, *op. cit.*, p. 71.

61 *Ibid.*, p. 73.

62 Miller and McLeroy were both members of CPT Hugh Shelton's SF team A-104 at Ha Thanh in Quang Ngai Province in the third quarter of 1967. McLeroy took Miller on his first combat patrol and saw then that he was recklessly fearless. SSG

Willie Swicegood, who served with Miller in the Mike Force, said he must have died happy at Ngok Tavak, because he loved the adrenaline rush of combat. Swicegood, Willie, telephone statement to McLeroy.

63 *Ibid.*, p. 213. Shulimson, *op. cit.*, p. 543.

64 *Ibid.*, p. 87. Makowski, Eugene, interview by Sanders, *op. cit.*

65 *Ibid.*, pp. 81–82. Ballard, Jack. *Development and Deployment of Fixed-Wing Gunships, 1962–1972* (Washington, D.C.: Office of Air Force History, 1982), pp. 22, 29–30, 37, 49, 52, 72.

66 Davies, *op. cit.*, pp. 82–85.

67 *Ibid.*, pp. 91, 97.

68 *Ibid.*, p. 85.

69 *Ibid.*, p. 86.

70 *Ibid.*, p. 89.

71 *Ibid.*, p. 87.

72 *Ibid.* pp. 90–91.

73 Davies, *op. cit.*, pp. 87, 90. Brady interview, *op. cit.*

74 Brady, *op. cit.*

75 *Ibid.*

76 Deleshaw, Jack, letter to Bill Schneider, undated. Matheney, Jack, interview by Sanders, San Antonio, TX, September 12, 2009. Brady, Patrick, email to Sanders, May 4, 2010.

77 Davies, *op. cit.*, pp. 95–97. Brady, Patrick. *Dead Men Flying* (Bennington, VT: Merriam Press, 2010), pp. 251–54, 257. Brady's email to Sanders, *op. cit.* White later stated that he ordered one of his Nung troops to shoot the men off Brady's helicopter. Cihak denies that they were shot at, but Schunck said he witnessed it. If so, the men in the helicopter probably would not have heard it due to the noise of the engine and the speed of the helicopter passing over the shooter.

78 Statement by White at a reunion of Kham Duc-Ngok Tavak battle veterans.

79 Davies, *op. cit.*, p, 97.

80 *Ibid.*, *op. cit.*, pp. 102, 135. On May 25, 1993, the Marine Corps headquarters propagated a fiction to hide the fact that eleven unburied Marine bodies were abandoned at Ngok Tavak. It was claimed that those men were killed when they returned to Ngok Tavak to look for Perry. That fiction, unrecognized as such by the U.S. Joint Task Force-Full Accounting, was conveyed to the families of the missing men, but was later acknowledged as false and retracted. Davies, *op.cit.*, p. 116.

81 Davies, *op. cit.*, pp. 100–01, 104. The four U.S. Special Forces men in White's column state that, contrary to White's claim, during their escape from Ngok Tavak (Davies, *op. cit.*, p. 101) they saw no napalm strikes and no burned areas. They praised White's strong leadership and said he deserved a U.S. Silver Star. Telephone and/or email statements of Makowski, Blomgren, and Deleshaw to McLeroy. White's Australian superior agreed and recommended him for the Australian equivalent award, but the Australian CG downgraded it to the equivalent of a U.S. Bronze Star. Davies, *op. cit.*, p. 215.

82 Davies, *op. cit.*, pp. 92, 101, 102–03, 108. Email of Flater to McLeroy.

83 *Ibid.*

84 "After Action Report [AAR], Ngok Tavak FOB, May 16, 1968", Mobile Strike Force Company C, 5th Special Forces Group Airborne, 1st Special Forces.

85 *Ibid.*

86 *Ibid.*

87 *Ibid.*

88 Davies, *op. cit.*, p. 108.

5

Reinforcements

"… nothing [is] more discouraging and enervating for seasoned troops … than immobility."

RICHARD HOLMES[1]

In 1968, the principle of war called "unity of command" was conspicuously absent in the organization of U.S. forces in I Corps, South Vietnam. The result was a complex and somewhat inefficient network of command relationships. At the top of the military organization chart was Army GEN William Westmoreland (COMUS-MACV), Commander of the Military Assistance Command, Vietnam, at his headquarters at Tan Son Nhut air base just north of Saigon.[2]

The Marine Corps units and conventional Army units in I Corps were commanded by Lieutanant General (LTG) Robert Cushman, CG of III Marine Amphibious Force (Third MAF), at his headquarters in Danang. In May 1968, he delegated the command of the conventional Army units in I Corps to his deputy, Army MG Richard Stilwell, at his headquarters in Phu Bai south of Hue. The CG of the Army 23rd Infantry Division (Americal) was MG Samuel Koster at his headquarters at Chu Lai on the coast south of Danang. Koster reported to Stilwell, who reported to Cushman, who reported to Westmoreland.

The Americal Division was responsible for the defense of all the SF camps in southern I Corps, but neither Koster nor Cushman commanded the SF troops in I Corps. All the overt SF troops in Vietnam were commanded by COL Jonathan Ladd, CO of the 5th SF Group at his headquarters at Nha Trang in II Corps. Although only a colonel, Ladd reported directly to GEN Westmoreland and was on the same level of the MACV organization chart as LTG Cushman.

The overt 5th SF Group troops in I Corps were commanded by LTC Daniel Schungel at his I Corps headquarters near Danang.[3] Schungel reported to Ladd, but was operationally under Cushman. In case of a conflict between Schungel's orders from his SF superior, Ladd, and those from his operational superior, Cushman, Schungel would obey Ladd's orders, and Ladd would work with Cushman to resolve the conflict. If they could not do so, Westmoreland would resolve it.

The covert troops of Operation 35 (Op 35), the top-secret cross-border reconnaissance and commando operations of the Studies and Observations Group (SOG), were assigned to the 5th SF Group as a cover, but were not commanded by Ladd or Schungel.[4] In I Corps they were commanded by LTC Lauren Overby, the CO of Op 35's FOB 4 near Danang. Overby reported to the CO of Op 35, COL William Johnson, at SOG headquarters in Saigon. Johnson reported to the CO ("Chief") of SOG, COL John Singlaub, at that headquarters.

Singlaub had been a senior staff officer in the 101st Airborne Division when it was under Westmoreland's command. In his conversation with Westmoreland on the morning of May 10 about the ongoing attack on Ngok Tavak, Singlaub did not request that Kham Duc be defended or claim that its abandonment would significantly affect Op 35's activities in Laos.[5] Unlike Ladd, Singlaub viewed the war from Westmoreland's macro perspective and was well aware of Kham Duc's notoriously bad weather as a cross-border launch site for helicopter operations.[6]

For reasons apparently more personal than professional, Ladd insisted that Kham Duc be defended at all costs, regardless of the questionable military value or disproportionate cost of doing so. His estimation of the value of all his SF camps was narrowly parochial, and he seemed to consider them his organizational fiefdom. He appeared to be at least as concerned (if not more so) for the camps themselves as he was for the SF, LLDB, and CIDG troops in them.

On the morning of May 10, Ladd went to Cushman's III MAF headquarters in Danang and urged him to send a multi-battalion force to defend Kham Duc from a pending attack by a much larger NVA force than the one that was attacking Ngok Tavak. Cushman said he had no spare battalions and did not think the remote camp was worth the large troop requirements and exceptionally difficult logistics requirements of defending.

Probably to avoid another inter-service scandal like the one caused by the NVA attack on Lang Vei SF camp[7] three months before, Cushman told MG Koster to immediately send one battalion of his American Division to defend Kham Duc's airstrip, until Westmoreland decided whether to reinforce the camp or abandon it. He also told Koster to determine how many C-130 flights would be needed to evacuate all the people, weapons, equipment, and supplies at Kham Duc.[8] He did not say that the SF A-team and their CIDG troops would be subordinate to the American battalion CO, much less the covert SOG troops.

One of the ironies of the battle was Ladd's reason for insisting on defending Kham Duc. Since its overt function as a basic training site for CIDG recruits could be conducted at other SF camps, his only justification for defending it was its covert function as a SOG launch site. The irony is that Ladd was strongly advocating an action on behalf of SOG that the CO of SOG, MG Singlaub, who was speaking directly with Westmoreland about it that day, did not advocate.

The American Division's designated reinforcement battalion for Kham Duc was the 1st Battalion, 46th [Regiment], 198th Light Infantry Brigade (1/46/198 LIB). At 0500 hours on May 10, the operations officer at the American Division headquarters at Chu Lai radioed the CO of the 1/46/198, LTC Garland Owens, at his headquarters on an artillery fire base named LZ Bowman. He only told Owens that Kham Duc was under attack and needed immediate reinforcements, but he did not have any information on the enemy situation.[9]

If the American Division headquarters had asked LTC Schungel's SF headquarters for an intelligence briefing on the recent activities of the 2nd NVA Division south of Kham Duc, the SF staff would have gladly provided it. With that data, the American staff could have estimated the likely size of the NVA force threatening Kham Duc, and Koster could have used that estimate to question Cushman's order to send only one battalion to reinforce the camp.

All of Owens's companies except one were then involved in a large operation from which they could not quickly disengage.[10] His only available troops were his headquarters reserve, A Company. He ordered its CO, 1LT Bobby Thompson, to quickly assemble his troops, put them in CH-47 Chinook helicopters, and take them to Kham Duc. He gave Thompson no information on the enemy situation there, because he had none.[11]

At 0800 hours on May 10, BG George Young, Assistant CG of the Americal Division, flew to LZ Bowman to brief Owens on what little he knew of the attack on Kham Duc and Ngok Tavak. Around 1000 hours, MG Koster arrived at Owens's headquarters to inform him that the 2nd Battalion, 1st [Regiment] of the 196th LIB (2/1/196) would be sent to Kham Duc instead of Owens's battalion, and Owens's A Company at Kham Duc would be attached to the 2/1/196.[12]

At 0930 hours, LTC Robert Nelson, CO of the 2/1/196, received the reinforcement order at his headquarters at an artillery fire base 24 miles northeast of Kham Duc named LZ Ross. His battalion was temporarily supporting a large operation near Hue, and his companies were operating around an artillery fire base named LZ Nola. Nelson was ordered to assemble his troops at LZ Nola, including the sixty-two men of the attached Battery A, 3rd Battalion, 82nd Artillery [Regiment]. He loaded them into CH-47 Chinook helicopters and took them to Phu Bai airfield south of Hue. From there three C-130 transport planes, which were too large to land at LZ Nola, took them to Kham Duc.[13]

When the NVA forces attacked the Kham Duc SF camp on the night of May 9/10 with mortar and rocket fire, they did not attack the engineer compound across the airstrip. At first light on May 10, twenty engineer troops supervised by an NCO loaded a 5-ton truck with tools and repair material and went to the south end of the airstrip to continue their work there, as usual. At 1000 hours, the NVA forces resumed their mortar attack on the SF camp, but the engineer troops again were not attacked, so they ignored the nearby mortar fire and continued working.

Then they noticed three NVA scouts camouflaged with foliage moving cautiously around the south end of the airstrip toward the CIDG trainee camp. The scouts were followed by other NVA troops, who apparently did not expect to see U.S. troops on the airstrip during the mortar attack on the SF camp. If those NVA troops had reached the CIDG trainee camp undetected, they could have killed the trainees occupying it and used the protection of its trenches and bunkers to attack the SF camp and airstrip at close range.

The engineer troops began to fire at them with their M–14 rifles, and the NVA troops fired back with AK–47 rifles. Then the engineer troops saw more NVA troops moving toward the CIDG camp and fired at them, hitting several. The NVA troops continued to fire back at the engineer troops, slightly wounding a few. The NCO in charge of the group radioed their CO, 1LT Waldo, and reported the ongoing skirmish.

Waldo ordered 1LT Bill Schrope and 1LT Lance Morris to take two enlisted men each, load two 5-ton trucks with weapons and ammunition, and rush them to the engineer troops on the south end of the airstrip. The M-60 machine guns and M-79 grenade launchers increased the firepower of the engineer troops, and after more than an hour of exchanging intermittent fire, the NVA troops retreated. Waldo then recalled all his work parties and put them in the trenches around Camp Conroy.[14]

At 1030 hours, LTC Schungel's Deputy CO, LTC William Smith, and CPT Robert Henderson, the former CO of the Kham Duc SF A-team, arrived at Kham Duc in a UH–1 helicopter. Henderson stayed there, while Smith went on to Ngok Tavak to coordinate the air support for White's company and provide an airborne radio link to Schungel's headquarters in Danang.[15] Shortly afterwards, A Company 1/46/198 arrived at Kham Duc amid sporadic NVA 60mm mortar fire.

When the A company CO, 1LT Thompson, learned of the NVA attack on Ngok Tavak and the skirmish of the engineer troops around the south end of the Kham Duc airstrip, he assumed that the NVA threat would be from that direction and deployed his troops there. His 81mm mortar platoon immediately began to return the NVA mortar fire.[16]

At 1100 hours, LTC Owens left his headquarters at LZ Bowman in a UH-1 helicopter and arrived at Kham Duc around noon. CPT Henderson informed Owens that LTC Schungel had sent him to Kham

Duc to replace the new A-team CO, CPT Silva, who had been wounded at Ngok Tavak and medically evacuated. Henderson answered Owens's questions about the SF camp, the engineer camp, the CIDG trainee camp, the CIDG troops, and the OPs, but Owens did not ask him about the enemy situation.[17]

Henderson naturally assumed that Owens had been briefed on that crucial topic before leaving his headquarters. He did not think it appropriate for an SF captain, a mere advisor to irregular indigenous troops, to offer unsolicited tactical advice to a regular Army lieutenant colonel in command of a conventional U.S. battalion on the deployment of his own troops.[18]

Consequently, Owens was unaware of the SF team's realistic estimate of the size of the enemy forces around the camp based on all the intelligence they had gathered in the previous four months from foot patrols, observation flights, and the interrogation of an NVA prisoner. After a brief overflight of the hilltop OPs, Owens ordered 1LT Thompson to send a squad to each of three of them.[19] The A/1/46/198 troops were taken to the hilltop OPs by helicopters and spent the night there.

At 1400 hours, LTC Nelson's operations officer, MAJ Donald Buchwald, arrived in a C-130 with an advance party of fifty-four men. Shortly afterwards, LTC William Smith returned to Kham Duc from Ngok Tavak to refuel his helicopter. At about the same time, MG Koster and MG Richard Stilwell arrived at Kham Duc in a UH-1 helicopter and landed on the tarmac across the airstrip from the SF camp.[20]

The separation between the conventional Army and the Special Forces at that time was so rigid that the two generals did not inform anyone in the SF camp of their arrival, and the SF men never knew they were there. MG Koster informed LTC Owens and 1LT Waldo that their troops would be attached to LTC Nelson's battalion, but he did not mention the estimated size of the NVA forces around them, because he was apparently unaware of it.

After Koster, Stilwell, and Owens left, MAJ Buchwald questioned Henderson about the defenses of the camps and OPs, but again did not ask him about the enemy situation. Henderson naturally assumed that Buchwald had also been briefed on it at his headquarters.[21] Buchwald was thus equally unaware of the well-informed SF estimate of the size of the NVA threat.

That afternoon, May 10, a three-man Air Force Combat Control Team (CCT) from the 834th Air Division headquarters at Tan Son Nhut airbase near Saigon arrived in a C-123. The CCT had a jeep and a trailer with powerful radios that enabled them to give the incoming and departing transport pilots technical and tactical data to facilitate their landings, takeoffs, and parachute supply drops.[22]

AF Technical Sergeant (TSGT) Morton Freedman and AF SSGT James Lundie were specially trained combat air controllers and had performed those duties under fire at Khe Sanh. The team CO, MAJ John Gallagher, was a C-130 pilot temporarily assigned to the CCT. He thought Kham Duc was a routine airlift mission, and when he saw that it was a combat situation, he asked his headquarters for permission to leave. His request was denied, but he never stopped trying to leave.

The first task of the CCT was to expedite the arrival of the remaining 2/1/196 troops. Before they could do so, their jeep and trailer were hit by an NVA mortar shell. The blast knocked them down and destroyed their radios, but did not wound them. They borrowed a radio from the SF team to contact their headquarters and request replacement radios. While trying to salvage some equipment from the wrecked jeep trailer, Lundie broke a bone in his hand, but despite the pain did not request evacuation.[23]

Later that afternoon, two men from A Company, 23rd Supply and Transport Battalion at Chu Lai arrived in a C-130 with two 500lb black rubber bladders of helicopter fuel and a pump. The engineer troops helped them unload the huge bladders and set up a refueling station for helicopters on the tarmac near the engineer camp.[24]

At 1830 hours on May 10, Nelson and half of his troops arrived in a C-130. Fifteen minutes later, another C-130 landed with the rest of his battalion. At 1900 hours, a third C-130 arrived with forty-six men of A Battery, 3rd Battalion, 82nd Field Artillery [Regiment] (A/3/82) attached to Nelson's battalion, three of their five 105mm howitzers and an ammunition supply.[25] With those forty-six men plus the sixteen artillerymen who arrived the next day, Nelson had 571 troops in his battalion. He also had the ninety-six infantrymen of A Company 1/46/198, the 122 combat engineer troops, and the two refueling men for a total force of 791 American troops.[26]

As soon as Nelson arrived, he went to the A-team TOC and announced that he was in command of everyone there, including the SF team and their CIDG troops, because he outranked them. The SF men knew that he was not in their chain of command and was not authorized to command them, but they said nothing. His hostile manner and arrogant attitude immediately alienated them and negated any inclination they might have had to offer him unsolicited tactical advice about the enemy situation.[27]

Nelson then went to the SOG sector of the camp to announce his supreme authority there. SSG M. C. Windley met him at the fence and respectfully informed him that it was a classified area, and no one was allowed to enter it without a security clearance from SOG. Nelson replied haughtily that as the ranking officer he could go wherever he pleased. Windley then slowly drew his pistol and respectfully told him that if he entered that restricted area, Windley would be required to respectfully shoot him.[28] Nelson abruptly left and did not return to the SOG area.

Most of the Americal troops were deployed in company enclaves around the airstrip. Buchwald later emphasized that, contrary to the After Action Reports of Nelson and one of his junior officers, the distance between the company positions was too great for a connected perimeter. The positions of each company were at least 30 yards from those of the next company, and most of the men were in trenches around the airstrip with no overhead cover.

Some companies had overlapping fields of fire, but most were separate enclaves, as were the CIDG trainee camp, the engineer camp, and the SF camp.[29] None of the Americal companies was connected to the SF camp, and none of them could even see the camp's most vulnerable perimeter facing the river gulch east of the SOG trench.

A Company 1/46/198 was on the southwest end of the airstrip, while A Company 2/1/196 was on the north side of the northeast end of the airstrip. B Company 2/1/196 was across from it on the south side of the northeast end of the airstrip, with C company 2/1/196 on the

I CORPS COMMAND CHART

MAY 1968

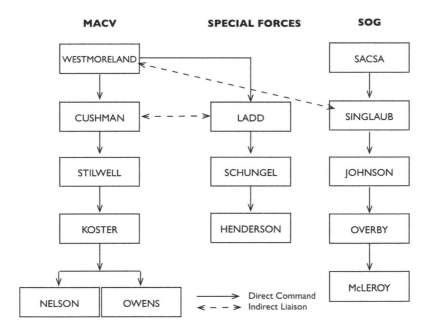

MACV   SPECIAL FORCES   SOG

WESTMORELAND — CUSHMAN — STILWELL — KOSTER — NELSON / OWENS

LADD — SCHUNGEL — HENDERSON

SACSA — SINGLAUB — JOHNSON — OVERBY — McLEROY

⟶ Direct Command
⟵ – – ⟶ Indirect Liaison

south side of the southeast end of the airstrip. D Company 2/1/196 was across from it on the north side of the southeast end of the airstrip, E Company 2/1/196 was on the northeast side of the airstrip parking area (tarmac), and the engineer company continued to occupy Camp Conroy.[30]

The 2/1/196 battalion's Tactical Operations Center (TOC) was on the southwest side of the tarmac. It consisted of two connected steel CONEX containers brought there separately under two CH-47 helicopters. The containers were partially buried in a hole dug by the engineer troops with a backhoe tractor and were connected by a roof of wooden beams covered with sandbags.

An engineer bulldozer leveled an area southwest of the TOC large enough for the five howitzers, their fire direction center, and their ammunition stack. It also leveled an area northeast of the tarmac large enough for the four 106mm recoilless rifles and four 81mm mortars of

E/2/1/196.[31] Neither position provided any protection from incoming enemy fire.

Buchwald suggested to Nelson that they simply walk across the airstrip and ask the SF team what they knew about the enemy situation, but Nelson refused to leave his TOC. He said they probably had no useful intelligence, and if they did, they had to come to him, because he outranked them.[32] He thus remained willfully ignorant of the enemy situation around the OPs.

At 1800 hours, NVA troops on the hills across the river east of the camp fired recoilless rifle rounds and mortar shells at the eastern part of the SF camp, but did not hit any SOG troops in the trench. The NVA stopped firing at nightfall to prevent the firing flashes from revealing their positions. Two UH-1 gunships ("Muskets") of the 176th Assault Helicopter Company arrived and remained at Kham Duc that night.[33]

On the night of May 10/11, all the Americal companies around the airstrip were totally vulnerable to simultaneous, battalion-size NVA assaults. The two reinforced NVA regiments surrounding them had more than enough troops for a mass attack that could have destroyed both the reinforcement troops and the CIDG troops in the SF camp, if they had chosen to do so. Even if the skies had remained clear and Spooky had been overhead before the attacks began, the C-47 gunship could not have supported all the U.S. troops and the SF camp at the same time.

The fact that the NVA did not choose to launch such an attack that night indicates either that their recently replaced CG and his key subordinates were incompetent or that their primary objective was not to capture Kham Duc. They seemed to be waiting for something to happen, either for the seasonal cloud cover to return and prevent close air support or else for more American reinforcements to arrive and increase the number of U.S. corpses and prisoners for them to film.

Tactically, the more U.S. troops they could divert from the lowland population centers, the more successful their attacks on those centers would likely be. Strategically, the more U.S. troops they could kill or capture at a remote outpost like Kham Duc, the more it would seem to the militarily ignorant and politically adversarial TV news gurus like an American Dien Bien Phu, as they had repeatedly tried to portray Khe Sanh.[34]

Late that night, AF LTC Reese Black, the senior FAC in I Corps, arrived at Kham Duc in an O-1 Cessna observation plane, landed in the dark, and spent the night there. The next day he requested and received a full briefing from the intelligence NCO of the SF team, SFC Richard Gill, on the estimated enemy situation.[35] Nelson and Owens could have had the same briefing at any time, if either of them had requested it.

The next morning, May 11, Nelson told Buchwald to conduct a helicopter reconnaissance of the surrounding jungle to locate potential evasion and escape routes, rally points, and LZs in case the airstrip was overrun. After spending most of the day doing so, Buchwald concluded that a mass escape attempt on foot through the jungle would be a chaotic disaster.[36]

At 0605 hours, two NVA mortar rounds landed on each side of the artillery battery. The Americal artillerymen immediately recognized it as a bracket for an NVA barrage between the two explosions. They fired 300 rounds of 105mm howitzer ammunition at the estimated NVA mortar position and prevented the NVA barrage from being fired. Then they moved their three howitzers to the position south of the battalion TOC that the engineers had leveled for them the previous afternoon. It was large enough for their five howitzers, but was equally unprotected.

Two members of the SF A-team took the CIDG recon platoon on a patrol southeast of the camp to search for NVA mortar positions. They saw two suspected mortar sites, radioed their map coordinates to the artillery battery, and returned safely to the SF camp. The artillery battery then fired on those positions.[37]

At 0930 hours, a C-130 arrived with the other sixteen artillerymen and their other two howitzers.[38] An AF NCO from the CCT headquarters at Tan Son Nhut air base also arrived with replacement radios for the CCT men.[39] Shortly afterward a second C-130 arrived with more 105mm ammunition and more fire direction equipment for the five howitzers.[40]

Later that morning, water from the tall hill west of the airstrip stopped flowing to the engineer camp. 1LT Waldo reported it to the battalion TOC, and MAJ Buchwald sent an infantry squad with an engineer squad to find and fix the water pipe.[41] He sent the two UH-1C gunships of the 176th Assault Helicopter Company ("Muskets"), who had spent the night at the SF camp, to cover the patrol.

While the patrol was moving toward the hill, one of the helicopter gunships was hit by NVA anti-aircraft machine-gun fire, and the pilot, Warrant Officer (WO) Ken Sykes, auto-rotated it down nearby. The water patrol troops guarded it, until a CH-47 Chinook arrived, lifted it on a sling, and hauled it back to Chu Lai. The patrol soon found the disconnected bamboo water pipe, reconnected it, and returned safely.[42] The other gunship returned to Chu Lai that night.[43]

Mortar explosions continued to hit the artillery battery and the SF camp every thirty to forty-five minutes, and several U.S. and indigenous troops were killed and wounded by them. The randomness of the sudden explosions caused constant apprehension and tension in most of the immobile defenders, who were forced to wait passively for the next potentially lethal blast.

At 1230 hours, a barrage of six 82mm NVA mortar rounds exploded on the artillery battery. Five infantrymen and one artilleryman were instantly killed, twenty-seven artillerymen were wounded, and two howitzers were destroyed. Nineteen of the most seriously wounded men were evacuated to Danang in a C-123. Despite their losses the battery fired 600 rounds that day at suspected NVA positions around the camp and fired 700 more rounds that night.[44]

On May 11, thirty B-52 bombers dropped more than 3,000 high-explosive bombs on probable NVA troop concentration areas around Ngok Tavak and Kham Duc.[45] Two FACs in a Cessna O-1 observation plane directing bomb strikes on suspected NVA troop locations, AF CPT Griffen Scarborough and AF 1LT Omar Jones, were shot down by NVA anti-aircraft fire and killed in the crash.[46]

Later that afternoon, Nelson called an outdoor meeting at the SF camp of all the unit leaders. He said he was going to send patrols around the perimeter the next day and asked for suggestions on where to send them. McLeroy waited until everyone else had spoken, then said he did not want any patrols near his perimeter. He said he knew where the NVA troops were and could see them on the hills across the river. He said he planned to attack them with air firepower, but could not do so if a U.S. patrol somewhere in front of his perimeter did not return for any reason and could not be contacted. No one would know whether they were dead or alive.

Nelson and McLeroy epitomized the radically different military cultures and missions of the conventional and unconventional Army officers in Vietnam. To Nelson, so conspicuously obsessed with his rank, it must have seemed outrageous that a mere 1LT from a part of the camp that he was not allowed to enter could openly challenge his tactical judgment and independently direct air strikes without his permission. Their mutual antipathy was silent but obvious.

Nelson sent three squads from his E Company to the hilltop OPs to replace the three squads of A/1/46/198, who through sheer luck had survived the night without being overrun. Some of the SF men watching the E Company troops load into the helicopters had the eerie feeling that they were seeing dead men leaving on a one-way trip. They could only exchange silent glances of disapproval and slowly shake their heads.

The SF men knew that the Army field manual on observation posts stressed that they should not be used as buffers to blunt an attack on their parent unit; that OPs should not be manned with less than a reinforced rifle platoon; that withdrawal plans for the OP troops should be prepared in advance; and that the OP troops should be briefed on those plans before their deployment.[47] Owens and Nelson undoubtedly were aware of those requirements, but chose to ignore them.

Nelson committed an even worse tactical blunder by deploying 106mm recoilless guns with anti-personnel ammunition on isolated hilltops defended only by squads. The SF weapons NCOs knew that the Army field manual on the deployment of 106mm recoilless rifles stressed that they should always be protected by at least a reinforced rifle platoon and only deployed where they can be quickly withdrawn to a defensive position of at least company size.[48]

Without consulting Henderson or even informing him, Nelson then arbitrarily changed the numbers of the three hilltop OPs where he sent his squads. SF OP 3 southwest of the SF camp became Nelson's OP 1; SF OP 1 due west of the SF camp became Nelson's OP 2; and SF OP 5 northwest of the village became Nelson's OP 3. The SF team, unaware of Nelson's changes, continued to refer to the OPs by their original SF numbers in their radio communications.[49]

That afternoon, a CH-47 helicopter arrived with a jeep, a sergeant, and three enlisted men from the headquarters of the 198th LIB at LZ Bayonet near Chu Lai. Their jeep had several types of radios, a teletype machine, and an encryption machine for encoding and decoding secure radio and teletype messages. They parked the jeep near the battalion TOC, erected two 16-foot poles, strung a wire antenna between them, and connected it to the jeep.

Radio messages to and from the TOC and the American headquarters at Chu Lai were then secure from NVA interception, but the equipment in the jeep could not be removed. After the incoming messages were decoded in the jeep, a team runner had to take them to the TOC, collect the outgoing messages from the American battalion, and take them back to the jeep for encryption and transmission to the American Division headquarters.[50]

At 1400 hours, another C-130 arrived with sixty-one Hre Montagnard CIDG troops from Ha Thanh SF camp in Quang Ngai Province under the command of an SF 1LT, an SF NCO, and an LLDB NCO. The troops of the 12th Mike Force Company and the survivors of the 11th Mike Force Company returned to Danang on the same C-130, and the Ha Thanh CIDG troops moved into the CIDG trainee camp. They were as tactically insignificant in the battle as the Kham Duc CIDG troops were.[51]

Later that day, MG Koster returned to Kham Duc to give LTC Nelson the evacuation sequence, if Westmoreland approved Cushman's and Abrams's recommendation to "relocate" (i.e., abandon) the camp. Koster said A/1/46/198 would be evacuated first, because they arrived before Nelson's battalion.[52] The 70th Engineer Battalion at Pleiku then radioed 1LT Waldo and told him his company would be evacuated first, since they arrived before the American troops.[53]

Three squads of E/2/1/196 were called the "recon" platoon. Like many others in the American Division, they were tough, brave soldiers, but they were not reconnaissance soldiers. Unlike the Long Range Reconnaissance Patrol (LRRP) teams attached to the American Division headquarters, they did not conduct clandestine patrols in enemy territory to collect intelligence data and direct artillery and air strikes on enemy forces. They were surveillance troops: regular infantrymen with no special training,

NVA soldier (Images from *North Vietnamese Army Soldier 1958–75* by Gordon Rottman © Osprey Publishing Ltd.)

NVA pack (Images from *North Vietnamese Army Soldier 1958–75* by Gordon Rottman © Osprey Publishing Ltd.)

7.62-mm AK-47 Automatic Rifle

7.62-mm RPD Machine Gun

RPG-7 Rocket Launcher

60-mm Mortar

82-mm Mortar

57-mm Recoilless Gun

12.7-mm Antiaircraft Machine Gun

52-mm Recoilless Gun

14.5-mm Antiaircraft Machine Gun

107-mm Mortar

NVA weapons (all sourced from Wikimedia Commons, except RPG–7 Rocket Launcher and 107–mm mortar—Russian dictionary)

Kham Duc valley

QL 14

1. USSF Team House
2. USSF Team House #2
3. USSF TOC, Commo & Medical Bunker
4. LLDB Team House
5. LLDB TOC/Commo Bunker
6. Nung Team House
7. a USSF Warehouse
7. b LLDB Warehouses

8. CIDG Troop Housing
9. Medical Dispensary
10. a Demolitions Bunker
10. b Ammunition Bunker
11. SOG TOC
12. SOG Latrine
13. USSF Latrine
14. Main Gate & Guard Shack

Kham Duc SF/CIDG camp

SF/CIDG camp

NVA roads

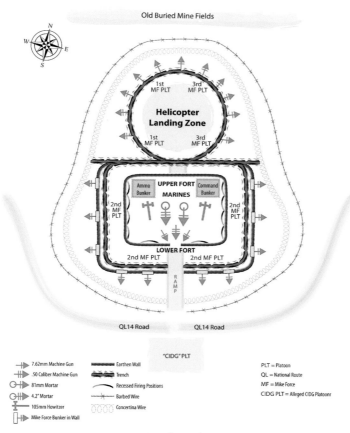

Ngok Tavak

Ngok Tavak

Americal Division fire bases

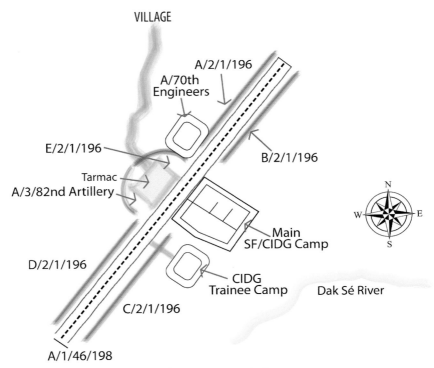

VILLAGE

A/2/1/196

A/70th
Engineers

A/2/1/196

E/2/1/196

Tarmac
A/3/82nd Artillery

B/2/1/196

N

W   E

S

Main
SF/CIDG Camp

D/2/1/196

CIDG
Trainee Camp

Dak Sé River

C/2/1/196

A/1/46/198

Americal Division troop deployment

Americal Division troops

U.S. WEAPONS

M-16A1 rifle, 5.56-mm

M-14 rifle, 7.62-mm

M-79 grenade launcher, 40-mm

M-60 machine gun, 7.62-mm

M-134 Minigun, 7.62-mm (hybrid)

M-72 LAW rocket launcher, 66-mm

M-2 machine gun, .50-caliber

M-1919A4 machine gun, .30 caliber

UH-1 helicopter gunship with Minigun (left),
rocket launcher (right), & M-60 machine gun (top)

M-40 recoilless gun, 106-mm

M-1 mortar, 81-mm

M-101 howitzer, 105-mm

M-30 mortar, 4.2-inch

M-26 hand grenade

Cast iron white
phosphorous grenade
(1968-era)

M-18 Claymore mine

Americal Division weapons (All sourced from Wikimedia Commons, except M-1 mortar, M-61 hand grenade, M-18 Claymore mine—US Militia Forum)

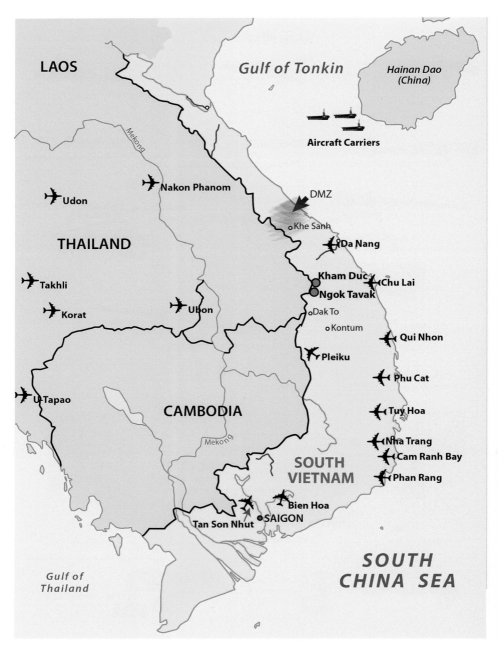

US military air bases

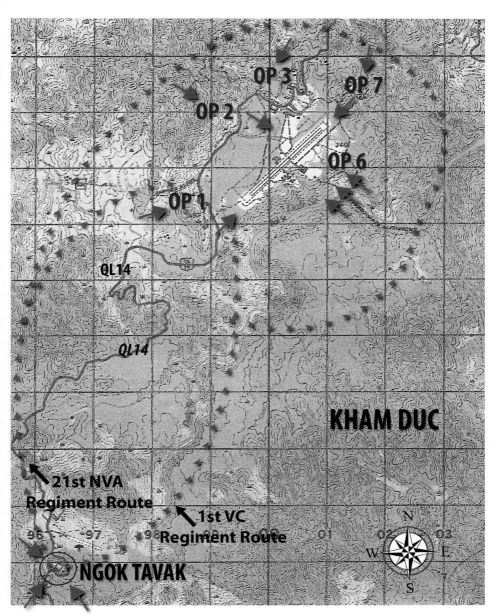

NVA advances

U.S. aircraft (from left to right): Cessna 0-1 Bird-Dog. (*US Air Force*); Cessna 0-2 Skymaster. (*US Air Force*); A-1 Skyraider. (*US Air Force*); F-105 Thunderchief. (*US Air Force*); F-100 Super Sabre. (*US Air Force*); F-5 Freedom Fighter. (*RVN Air Force*); B-52 (*US Air Force*)

U.S. aircraft (from left to right): A-4 Skyhawk. (*US Navy and Marine*); A-6 Intruder. (*US Navy*); F-8 Crusader. (*US Navy*); F-4 Phantom. (*US Air Force, Navy and Marine*); North American RA-5 Vigilante. (*NASA*); C-123 Provider. (*US Air Force*); CH-47 gunship. (*US Air Force*); C-7 Caribou. (*US Army*)

US aircraft (from left to right): C–130 Hercules. (*US Air Force*); CH–46 Sea Knight. (*US Navy and Marine*); CH–47 Chinook. (*US Army*); H–3 Jolly Green Giant. (*US Air Force*); KC–135 Stratotanker. (*US Air Force*); SR–71 Blackbird. (*US Air Force*); UH–1 Iroquois transport. (*US Army*); UH–1 Iroquois gunship. (*US Army*)

who passively observed the terrain from static outposts and reported by radio any enemy activity they happened to see.

The SF men watching them load into the helicopters knew they had not received a realistic briefing on the enemy situation, because otherwise they would not have been sent to those indefensible OPs. The SF men also knew that inadequate little squads on indefensible OPs had little or no military value for the defenders, and the NVA forces would inevitably overrun them any night they chose. By making three 106mm recoilless guns and their anti-personnel ammunition virtual gifts to the NVA attackers, Nelson's tactical incompetence actually increased the danger to the American troops in the camp and around the airstrip.

OP 1 (SF 3) was on a ridge about a mile southwest of the south end of the airstrip and some 400 feet above it. It was an equilateral triangle of about 140 feet on each side, with the southeast side overlooking QL 14's southern approach and the northeast side overlooking the Kham Duc valley. On the northeast and southwest ends of the triangle were two concrete bunkers with concrete blast walls in front of their entrances and cement floors a few feet below ground level to allow the men in them to stand upright.

On the third point of the OP triangle was a large foxhole surrounded by sandbags with a sheet metal roof covered by sandbags. The bunkers and foxhole were connected by earthen berms 4 feet high. The concrete bunkers provided protection from mortar, rocket, and artillery shrapnel, but the roof of the foxhole with no walls only provided some protection from the sun and rain. A UH-1 helicopter took the nine members of the 1st squad, a 106mm recoilless rifle, and a supply of anti-personnel ammunition to the OP in two lifts. The NVA scouts nearby must have seen the helicopter both times and could have fired at it either time, but chose not to do so.

The leader of the 1st squad, SGT Joe Simpson, was a tough former Marine with a prior Vietnam tour. In the southwest bunker he found six CIDG troops with an A/N PRC-25 FM radio. He took their radio and used it to send hourly situation reports to the battalion TOC. SP4 Bill Wright carried the squad's PRC-25 FM radio to transmit and receive messages to and from the E Company headquarters near the airstrip.

PFC Harry Coen and SP4 Julius Long manned the 106mm recoilless rifle, PFC Antonio Guzman had an M-60 machine gun, and SP4 Orlando Vasquez had an M-79 grenade launcher. SSG Johnny Carter from the E Company mortar platoon was sent to OP 1 with Simpson's squad to spot NVA mortar positions. When he refused to perform guard duty, Simpson sent him to OP 2 (SF 1) with the second helicopter.[54]

The steep slope on the OP's western side had been booby-trapped by the CIDG squad, and Vasquez placed claymore mines outside the OP's eastern perimeter facing the airstrip. A double strand of concertina wire was strung around the OP's perimeter and a second row was strung 50 feet below it. The foliage between the two rows had been cut down. The OP's gate was made of X-shaped timbers and wrapped with concertina wire. Wright found some unused roles of concertina wire, and he and a few other men strung them outside the gate.[55]

The platoon CO, 2LT Fred Ransbottom, took twelve men of the second squad to OP 2 (SF 1) in two lifts by a UH-1 helicopter. They brought with them a 106mm recoilless gun and a supply of anti-personnel ammunition. As with the helicopter transfer of Americal troops to OP 1 (SF 2), NVA scouts must have seen the helicopter taking those men to OP 2, but again chose not to fire at it.

OP 2 (SF 1) was in a cleared area on a jungle-covered ridge 2,100 yards west of the artillery battery and 300 yards above it. The OP was a rectangle of 100 by 250 feet surrounded by a double row of concertina wire. The vegetation around the perimeter was cleared, and outside the wire on the north end of the OP was a small helicopter LZ. On the east side of the hill a switchback path led up to the OP from the airstrip.

Inside the perimeter wire were large outcroppings of rock and three foxholes 8 feet wide, 9 feet long, and 4 feet deep spaced 40 yards apart. One foxhole was on the north end of the OP, one was on the eastern crest of the hill, and one was on the western crest of the hill. They had slanted tin roofs with a layer of dirt and sandbags on them, but were not fortified. The 106mm recoilless rifle and anti-personnel ammunition were placed in the center of the OP.

The platoon leader, 2LT Ransbottom, had been with E Company only a few weeks, but he was not new to the battalion. During the first three months of his Vietnam tour he had been a platoon leader in A Company. He, PFC Randall Lloyd, PFC William Skivington, PFC Danny Widner, SP4 Richard Bowers, and SP4 Maurice Moore occupied the foxhole facing west. SSG Johnny Carter, SP5 John Stuller, PFC Imlay Widdison, and PFC Roy Williams were in the foxhole on the southern perimeter. Eight CIDG troops occupied the foxhole facing north.

The leader of the second squad, SSG Edward Sassenberger, together with PFC John Colonna and SP4 Wilbert Foreman, occupied the foxhole facing east. Sassenberger had more experience than the others, having served two years in Korea and nine months in Vietnam. A slightly built man, he was suffering from an intestinal infection that left him weak from diarrhea and vomiting.[56]

OP 3 (SF 5) was on a ridge a mile northwest of the north end of the airstrip on roughly the same elevation as Nelson's OPs 1 and 2. It overlooked the village and the northern approach on QL 14. Like Nelson's OP 1, it was an equilateral triangle of 170 feet on each side. On each of the OP's three points was a concrete bunker connected to the other two by earthen berms and trenches with recessed firing positions. The third squad leader, SGT Wayne Wietting, took his twelve men with a 106mm recoilless gun and anti-personnel ammunition to the OP in two lifts in a UH -1 helicopter. The NVA troops undoubtedly saw it, but again did not fire at it.[57]

Meanwhile, COL Ladd kept trying to obtain higher-level support for defending Kham Duc. At a meeting in Danang with GEN Creighton Abrams, LTG Cushman, and MG Koster, Ladd proposed another reason for doing so. He argued that if the NVA forces captured or killed the Kham Duc defenders just before the start of the peace negotiations in Paris, the NVA could use that victory as propaganda in America and possibly gain negotiating leverage with it in Paris.

Abrams agreed, but neither he nor Cushman was willing to divert any large U.S. unit to the sparsely populated mountains, while more than a hundred lowland population centers were under attack in the second phase of the NVA's 1968 General Offensive ("Mini-Tet"). Cushman recommended that the camp be "relocated" (i.e., abandoned), and again Abrams agreed, but said only Westmoreland could make that decision.

Ladd repeatedly tried to speak directly to Westmoreland in Danang, but COMUS-MACV seemed to be avoiding him.[58] Westmoreland knew that Abrams, who would replace him the next month, did not want to inherit a large, unnecessary battle in a place even more remote and isolated than Khe Sanh, yet he continued to delay his approval of the evacuation plan.[59]

He finally approved the evacuation order apparently between 2300 and 2400 hours on Saturday, May 11. MACV headquarters sent the order to III MAF headquarters, who sent it to the Americal headquarters, Schungel's SF headquarters, and SOG's FOB 4. At 0030 hours, Schungel's headquarters sent it to Henderson, and FOB 4 sent it to McLeroy at Kham Duc.[60]

The evacuation plan was based on the calculation that up to 1,200 people and 50 tons of engineer equipment and construction materiel at Kham Duc could be evacuated in twenty-five flights of C-130s, five in the morning and five in the afternoon, for the next two-and-a-half days.[61] That calculation was based on two key assumptions: clear skies over Kham Duc and a delay of the main NVA attack for three more days. The first assumption was unlikely; the second was unrealistic.

Notes

1   Holmes, Richard. *Acts of War* (NY: The Free Press, 1985), p. 230.

2   In February 1968 Westmoreland established a branch of his MACV headquarters in I Corps called MACV FORWARD commanded by his deputy, GEN Creighton Abrams. It controlled all the U.S. ground forces in the two northernmost provinces. It later became a provisional Army corps, then the permanent Army XXIV Corps. Although subordinate to III MAF, it was under an Army LTG with a rank equal to the Marine LTG commanding III MAF.

3   The SF I Corps headquarters and the SOG FOB 4 headquarters were about a mile from each other on China Beach in the Marble Mountain area of the Tien Sha Peninsula east of Danang.

4   Singlaub, John. *Hazardous Duty* (NY: Summit Books, 1991), pp. 292–93.

5   Statement of Singlaub to McLeroy at the 1999 reunion of the Special Operations Association.

6   *Ibid.*

7   Lang Vei was an SF/CIDG camp 5 miles west of Khe Sanh and 1½ miles from the Laotian border. On the night of February 7, 1968, it was attacked by Soviet light tanks supported by NVA infantry. The Marine CO at Khe Sanh, who was

responsible for reinforcing Lang Vei, refused to do so and ignored the desperate, repeated radio pleas of the SF team CO. It infuriated Ladd and all the SF men in I Corps. cf. Phillips, Willliam. *Night of the Silver Stars* (Annapolis, MD: Naval Institute Press, 1997). Shulimson, Jack *et al*. *U.S. Marines In Vietnam: The Defining Year, 1968* (Washington D.C.: History and Museums Division, Headquarters, U.S. Marine Corps, 1997), p. 276.

8   Ladd, Jonathan, Message, CO, 5th Special Forces Group; Nha Trang, to Director I &CA, ODCSOPS, DA 2208257 May 68; attachment to Fact Sheet, "Attack On Kham Duc."

9   Statement of Owens, Garland (undated). Statement of Thompson, Bobby, in interview by McLeroy, Fort Knox, KY, November 1995; and by Sanders, San Antonio, TX, October 2008. Every battalion in a U.S. Army brigade has a number identifying it with its historic parent regiment, even though that regiment is no longer an active unit. 2/1/196 LIB means the Second Battalion of the First Infantry [Regiment] of the 196th Light Infantry Brigade (LIB). 1/46/198 means the First Battalion of the 46th Infantry [Regiment] of the 198th LIB.

10 Owens, *op. cit.*

11 Thompson interviews, *op. cit.*

12 Owens, *op. cit.* Statement of Nelson, Robert (undated). Statement of Buchwald, Donald (undated).

13 Nelson, *op. cit.*; Buchwald, *op. cit.*

14 Waldo, Daniel, Jr, "After Action Report", Company A, 70th Engineer Battalion (Combat), Department of the Army, May 19, 1968. Email statement of William Shrope to McLeroy, February 2016.

15 Schungel, Daniel, "After Action Report Battle of Kham Duc", Company C, 5th Special Forces Group (Airborne), 1st Special Forces, May 31, 1968. Henderson, Robert, interviews by McLeroy, San Antonio, TX, December 1995 and May, 1997; and interview by Sanders, San Antonio, TX, September, 2009.

16 Thompson statement, *op. cit.*

17 Owens statement, *op. cit.* Henderson statement, *op. cit.*

18 Henderson interviews, *op. cit.*

19 Thompson statement, *op. cit.*

20 Buchwald statement, *op. cit.*

21 Henderson interviews, *op. cit.* Waldo, *op. cit.* Owens, *op. cit.*

22 Freedman, Morton, email to McLeroy, August 1999.

23 Gropman, Alan. *Airpower and the Airlift Evacuation of Kham Duc* (Washington D.C.: Office of Air Force History, United States Air Force, 1985), pp. 57–58.

24 Telephone interview of SP4 Noe Bollard by Sanders, August 2009. The other man was SP4 Wolfgang Richter.

25 Buchwald statement, *op. cit.*

26 Almost none of the combat units in Vietnam fought at full strength due to deaths, wounds, sickness, R&R leave, administrative chores, tour rotations, etc. The authorized troop strength of the Americal Division was 24,163 men, but in May

1968 its actual strength was 15,825 men. The authorized strength of an Army infantry company was 230 men, but Nelson's companies averaged about 100 men at Kham Duc.

27 Statement of Richard Gill, former intelligence NCO of the Kham Duc SF A-team, to McLeroy, June 1997.

28 Statement of M. C. Windley, former launch site NCO, to McLeroy, June 1997.

29 Statement of Buchwald to McLeroy. Sanders' interviews of Karl Mays, Richard Newell, and Roy Obrigewitch, San Antonio, TX, September 2009.

30 Buchwald statement, *op. cit.*

31 Schrope statement, *op. cit.*

32 Buchwald letter to McLeroy, November 18, 1997.

33 Richardson, Don. "Kham Duc Revisited: A Chronological Study of the Evacuation of Kham Duc, May, 1968", donscott619@aol.com. This is an extensive, detailed, unpublished compilation of primary-source documents.

34 Eleven of thirty-one filmed television reports on the battle of Khe Sanh treated it as a potential disaster comparable to Dien Bien Phu. Hallin, Daniel. *The "Uncensored War* (Berkeley, CA: University of California Press, 1986), p. 173. The Dien Bien Phu comparison was the prevalent theme of all U.S. reporting on Khe Sanh. Braestrup, Peter. *Big Story* (Novato, CA: Presidio Press, 1983), pp. 256–65, 278–81, 284–87, 290, 303–04.

35 Statement of LTC Reese Black, May 16, 1968. In his report McLeroy's name is misspelled as "McElroy." There was no lieutenant McElroy at Kham Duc on May 12, 1968.

36 A comparable case was the battle of A Shau SF camp 30 miles north of Kham Duc. On March 9 and 10, 1966, fog and low clouds prevented close air support, and it was overrun by three NVA battalions. On March 10, sixty-nine survivors were extracted by helicopter. Others escaped into the jungle and evaded the NVA for two days, until extracted by helicopter. Only 186 of the 434 people in the camp survived. Blair, John D. "After Action Report—Defense of Camp A Shau," Fort Benning, GA, 1968, pp. 10, 16–17. Sams, Kenneth. Project CHECO Report "The Fall of A Shau," Tactical Evaluation Center, HQ PACAF, 1966.

37 Henderson interviews, *op. cit.*

38 Bernard, Kenneth. "After Action Report (A Battery, 3d Bn., 82d Artillery)," May 14, 1968. Sanders' telephone interview of Pelkey, Chris.

39 Freedman email, *op. cit.*

40 Bernard, *op. cit.* Pelkey interview, *op. cit.*

41 Waldo, *op. cit.*

42 Richards, *op. cit.*

43 Waldo, *op. cit.*

44 Gropman, *op. cit.*, p. 9.

45 Hobson, Chris. *Vietnam Air Losses* (Hinckley, UK: Midland Publishing, 2001), pp. 148–49.

46 The KIAs were: SSG Pearl "Randy" Bush in the artillery battery; SGT Edward Pigg in E Company 2/1/196; PFC Robert Bennett and PFC Robert Salmela in B Company 2/1/196; PFC Randall Lloyd and SP4 Juan Jimenez in A Company 2/1/196. Salmela was mortally wounded and died in hospital the next day. Jimenez's body was inadvertently left at Kham Duc in a body bag and was undoubtedly destroyed in the bombing around the airstrip after the evacuation. Bush was originally identified mistakenly as "Buck." Bernard, *op. cit.* Email of Bill Schneider to McLeroy. Pelkey, Chris, letter to Mr and Mrs C. J. Pelkey, May 15, 1968. Telephone interview of Ron Price by Sanders, August 15, 2010.

47 Army Field Manual 7–11. *Rifle Company, Infantry, Airborne, and Mechanized* (Washington, D.C.: Headquarters, Department of the Army, 1965).

48 Army Field Manual 23–82. *106mm Recoilless Rifle* (Washington, D.C.: Headquarters, Department of the Army, 1965).

49 Buchwald statement, *op. cit.* Henderson interviews, *op. cit.*

50 The men in the encryption squad were SGT Jerry Bodine, SP4 Calvin Mayhue, PFC Jerry Merkle, and SP4 Mike Laughlin. Sanders' telephone interview with Merkle, July 30, 2009.

51 Most of the CIDG troops and some of the American troops around the airstrip were never directly attacked and were passive spectators at the battle.

52 Buchwald, *op. cit.*

53 Waldo, *op. cit.*

54 Wright interviews, *op. cit.* The other men in the OP 1 squad were SSG Harry Sisk, PFC Harry Chandler, PFC Andrew Craven, and PFC Richard Hill.

55 *Ibid.*

56 Statement by Sassenberger, Ron, interview by McLeroy, Key West, FL, July 1995. Statement by Foreman, Wilbert, interview by McLeroy and Cox, Waco, TX, February 1, 1997.

57 Weber, Jeffery, interview by Sanders, San Antonio, TX, July 15, 2007; telephone interview by Sanders, September 12, 2009. The other men in the OP 3 squad were SGT Freddie Bostick, SGT Jeffery Weber, SP4 William Bledsoe (a medic who had just been assigned to the squad), SP4 Virgilio Cruz, SP4 Willie Lamar, SP4 Philip Peltier, SP4 Ed Pierce, SP4 Paul Ternullo, SP4 Bernard Zacherson, PFC Earl Theriot, PFC Charles Cunningham, and PFC Travis Whitfield.

58 Ladd, *op. cit.*

59 "All plans included several options, with a final decision to be made … just before the operation began." "As always, I made the final decision only at the last minute lest conditions should change." Westmoreland, William. *A Soldier Reports* (Garden City, NY: Doubleday, 1976), pp. 156, 271.

60 Statement by Robert Henderson dated June 10, 1968, attached to Schungel, Daniel, "After Action Report Battle of Kham Duc," Company C, 5th Special Forces Group (Airborne), 1st Special Forces, May 31, 1968.

61 Waldo, *op. cit.*

6

Mother's Day

"That was a damn [close] thing, sir, the nearest-run thing you ever saw in your life."

WELLINGTON[1]

The kaleidoscope of events at, around, above, and about Kham Duc on Sunday, May 12, 1968 (Mother's Day in America) was a classic example of the "fog of war" cliché. It was an extremely "foggy" battle: unusually complex and largely improvised. For many participants, direct and indirect, those disjointed events were far more confusing as they were happening than this chronological narrative of them may be for the reader.

Communications

The normal fog of war was thickened by an almost constant communication overload. Nine types of units were trying to communicate with their headquarters or with each other, often at the same time: 1) the Americal Division battalion; 2) the Army engineer company; 3) the SF A-team; 4) the SOG detachment; 5) the Air Force transport crews; 6) the Army and Marine helicopter crews; 7) the Air Force, Marine, Navy, and Vietnamese attack pilots; 8) the Air Force FACs; and 9) the Air Force Airborne Battlefield Command and Control Center (Hillsboro).

The ground troops had FM radios; the fixed-wing planes had UHF and VHF radios; and the troop-carrying and gunship helicopters had UHF, VHF, and FM radios. Different units with the same PRC-25 FM radios used different frequencies among its 920 frequencies. The frequencies were often clogged by the desire of many rear area officers to vicariously participate in the battle. Any radio silence seemed to cause an intolerable tension in their minds. Some insisted on maintaining almost constant radio contact with their units at Kham Duc, while the latter were trying to understand and cope with the evolving battle.

Different headquarters had different interests and priorities and most of them were less concerned with the battle itself than with the current status of their own units. Their demands for the latest detailed information, whether for their unit's reporting requirements or for their own voyeuristic curiosity, were almost constant. Most participants' view of the battle was limited to their perception of their individual situation or their unit's situation at the moment. They were seeing and hearing different aspects of different events from different viewpoints under different conditions of stress, uncertainty, and fatigue.

The result was occasional discrepancies in the status reports of the ongoing events, and that confusion made it difficult for rear area units to understand the actual status of the combat. The distortion of reality caused by orally relaying confusing information in an evolving situation was exacerbated by the need of rear area units to quickly translate incomplete or inaccurate oral reports from Kham Duc into specific actions.

MACV

Westmoreland was keenly aware of the potential political and diplomatic ramifications of losing Kham Duc at that critical juncture in the war. He knew that if the camp's defenders were killed or captured just before the start of the Paris peace talks, that anomalous defeat would be sensationally publicized in America and might give the North Vietnamese delegation in Paris a significant negotiating advantage. He did not know that an NVA camera crew from Hanoi was already waiting near Kham Duc to film the anticipated NVA victory for a propaganda film with that strategic potential.[2]

On May 12, 1968 Westmoreland telexed two current status reports on the Kham Duc battle to his superior, Admiral Sharp, in Hawaii, with copies to GEN Wheeler, Chairman of the Joint Chiefs of Staff, and LTG Andrew Goodpaster, the senior military officer on the American negotiating team in Paris. With a euphemism for the military and political risk of the situation, he warned them that the evacuation of all the defenders and civilians at Kham Duc that day could be "sticky business." Wheeler immediately sent the cables to the National Security Advisor, Walt Rostow, who sent them directly to the President at the LBJ ranch in Texas.[3]

Westmoreland was, in effect, using the camp as passive bait for the mass attrition of a major NVA force, but he was determined to evacuate all its defenders and civilians before they were killed or captured. He ordered his Deputy CG for Air, AF GEN William Momyer, to use his full authority as the new Single Manager for Air to complete the mass air evacuation at all costs. Momyer had recently been given personal authority to directly control more than 600 fixed-wing aircraft operating in Vietnam, regardless of their service branch or home base.[4]

His command authority included 120 Air Force and Marine fighter-bombers and tactical bombers at 11 bases in South Vietnam, 110 Air Force fighter-bombers and tactical bombers in Thailand, and nearly 300 Navy and Marine fighter-bombers at six bases and tactical bombers on three aircraft carriers in the Gulf of Tonkin. He also controlled all the Army helicopters in Vietnam, and he indirectly controlled more than 100 Air Force B-52 strategic bombers in Thailand, Guam, and Okinawa.[5]

OP 2

Shortly after midnight on Nelson's OP 1, SP4 Orlando Vasquez caught a glimpse of a shadowy figure between the inner and outer perimeter wires. He fired at it five times with his 40mm grenade launcher and the figure disappeared.[6] For almost the next three hours, the hilltop OPs were ominously quiet.

At 0245 hours, Nelson's OP 2 received a mortar and rocket barrage followed by an assault on the southern perimeter by an estimated platoon of NVA sappers. Stunned by the deafening explosions and disoriented in the chaotic darkness, SSG John Carter, SP5 John Stuller, PFC Imlay Widdison, and PFC Roy Williams ran from their foxhole on the southern perimeter to the foxhole on the eastern perimeter and jumped into it on top of SSG Edward Sassenberger, PFC John Colonna, and SP4 Wilbert Foreman.

The attackers threw two hand grenades into their foxhole, and the first blast killed Widdison. The second blast killed Williams, fatally wounded Stuller, wounded Foreman's hand, wounded Colonna's knee, and blew off part of the roof. Stuller was lying on top of Foreman, and when Foreman told him to get off, Stuller weakly replied, "I can't … I'm dying."[7]

From under the bloody pile Sassenberger laboriously disentangled himself and his rifle, pushed his head and arms out of the hole in the roof, and shot four attackers. A bullet grazed him, and he ducked back into the foxhole, bleeding. Then he crawled out the north side of the foxhole and pulled Foreman out, while Colonna crawled out of the south side of it.

Carter was about to crawl out of it, when he was shot. Colonna tried to pull him out, but the attackers threw a third grenade into the hole, killing Carter.[8] The other two men on the southern perimeter—SP4 Richard Bowers and SP4 Maurice Moore—were either killed there or ran to the foxhole on the western perimeter occupied by 2LT Fred Ransbottom, PFC Randall Lloyd, PFC William Skivington, and PFC Danny Widner.

At the same time, CPT John Connolly, the American battalion's assistant operations officer, radioed an AC-47 nighttime gunship, radio name Spooky, to request emergency air support for OP 2. Buchwald or Connolly had to send most of the radio transmissions from the TOC, because Nelson became nervous and confused when talking into a microphone with a cigar in his mouth.[9] Simultaneously and independently, the radio NCOs of the SF A-team and the SOG launch team were reporting the attack to their respective headquarters near Danang.[10]

At 0300 hours, Spooky arrived and began dropping magnesium parachute flares around OP 2. They burst with a pop and burned for three minutes with two-million candlepower. Spooky also had three Miniguns and 43,500 rounds of 7.62mm ammunition,[11] but the pilot could not use his guns on the OP, because he could not clearly see it through the fog.

Even if the pilot could have seen the OP, he was not allowed to fire on a target unless the ground CO requested it either directly or through a FAC who authorized it.[12] No FAC was there, Spooky did not have

Ransbottom's radio frequency, and Ransbottom did not have Spooky's radio frequency. Ransbottom was desperately radioing the battalion TOC for artillery support, when his voice was suddenly cut off. He was never heard from again.

Two UH-1 helicopter gunships ("Muskets") of the 176th Assault Helicopter Company (AHC) at Chu Lai took off for Kham Duc, but one developed mechanical problems and had to return. It was replaced by a UH-1 gunship from the 123rd Aviation Battalion ("Warlords").[13] They also could not provide fire support to OP 2, because the pilots could not clearly see it. The parachute flares produced a "bowl" visual effect in the fog that made the terrain seem to curve around the pilots' eyes.

One of the pilots, WO Bob Smith, radioed OP 2 and told the frightened soldier on the radio to shine a flashlight upward to mark his position, but the man said he had no flashlight. Smith then told him to fire tracer rounds upward to mark his position, but the man said he had no tracer rounds. Smith finally told him to adjust the red tracer fire from his helicopter. The man said he could see the red tracers, but did not know how to adjust them, because he had no compass and no sense of direction in the foggy darkness.[14]

OP 1

The men on OP 1, seeing and hearing the attack on OP 2, prepared for the inevitable attack on themselves as best they could. At 0320 hours, they were hit by a barrage of mortar and rocket fire followed by an NVA ground assault. Spooky dropped more parachute flares in the darkness around the fog-covered OP. In the hazy, oscillating light PFC Harris Chandler, PFC Richard Hill, and PFC Andrew Craven saw a group of NVA troops trying to get through the concertina wire on the eastern perimeter. They shot the attackers with automatic bursts from their M-16 rifles, and the NVA bodies piled up on the wire.

The CIDG squad tried to escape into the jungle below, but the attackers killed all but two of them. Another explosion blew the OP gate open, and several attackers got within 10 feet of it, but became entangled in the concertina wire that Wright and others put there the previous day. Wright shot most of them with automatic bursts of his M-16 rifle, and the few NVA survivors retreated down the hill to reorganize for another assault.[15]

I DASC

At 0400 hours, the American Division headquarters at Chu Lai and the SF headquarters in Danang independently radioed the Air Force I Corps Direct Air Support Center (I DASC) in Danang, told them Kham Duc was under attack, and requested maximum air support. I DASC immediately sent an AF forward air controller to the camp and began to organize attack aircraft to send.[16]

At 0445 hours, four crews of the 178th Assault Support Helicopter Company (ASHC), radio name "Boxcars", were alerted for a tactical emergency mission. Their operations officer, CPT Joe Sturdevant, hastily assembled the four Chinook crews and informed them that everyone at Kham Duc had to be evacuated that same day.[17]

The First FAC

At 0515 hours, CPT Wilbert (Herb) Spier, an AF FAC attached to the Americal Division in Chu Lai, took off for Kham Duc in a Cessna 0–2 observation plane. By 0600 hours, the low clouds on the hilltops had dissipated, and in the distance he could see tracer fire and explosions in and around the camp and the OPs. Against the dark sky it looked like the largest fireworks display he had ever seen.[18] Orbiting near the valley at between 2,000 and 3,000 feet, Spier received a radio briefing on the situation from the Americal battalion TOC. Soon a C-130 flare ship arrived to replace Spooky, who had used all his flares.

I DASC also sent ten Air Force F-4 fighter-bombers from Danang, ten Marine A-4 tactical bombers from Chu Lai, and eight B-52 strategic bombers from Thailand. As each pilot arrived overhead, he radioed Spier and reported his ordnance.[19] By then, the attackers were so intermingled with the U.S. troops that Spier could not put air strikes on the OPs for fear of killing any surviving American troops, but he could put air strikes around the OPs, airstrip, and SF camp.

His plane carried fourteen white phosphorous rockets, and he told the pilots of the attack planes to put their bombs either on his rocket smoke or at a certain distance and direction from it. After identifying his bright-white smoke as the reference point, each pilot could make up to eight passes on the indicated targets. As the warmth of the predawn sun met the cool night air, ground fog began to cover the valley, and the pilots could no longer see the rocket smoke.

Spier retained a mental image of the terrain and improvised a tactic to continue providing fire support through the fog. He assigned altitudes to each attack pilot, told the pilot to follow his FAC plane, then told him when to release his bombs.[20] The Air Liaison Officer (ALO) at the SF camp, AF CPT Willard Johnson, could not see the attack planes through the fog, but could hear the impact of the bombs. Talking to Spier on his UHF radio, Johnson guided him in, bringing the bombs to within 600 yards of the camp and OPs.[21]

OP 1

With shrill whistles and shouts, the NVA troops renewed their assault on OP 1, but became entangled in the concertina wire surrounding it. PFC Craven detonated the claymore mines on the perimeter, killing many attackers, but also blowing gaps in the wire. Other attackers ran through the gaps, throwing hand grenades and firing RPD machine guns and AK-47 rifles.

After firing all his 40mm grenades with his M-79 grenade launcher, SP4 Orlando Vasquez somehow lost his weapon in the chaotic darkness. Seeing PFC Antonio Guzman on the roof of the southeast bunker firing an M-60 machine gun, Vasquez ran to it, climbed onto the roof, and assisted Guzman by feeding linked ammunition into the gun. Their fire forced the NVA attackers to retreat into the northwest bunker, until the machine gun jammed. After attempting unsuccessfully to clear it, Vasquez and Guzman retreated into the bunker below, where Wright, Simpson, and the two surviving CIDG troops were sheltering.[22]

SP4 Julius Long was running toward that bunker, when he saw PFC Coen lying on the ground. Long tried to help him get up, but saw that Coen's abdominal wound was causing some of his intestines to protrude.

Coen pushed his intestines back into his abdominal cavity and held them there as best he could, while Long helped him into the bunker.[23]

OP 3

To prevent OP 3 from being overrun, MAJ Buchwald in the battalion TOC radioed SGT Wayne Wietting on OP 3 and told him to fire his ammunition for the 106mm recoilless gun, destroy it, and withdraw his squad to the airstrip.[24] Wietting fired the ammunition, destroyed the breach of the gun with a thermite grenade, then cautiously began to move his squad down the south side of the dark, jungle-covered hill.

Nearing the village, they suddenly met an NVA platoon in the darkness and exchanged fire with them. The point man, SP4 Edward Pierce, was hit in the arm, and the squad medic, SP4 William Bledsoe, heedless of the enemy fire, ran to the front of the column to treat his wound. The NVA troops broke contact, and Wietting's squad continued down the hill to the airstrip.[25]

As they approached it, they saw one of the howitzers in the artillery battery receive a direct hit from an NVA mortar shell, wounding several artillerymen. Again Bledsoe fearlessly ran forward and began treating them, until another mortar explosion seriously wounded him. Despite the shock and pain of his wound, he continued giving emergency first aid to the other wounded men.[26]

OP 1

The long antenna on the radio that SGT Simpson commandeered from the CIDG squad was broken and could only transmit for short distances. At 0430 hours, he used Wright's radio with its long antenna to call the battalion TOC and ask Buchwald to have Spooky fire directly on the northwest bunker of his OP, which was occupied by NVA troops. Instead, Buchwald ordered him to abandon the OP and bring the survivors back to the airstrip.

Simpson told Wright and Vasquez to take the radio with the long antenna down the west side of the hill with the two surviving CIDG men, while he, Long, and Guzman took the CIDG radio with the short antenna and helped Coen go down the east side. Craven, Hill, and Chandler were also trying to escape down the east side of the OP in the darkness, but they had no radio and could not communicate with anyone.

When Guzman peered out of the bunker to see if Wright and Vasquez had escaped, he was shot in the head and instantly killed. His body was left there and undoubtedly was destroyed by the subsequent bombing and artillery fire on the OP. Wright saw Sisk lying on the ground and verified that he was dead. Following the two CIDG troops, Vasquez and he then climbed over the OP berm. Wright had his M-16 rifle and twenty-one magazines of ammunition, but Vasquez had no weapon.

As they moved through the first strand of concertina wire, one of the CIDG troops tripped a booby trap. The explosion killed both CIDG men, wounded Wright and Vasquez, and left them lying unconscious on the ground. Wright was bleeding from shrapnel in his legs, and Vasquez was bleeding from a gaping neck wound.

When Wright regained consciousness, he grasped the still unconscious Vasquez by the collar, and pulled him through the second strand of wire to the edge of the western slope of the hill. They rolled off the edge, slid 25 yards down the hill, and became separated in the thick underbrush. Hearing Vasquez's groans, Wright groped for him in the darkness, found him, and dragged him 40 yards farther down the hill into a grove of banana trees.

He was bandaging Vasquez's wound with his field dressing, when artillery shells from the American battery below crashed into the banana grove. Wright frantically radioed the battalion TOC and told Buchwald to stop the artillery. Buchwald said they had to keep firing at the OP, because the NVA anti-aircraft machine guns in the northwest bunker had to be destroyed before the wounded men in the southeast bunker could be evacuated.

To hit the NVA on top of the hill, the artillerymen had to first bracket it on the far and near sides, then fire at the center of the bracket. He told Wright to adjust the artillery fire onto the OP, but Wright said he did not know how and did not want artillery fire on the OP, because he feared it would kill the Americans there.

Simpson's radio with a short antenna could receive and transmit to Wright's radio, as long as Wright was relatively close to Simpson's bunker. He radioed Wright and told him NVA troops were throwing hand grenades into the bunker. He and the others there were wounded and urgently needed evacuation. Wright realized then that unless the NVA troops in the northwest bunker were killed, the U.S. troops in the southeast bunker soon would be.

Coached by Buchwald, Wright observed where each shell landed and reported it to him by radio. Buchwald told the artillerymen to adjust their fire accordingly. The 105mm rounds landed very near the northwest bunker, but were not powerful enough to destroy the concrete walls and kill the NVA troops inside.

By 0735 hours, the ground fog had dissipated, and from Wright's position on the side of the hill below OP 1 he saw an NVA platoon carrying supplies up the hill toward the northwest bunker. He reported it to Buchwald, who ordered the artillery to fire on the platoon. Wright again adjusted their fire by radio, until most of the NVA troops were killed. The few survivors dropped their cargo and scattered.

Buchwald then told Wright to move to another hill west of OP 1. When Wright reported that he had done so, Buchwald gave him the radio frequency of an AF FAC. He told Wright to radio the FAC and follow his instructions for putting an air strike on OP 1. Wright again refused, fearing that the bombs would kill the members of his squad in the southeast bunker. The FAC assured him that they would not use napalm, and the force of the high-explosive blasts would be toward the northwest bunker, not the southeast one.

The FAC marked the target with a smoke rocket, Wright confirmed it, and two F-4 Phantoms swooped in and dropped 500lb bombs near the northwest bunker. The blasts did not destroy the concrete bunker walls or kill the NVA troops inside, but the deafening shock waves stunned and silenced them for a while.

Wright urgently radioed Simpson in the southeast bunker to confirm that they had survived the bombs. Simpson heard his message and tried to respond to it, but Wright was beyond the range of Simpson's short-antenna radio. Hearing no reply, Wright thought the bombs he helped put on OP 1 had killed his comrades, and that secret guilt haunted him for years.[27]

Buchwald ordered Wright and Vasquez to get back to the airstrip any way they could. As the two men worked their way down the south slope of the hill, they saw a long column of NVA troops moving toward the airstrip. Wright counted them to a hundred and saw that there were many more in the column.

He radioed Buchwald, who told him to radio the FAC and give him their location. Wright did so, and the FAC marked the head and tail of the column with white phosphorus rockets. Two F-4 Phantom fighter-bombers then streaked in and dropped napalm bombs on the whole column, enveloping it in roaring fire clouds burning at 2,000-degree Fahrenheit.[28]

The SF Camp

The SF A-team and the SOG troops were not in direct radio contact with the U.S. troops on the hilltop OPs, but they monitored the FM radio traffic between the OPs and the Americal TOC. Seeing the explosive flashes and firing on OP 1 and 2, they knew what was happening there at the same time the Americal TOC did. Some of the SF A-team men were firing 81mm mortars, a 106mm recoilless gun, and a .50 caliber machine gun at the NVA troops on OPs 1 and 2. The ALO, AF CPT Willard Johnson, recorded the battle sounds on a small tape recorder, and his comments reveal his growing apprehension about the defenders' fate, if they were not evacuated before nightfall.[29]

At 0640 hours, SF SSG "Mac" Woodard and two Nung crewmen in the SF A-team's part of the camp were firing an 81mm mortar, when they received a direct hit from an 82mm NVA mortar. The explosion instantly killed one Nung, mortally wounded the other, and hurled Woodard's unconscious body out of the pit. He miraculously survived and was later medically evacuated, but remained dazed and confused from the brain damage of a severe concussion.[30]

Two SF officers, CPT Bud Williams and 2LT Lee Purdy, were in the SOG trench, but the morale and combat-readiness of the SOG troops did not require the personal leadership of any officer. They were well-armed volunteers emotionally primed for close, high-risk combat. The only leadership they needed was Windley's cheerful, fearless example, and the only leadership their indigenous troops needed was the steady presence of their SF NCOs.

Hillsboro

At 0630 hours, the 7th Air Force Tactical Air Control Center (TACC) at Tan Son Nhut air base near Saigon diverted a C-130 control aircraft, radio name "Hillsboro", from its daytime operating area over Laos and sent it to Kham Duc's map coordinates. It could fly for sixteen hours without refueling, and its large interior module carried a ten-man technical crew with data processing equipment that enabled them to simultaneously coordinate large numbers of aircraft. The duty controller, AF CPT Medley Gatewood, had performed the same function at the battle of Khe Sanh three months earlier.[31]

Hillsboro began diverting attack aircraft from all over South Vietnam and Thailand to Kham Duc. The pilots were given Hillsboro's map coordinates and radio frequency and told to report to it, when they arrived in the area. Gatewood inventoried the ordnance of each plane and sent it to one of several high-altitude parking orbits. Large AF KC-135 tanker planes were also orbiting nearby to give the attack planes all the fuel they needed to stay on station indefinitely.[32]

The FACs

AF Forward Air Controllers were fixed-wing attack pilots with the technical skill and flying experience to direct the pilots of other fixed-wing attack planes. They were a vital communication link between the ground troops and the fixed-wing planes supporting them. Flying low and slow in small, piston-engine observation planes, the FACs were frequently exposed to lethal ground fire, and several FACs were shot down and killed during the war.

Ten AF FACs flew over Kham Duc on May 12, working two-hour shifts in teams of three. Two low FACs flew on each side of the airstrip, and a high FAC flew above them. Based on a low FAC's need for specific ordnance, Hillsboro selected the planes carrying that ordnance and released them to the high FAC, who briefed the attack pilots on the type and location of the target and released them to one of the low FACs. The low FACs worked directly with the ground troops to attack the target as many times and in as many ways as necessary.[33]

The First CH-47 Crash

Four CH-47 Chinook transport helicopters (radio name "Boxcars") had been orbiting over the airstrip for nearly an hour, waiting for the ground fog to clear enough for them to see it. At 0710 hours, LTC Ray Carson, CO of the 14th Combat Aviation Battalion, arrived over Kham Duc in a UH-1 transport helicopter, saw the situation, and sent the four CH-47s to LZ Ross to refuel and await orders. Twenty-five minutes later the ground fog cleared, and he ordered the helicopter evacuation to resume.[34]

At 0800 hours, the first CH-47, commanded by CPT Joe Sturdevant, was descending over the airstrip at about 400 feet when anti-aircraft machine-gun bullets ripped into it. They destroyed the hydraulic system and started a fire in the cargo bay that spread to the cockpit. As the NVA gunners poured more bullets into it, the burning helicopter fell hard on its back wheels and began to careen down the airstrip.

Frantically attempting to escape the fire, the three crewmen jumped out. Two of them landed on their feet and rolled, but one landed on his knees, breaking them.[35] Four American infantrymen, seeing the man lying helplessly and in pain on the fire-swept airstrip, ran out, picked him up, and carried him back to their place in the drainage ditch around the airstrip.

The front wheel of the CH-47 then slammed down, causing the burning helicopter to flip forward, twist in the air, crash down on its right side, and skid to a stop near the middle of the airstrip with an enormous column of black smoke billowing out of it. Sturdevant and his co-pilot, WO Bill Eoff, scrambled out through the cockpit door, as NVA machine-gun fire shattered the instrument panel and the Plexiglas chin bubble, splattering them with fragments.[36]

The Engineers

The burning helicopter on the airstrip was not only preventing the fixed-wing transport planes from landing, but was damaging the airstrip by beginning to burn a hole in the asphalt. A brave engineer soldier, SP4 John Powell, spontaneously climbed on a bucket loader (aka front loader) tractor and started it, although he had never driven one before. Seeing what Powell was about to do, one of the engineer officers, 1LT James Lanier, climbed onto it with him.[37]

Powell drove the tractor out onto the airstrip, scooped up the burning engine with the huge bucket, and dumped it off on the side of the airstrip. As he backed up to push more burning wreckage off, he inadvertently drove into the fire, igniting the tractor's tires and hydraulic fluid and forcing Powell and Lanier to abandon it. The burning wreckage partially blocked the airstrip, but other brave engineer soldiers drove a water truck onto the airstrip and put out the fire.[38]

The engineer company's two D-7 bulldozers were disassembled for loading onto C-130s, but 1LT Waldo ordered the blade and push arms quickly reattached to one of them. Matching Powell's courageous example, SP5 Donald Hostler alone drove the bulldozer onto the airstrip and pushed the remaining wreckage off.[39] To the onlookers around the airstrip and in the SF camp it seemed incredible that he was not shot. Only his conspicuously valiant action enabled the evacuation by fixed-wing aircraft to begin.

Over the Airstrip

At 0800 hours, the pilot of an A-1E Skyraider, AF LTC James Swain, saw an NVA anti-aircraft machine gun firing from the abandoned CIDG OP east of OP 3 on the northeast end of the airstrip. He attacked it with the rasping growl of his 20mm automatic cannons and the rippling crackle of his CBU bombs. The NVA gunner's body was flung into the air like a rag doll, but soon another fearless NVA gunner with another anti-aircraft machine gun replaced the first one and resumed firing at Swain's plane.

Swain dove on the position again and dropped another bomb on it, but before the second gunner was killed, he riddled Swain's plane with .51 caliber bullets. As Swain pulled out of the dive and started to climb, his plane began to stream black smoke. The U.S. troops watching it climb heard the rpms of its piston engine whining higher and higher, as it strained to gain enough altitude for the pilot to bail out before it burned up and fell out of the sky.

Swain ejected and fell free for three seconds, then his parachute blossomed, and he began to float down over scores of NVA troops firing at him. He landed on the side of a jungle-covered hill 100 yards from the south end of the airstrip. WO Edward Fitzsimmons, a UH-1 pilot from the 176th Assault Helicopter Company ("Minutemen"), saw where he landed and raced to rescue him. Two UH-1 gunships spontaneously accompanied Fitzsimmons.

One was from the 176th AHC ("Muskets") commanded by WO Coburn and piloted by WO Ron Blohm. The other was from the 123rd Aviation Battalion ("Warlords") commanded by WO Ezell and piloted by 1LT David Ewing.[40] The two gunships killed many of the NVA troops with their 7.62mm Minigun rounds, 2.75inch rockets, and 40mm grenades. Other enemy troops fearlessly fired back at them, hitting both gunships repeatedly.

Hovering his helicopter near the parachute hanging in the trees, Fitzsimmons used his rotor blades to cut through the foliage, while his crew chief fired an M-60 machine gun at the NVA troops. His door gunner, SP4 Ray Cyrus, and his pilot (an unidentified lieutenant) jumped out and ran to recover Swain, who was limping toward them on an injured ankle. They threw him into the helicopter and flew him to Chu Lai, where he cleaned himself up and hitched a plane ride back to his base at Pleiku. Fitzsimmons made two more trips from Chu Lai to Kham Duc that day, carrying ammunition in and bringing wounded men out.[41]

The two badly shot-up UH-1 gunships flew to the nearest fortified LZ, Fire Base Ross, 20 miles northeast of Kham Duc. When they landed, they saw that the tail rotor cable of one helicopter was nearly severed, and both gunships had so many bullet holes in them that they were rated inoperable. The pilots and crews returned to Chu Lai in a CH-47 helicopter.[42]

The Grand Slam

At 0830 hours, AF GEN William Momyer, Westmoreland's Deputy CG for Air, declared Kham Duc a Grand Slam emergency. It was the first time he used his new authority as the Single Manager for Air to command all the Air Force, Marine, and Navy fixed-wing aircraft and all the Army rotor-wing aircraft in Vietnam, regardless of their parent unit or home base.[43]

On May 12, Hillsboro diverted 120 Air Force fighter-bombers and tactical bombers (F-4s, F-100s, F-105s, and A-1s) based in South Vietnam and Thailand, sixteen Marine A-4s based in South Vietnam, six Vietnamese Air Force A-5s, and two non-specified Navy fighter-bombers and/or tactical bombers (F-4s, F-8s, A-4s, and/or A-6s) based on one or more of the three aircraft carriers on Yankee Station in the Gulf of Tonkin 100 miles northeast of Danang.[44]

Most readers, including most Vietnam battle veterans, have no concept of the magnitude of destructive power inflicted on the massed NVA troops at Kham Duc on May 12, 1968. No U.S. troops in Vietnam ever experienced an enemy air attack, and no VC or NVA troops except those near Khe Sanh three months earlier ever experienced a mass air attack like the one suffered by those two NVA regiments that day.

- The A-1 Skyraiders had four 20mm automatic cannons and carried 8,000 pounds of 500lb bombs, 750lbbombs, napalm bombs, white phosphorous bombs, and cluster bombs.
- The A-4 Skyhawks had two 20mm automatic cannons and carried 8,200 pounds of 500lb bombs, 750lb bombs, and 2.75inch rockets.
- The A-6 Intruders carried 18,000 pounds of 250lb bombs, 500lb bombs, 750lb bombs, napalm bombs, cluster bombs, 2.75inch rockets, and 5inch rockets.
- The F-4 Phantoms had a 20mm automatic cannon and carried 16,000 pounds of 500lb bombs, 750lb bombs, napalm bombs, and 2.75inch rockets.
- The F-5 Freedom Fighters had two 20mm automatic canons and carried 3,500 pounds of 500lb bombs, 750lb bombs, napalm bombs, cluster bombs, and 2.75inch rockets.

- The F-8 Crusaders had four 20mm automatic cannons and carried 5,000 pounds of 500lb bombs, 750lb bombs, and 2.75inch rockets.
- The F-100 Super Sabers had four 20mm automatic cannons and carried 7,500 pounds of 500lb bombs and 750lb bombs.
- The F-105 Thunderchiefs had a 20mm automatic cannon and carried eight 750lb bombs and thirty-eight 2.75inch rockets.45

A 500lb high-explosive bomb bursting on a relatively level surface can produce a crater 15 feet deep and 30 feet wide. A 750lb high-explosive bomb bursting on the same kind of surface can produce a crater 30 feet deep and 45 feet wide. In unobstructed areas both sizes of bombs can hurl lethal shrapnel up to 700 feet.[46]

A napalm bomb contains 125 or more gallons of a flammable petroleum gel. Dropped at low altitudes, it explodes on contact, deoxygenates the air, and scatters particles of gel burning at 2,000 degrees Fahrenheit. The gel sticks to anything it touches and cannot be extinguished until consumed or deprived of oxygen.[47]

A cluster bomb unit (CBU) is a bomb case with hundreds of 1lb, baseball-size bomblets. It opens at a pre-determined altitude and scatters the bomblets in all directions. They explode with the force of a hand grenade either on contact or as pre-timed, and release 180,000 steel pellets flying at the speed of a bullet.[48]

A 2.75inch rocket has a warhead that explodes with the force of a 75mm artillery shell. It hurls metal fragments or phosphorous particles in a lethal radius of 10 yards and a danger radius of 50 yards.[49]

The U.S. weapon most feared by both VC and NVA troops was an attack by B-52 long-range bombers (code named "Arc Light"). The internal radar of B-52s combined with the AF TPQ-10 and MSQ-77 ground radar systems enabled them to bomb area targets (not point targets) in zero visibility from 35,000 feet with a 100-yard margin of error. Three-plane cells, flying unseen and unheard at an altitude beyond sight and sound on the ground, located their area target by radar and simultaneously released all their bombs on it.

With no warning, an area 3 miles long and half a mile wide suddenly erupted in the rippling shock waves of more than 300 simultaneous explosions from one cell of three B-52s. Anyone above ground was suddenly obliterated by hurricane-force storms of hot metal, wood, dirt, and rock shrapnel. Even those protected from the shrapnel in deep trenches and bunkers were not safe from an Arc Light attack.

Hundreds of high-explosive bombs detonating almost simultaneously in the same area cause temporary vacuums in the air. Air molecules rushing into the vacuums at 900 miles per hour create winds moving in the opposite direction at the same speed. The whiplash wind forces can burst eardrums, collapse lungs, explode bladders, compress spleens, destroy neural networks, and tear blood vessels in the face, eyes, ears, and brain. The destruction of blood vessels in the lungs alone can cause the victims to drown in their own blood.[50]

The NVA troops not killed or wounded by the thousands of explosions were deafened and disoriented by the ear-splitting noise and concussed by the pounding, earth-shaking shock waves.[51] On May 12, eight B-52s dropped 800 high-explosive bombs around Kham Duc before the morning fog lifted, and during that day, twenty-four additional B-52s dropped 2,400 more high-explosive bombs on suspected NVA positions around the valley.

On May 13 and 14, 120 sorties of B-52s dropped more than 12,000 high-explosive bombs on potential NVA assembly areas and withdrawal routes around Kham Duc. The bombs caused 130 secondary explosions that were three to ten times larger than the bomb blasts. One B-52 mission alone caused seventy-eight secondary explosions.[52] They revealed the huge amount of ordnance the two reinforced NVA regiments stockpiled around Kham Duc, evidently in the expectation of a much larger and/ or longer battle.

The Second Ground Attacks

The attack aircraft were orbiting so high and the orbits were so dispersed that no one on the ground could see how numerous they were. The defenders did not realize that a virtual air armada was lurking overhead to give them all the close air support they wanted, as long as the pilots could see their targets. The attackers did not realize that they could never capture the camp and its defenders, as long as the May sky over Kham Duc remained abnormally clear. The more they massed to attack in the open, the more they were slaughtered by a seemingly inexhaustible concentration of air firepower.

Among the scores of aircraft diverted to Kham Duc were two Air Force F-105 fighter-bombers from Takhli, Thailand, flying at 15,000 feet toward a target north of the DMZ. When they arrived over Kham Duc, Hillsboro turned them over to the high FAC, who told them to put all their bombs on the area marked by his smoke rocket half a mile southwest of the south end of the airstrip, where a large number of NVA troops were forming for a mass assault.

Each F-105 made a steep dive toward the area, released its eight bombs at 6,500 feet, and streaked away. The almost simultaneous impact of sixteen 750lb high-explosive bombs on that relatively small area pulverized the massed NVA troops and caused such a gigantic eruption of fire, smoke, dirt, and foliage that the American troops on the south end of the airstrip thought it was a dangerously close B-52 strike.[53]

At 0936 hours, other NVA troops launched multi-company assaults on the north and west sides of the airstrip across flat, open ground in clear daylight. Before they could reach the U.S. troop positions, most of them were disintegrated by a deluge of airstrikes and direct artillery fire. The stunned survivors retreated in disorder, some dragging NVA bodies with them.

OP 2

The U.S. troops around the airstrip saw the NVA troops on OP 2 loading the 106mm recoilless gun that the overrun American squad did not have time to destroy.[54] As the SF men feared, the attackers were using a U.S. weapon to fire U.S. ammunition at U.S. troops as a direct result of Nelson's tactical incompetence. Owens's blunder in putting inadequate squads on the hilltop OPs without consulting the resident SF team on the enemy situation was thoughtless. Nelson's blunder was willful—not only putting squads there without consulting the SF men on the enemy situation, but sending 106mm recoilless guns and anti-personnel ammunition with them, which they obviously could not defend in a sudden night attack by a superior enemy force.

The First C–130

At 1000 hours, a C–130 commanded by AF LTC Darryl Cole and piloted by AF MAJ Walter Farrar was diverted to Kham Duc from a routine mission with no warning of what to expect there. Escorted by an A–1E Skyraider and an F–4 Phantom, they landed safely and taxied onto the tarmac. When the loadmaster lowered the rear ramp, scores of terrified Vietnamese civilians from the village and some CIDG deserters in civilian clothes ran from the drainage ditches on the west side of the airstrip and crowded into the cargo bay.[55]

Following the order of withdrawal from III MAF headquarters, Buchwald told the CO of A Company 1/46/198, 1LT Thompson, that his troops would be the first ones evacuated, since they arrived before Nelson's battalion.[56] Then MG Koster, the CG of the American Division, decided that the engineer troops should be the first ones evacuated, since they arrived before the American troops. The American headquarters informed the headquarters of the engineer company at Pleiku that their troops would go out first, and the engineer headquarters informed the CO of their A Company, 1LT Waldo.[57] Buchwald was apparently not informed of the change.

When the first C–130 landed, Buchwald told the CO of A/1/46/198 to take his troops from their defensive position on the south end of the airstrip to a position near the tarmac and prepare to board the plane.[58] Some of the SF NCOs, who did not know that those troops were told to leave their position, saw their action as a cowardly lack of discipline, and that erroneous impression was later propagated in a published account of the battle.[59]

Some of the engineer troops and some of the A/1/46/198 troops, including at least one U.S. platoon leader, crowded into the cargo bay with the civilians. Cole taxied the C–130 onto the airstrip and tried to take off, but with the weight of so many passengers and the unloaded cargo he could not develop enough speed. They returned to the tarmac, while mortar shells exploded around the plane. One landed only 10 yards from it, shattering two cockpit windows. Other mortar shells and machine-gun bullets punctured a wing fuel tank and flattened a tire.[60]

As soon as the rear ramp was lowered, the panicked civilians, CIDG deserters, and a few American troops ran out of the plane and back into the ditches along the airstrip. One woman handed her baby to a U.S. lieutenant on board, evidently thinking it was safer with him. He jumped off the ramp with the baby in his arms, gave it to the first woman he saw, and rejoined his platoon.[61]

Despite the enemy fire, the C-130 crewmen were trying to cut the flat tire off the wheel with a bayonet, but could not cut through its steel belting. Seeing their problem, two engineer troops drove an equipment truck onto the tarmac and cut off the tire with a blowtorch.[62] At the same time, an NCO in the SF camp, SSG Mac Woodard, raced across the airstrip in a jeep, picked up Cole and Farrar, and raced back across the airstrip to the camp.

The ALO at Kham Duc, CPT Johnson, radioed the I DASC in Danang and reported that a CH-47 helicopter and an A-1E attack plane had been shot down, and the first C-130 that landed was so badly damaged by enemy fire that it could not take off. I DASC relayed his message to GEN Momyer, who ordered BG McLaughlin, the CG of the 834th Air Division, to cancel future C-130 landings at Kham Duc.[63]

I DASC received the order and relayed it to Johnson, who informed Henderson and Nelson that the air evacuation was suspended. When Cole and Farrar were told they might have to evacuate with the Americal troops on foot, they decided to attempt another takeoff.[64] Cole invited the other four Air Force men—the three CCT men and the ALO, Johnson—to leave with him. Johnson and MAJ Gallagher, the CO of the CCT, eagerly accepted.

The two CCT NCOs, Freedman and Lundie, protested that they could not leave the ongoing battle, regardless of the cancellation of the C-130 evacuation. They knew that they had to stay there until it was either resumed or replaced by a parachute supply mission, both of which would require their assistance. Their CO ordered them to either leave with him then or face a court martial for refusing to obey his direct order. The two CCT NCOs then reluctantly boarded the plane.[65]

With one tire removed and the loss of 4,000lb of fuel from the left wing tank, the C-130 was dangerously unbalanced. Cole feared to start the fourth engine on that wing because of the danger that the heat would ignite the fuel pouring out of it. As the C-130 taxied off the tarmac onto the airstrip, the leaking wing tank sprayed fuel on the CIDG deserters and village civilians in the nearby drainage ditch.[66]

The Americal and engineer troops watching it feared that if it could not take off, all future transport flights would be cancelled. As the C-130 lumbered down the airstrip, Cole started the fourth engine, and the troops along the side chanted "Go! Go! Go!" until it cleared the ridge at the south end of the airstrip.[67] With fuel still streaming out of the punctured wing, Cole and Farrar flew the C-130 to Cam Ranh Bay and landed it on a foamed runway.[68]

Preparing for the Worst

When Buchwald learned that all C-130 landings had been cancelled, he realized that the defenders might have to escape on foot through the jungle. He ordered the 2/1/196 troops, the A/1/46/198 troops, and the engineer troops to destroy all their equipment except their helmets, belt-and-suspender harnesses, canteens, personal weapons, and ammunition. The infantry and engineer troops began to stack or throw their other equipment into piles and burn it.

Protective vests, backpacks, collapsible shovels, rubberized ponchos, nylon poncho liners, smoke grenades, trip flairs, signal flares, medical kits, claymore mines, pieces of C-4 plastic explosive, detonation cord, fuses, firing devices, AN/PRC-25 FM radios, radio batteries, gas masks, canned rations, wound dressings, toilet articles, ID cards, and all other papers were thrown onto the bonfires.[69]

The encryption team destroyed their radios with thermite grenades, broke the circuit boards of their encryption and teletype machines, threw them into a pile, poured gasoline on the pile, and burned it.[70]

The engineers disabled the engines of their vehicles with thermite grenades, and the infantrymen used thermite grenades to destroy the firing mechanisms of their recoilless guns and mortars.

The artillery battery continued to fire at suspected NVA targets and by 1530 hours had fired 720 rounds. 1LT Chris Pelkey, 2LT Gary Cutler, and two gun chiefs fired as many of the secret "Firecracker" anti-personnel rounds as possible, until the battery was ordered to prepare for evacuation. They stacked the remaining 105mm rounds for burning, but much of the secret ammunition had to be left for later destruction by bombing.[71]

Buchwald told the engineer CO, 1LT Waldo, to leave his .50 caliber machine guns, 81mm mortar, 7.62mm machine guns, and the ammunition for them in his camp for the American infantrymen who would occupy it and defend that portion of the camp after the engineers left.[72] When the Americal troops moved into the engineer camp and saw those weapons there, they mistakenly thought the engineer troops had abandoned them in a cowardly rush to escape.

The SF Commanders

At 0930 hours, a UH-1 from Danang landed in the SF camp with LTC Schungel, CO of the 5th SF troops in I Corps, and LTC Overby, CO of SOG's FOB 4 near Danang. With them came SF CPT Warren Orr, six SF NCOs, and Schungel's LLDB Vietnamese counterpart.[73] The *beau geste* arrival of the two SF commanders sent a powerful nonverbal message to the SF and SOG men: if they were killed or captured at Kham Duc, the senior SF officers who sent them there would voluntarily die or be captured with them.

More importantly, Schungel's arrival radically changed the command structure at Kham Duc. No one in the American Division, including its CG, had the authority to tell him he was subordinate to Nelson. Since Nelson was no longer the ranking U.S. officer, he could not issue any orders to the SF men or make any decisions about their CIDG troops. Schungel did not command the SOG men, but the camp was part of his command, and LTC Overby willingly cooperated with him.

After a brief stop at Nelson's TOC to announce his arrival, Schungel returned to the SF camp and stood outside the TOC, monitoring the FM radio traffic and occasionally talking to the FACs. SFC Sidney Sheeler in the A-team communication bunker encrypted Henderson's status reports, and SGT Robert Aycock sent them in Morse code to the 5th SF Group headquarters in Danang.[74] LTC Overby went to the SOG TOC to monitor the radios and send status reports to SOG headquarters and his own FOB 4 headquarters.

McLeroy then joined the SOG troops in the trench and took over Windley's FM radio contact with the FAC flying over the SF camp at that time. AF LTC Reese Black had been at Kham Duc a few weeks before the battle and knew that McLeroy was the OIC of the SOG site. They recognized each other's voices from their brief radio conversation at that time.[75]

On the Airstrip

Hillsboro and the FACs attempted to match the flight paths of the landing airlift planes with pairs of fighter-bombers and/or tactical bombers to provide armed escorts for them. Some of the escort planes flew as close as 100 feet from the wing tips of the incoming transports. At 1100 hours, a C-123 piloted by AF MAJ Ray Shelton and escorted by two attack planes landed.

As soon as the rear ramp was lowered, forty-nine engineer troops and twenty-one frantic civilians ran into the cargo bay. The engineer troops boarded in a reasonably orderly manner, but the civilians were semi-hysterical, and the loadmaster could not control them. A wounded CIDG soldier was holding part of his intestines in his hands. Other terrified civilians tried to force their way into the cargo bay designed for thirty-two U.S. soldiers and their gear.

Shelton tried to push them away from his plane by locking the brakes and revving the two engines up to their maximum rpms to generate powerful wind blasts. It dislodged most of them, but as he began to roll down the airstrip and his loadmaster started to close the rear ramp, two desperate CIDG deserters grabbed the edge of the ramp and tried to climb into the plane. The loadmaster pulled them into the cargo bay, as Shelton took off in a hail of NVA fire.

He narrowly avoided a mid-air collision with a low-flying F-4 Phantom fighter-bomber, then almost collided with a damaged Cessna 0–2 FAC plane making an emergency landing at the same time. Despite all the explosions around his plane, it was never hit. Shelton considered his incredible escape from so much enemy fire and two near mid-air crashes literally miraculous.[76]

The Accidental ALO

The Cessna 0–2 that nearly hit him was piloted by AF CPT Phillip Smotherman, whose plane had been hit by anti-aircraft fire. The tip of one wing was shot off and the controls were damaged. He was trying to land it on one end of the airstrip with only his rudder for control, when he saw Shelton's C-123 taking off directly toward him. He quickly slid his plane over to the side of the airstrip to avoid the C-123, then used his rudder to slide his plane back over the airstrip, land it, and steer it safely to the side.

SF SSG Mac Woodard again raced out in a jeep, picked up Smotherman, and took him into the SF camp. Henderson assigned him to the bunker formerly occupied by the CCT men. Smotherman used one of their abandoned radios to contact the I DASC in Danang and report the departure of the Air Liaison Officer and the three CCT men. I DASC sent his report to MACV headquarters, and AF GEN Momyer ordered I DASC to tell him to remain at Kham Duc as the new ALO.

With the CCT radios Smotherman was able to keep the American Division Tactical Air Control Center in Chu Lai informed of the number of people waiting to be evacuated. Between reports he helped direct some air strikes. When the radios in the battalion TOC were destroyed, MG Koster, the American CG, temporarily lost radio contact with the battalion and feared it had been overrun. With a VHF radio left by the CCT men, Smotherman informed him of the true situation.[77] Smotherman's accidental presence and extemporaneous function as an emergency ALO at Kham Duc proved extremely fortuitous.

Army and Marine Helicopters

On May 12, forty-one flights of Army CH-47 helicopters, thirty flights of Marine CH-46 helicopters, and twelve flights of Army UH-1 helicopters evacuated hundreds of people, civilian and military, American and Vietnamese.[77] Some of the helicopter pilots decided they could not land safely and flew away. Others landed, realized the danger, and took off empty. Many others landed, waited until they were loaded with as many people as they could carry, evacuated them, and returned several times to repeat the extremely hazardous process.

No systematic coordination of the attack planes with the helicopters was possible. The senior controller aboard Hillsboro, CPT Medley Gatewood, was a fighter pilot with no helicopter experience and did not know the radio frequencies of the helicopters. The FACs were also fighter pilots or tactical bomber pilots, who did not know the helicopters' radio frequencies and were fully occupied with coordinating air strikes by more than a hundred fixed-wing attack planes.

With so many helicopters landing and departing in an overcrowded, unregulated air space at the same time that large, fixed-wing transport aircraft were landing and taking off in the same space, the danger of a mid-air collision was extreme and constant. Fortunately, the CO of the 14th Combat Aviation Battalion, LTC Ray Carson (radio name "Arab 6") and his operations officer, MAJ John Todd, in a UH-1 helicopter assumed the critical role of airborne helicopter controllers.

They used an FM and a UHF radio to inform the incoming Army CH-47 helicopter pilots, some of the Marine CH-46 helicopter pilots, and some of the C-130 pilots of the best approach routes, flight tactics, and departure routes to avoid known NVA anti-aircraft areas. They also directed seventy bomb strikes against NVA targets through the AF FACs. As each helicopter departed, Carson and Todd tried to keep a running account of its radio name, aircraft type, unit, and estimated number and type of evacuees on it. They also kept the American headquarters in Chu Lai informed of the current status of the evacuation.

When they had to leave to refuel, WO Leon Bradford and WO George Schultz ("Boxcar 23") of the 178th ASHC assumed their role in a CH-47 helicopter.[78] The spontaneous leadership of those two officers and two warrant officers was crucial in preventing potentially disastrous collisions of the helicopters with each other and with the fixed-wing aircraft on and over the Kham Duc airstrip on May 12.

The CCT

When Cole's C-130 landed at Chu Lai, the three CCT men were taken to a nearby room, where the CG of their unit, AF BG McLaughlin, furiously awaited them. Livid with rage, he excoriated them in loud, profane, insulting language for their unauthorized departure from the battle and bitterly reminded them that the survival of his air crews and all the people at Kham Duc depended on his planes being able to land and take off in that hostile, crowded air space.

With biting sarcasm he informed them that the mission of a Combat Control Team is to stay at a battle as long as necessary to facilitate the take-offs, landings, and cargo delivery of all the planes involved, regardless of the combat circumstances. When he finally allowed the senior NCO to speak, he realized that the team CO was solely responsible for their premature departure.

He then focused his wrath on the CCT commander, who claimed he could not perform his duties at Kham Duc, because his radios had been destroyed. Whether or not McLaughlin knew that those radios had been replaced on May 11, he ordered the CCT men to immediately return to Kham Duc on the next available aircraft. Then he took command of a C-130 and flew to Kham Duc to personally supervise the rest of the evacuation.[79]

A C-130 piloted by AF MAJ Jay Van Cleeff that was about to depart for Danang was ordered to take the three CCT men to Kham Duc first. In Freedman's haste to board the plane, he did not have time to find a radio to replace the one he left at Kham Duc. He thought that if it was not there or was destroyed, he would use the small emergency UHF/VHF radio in his pocket. He and Lundie had their M-16 rifles, .38 caliber revolvers, and eleven magazines of 5.56mm rifle ammunition, but their CO considered himself a non-combatant and refused to carry a weapon.[80]

He kept trying to convince anyone who would listen that there was no need for him to return to Kham Duc, since everyone who could be evacuated must have been by then. Even if not, he claimed he could not assist the evacuation aircraft, because he had no radio. Someone finally told him to get off the air. The CCT NCOs, having been vindicated by their own CG, no longer considered him their CO and ignored him. He had no choice but to meekly follow them.[81]

OP 1

Meanwhile, Craven, Chandler, and Hill were trying to escape from OP 1. As they slowly made their way through the jungle below, they suddenly ran into a platoon-size NVA unit. The point man, PFC Andrew Craven, opened fire on them, but was shot in the chest and killed. Hill and Chandler escaped into the jungle and eventually found their way back to the airstrip.[82]

Wright and Vasquez continued to move down the south side of their hill. When they reached the bottom, they worked their way around the east side of it, then turned north back toward the airstrip. Wright radioed Buchwald in the TOC to report their position and ask for instructions on what to do. Buchwald told him to return through the position of A Company 1/46/198 on the southwest side of the airstrip.[83]

As soon as Wright and Vasquez emerged from the tree line, some of the A/1/46/198 troops, mistaking them for NVA, fired 40mm grenades at them. The two men ran back to the tree line, radioed Buchwald again, and told him what happened. Buchwald told the CO of A/1/46/198, 1LT Thompson, to send some of his men to escort the OP survivors into their position. SP4 Cowburn and a few others ran out between the air strikes and brought the two survivors safely back to the airstrip.[84]

Two UH-1 Crashes

At 1350 hours, two UH-1 gunships from F Troop ("Blue Ghosts") of the 8th Cavalry [Regiment] attached to the Americal Division arrived from Chu Lai to replace the two damaged UH-1 gunships ("Muskets") of the

176th Assault Helicopter Company. One of the replacement gunships was armed with fourteen 2.75inch rockets and two 7.62mm Miniguns. The other was armed with two 7.62mm Miniguns and an automatic 40mm grenade launcher.[85]

Earlier that morning the 176th crews had tried unsuccessfully to destroy the anti-aircraft machine guns on OP 1. The two new gunships escorted a UH-1H Dust Off medical evacuation helicopter in another attempt to rescue the wounded men in the southwest bunker on OP 1. They attacked the concrete bunker with all their ordnance, but were ineffective against it. The NVA anti-aircraft machine guns in the bunker shot both helicopters repeatedly and seriously wounded one of the co-pilots, WO Glen Opheim. The pilot, Chief WO Terry Rippy, managed to crash-land it on the east side of the airstrip.[86] The other damaged helicopter lost all its power, and its pilot, 1LT Jack Reed, auto-rotated it down between the airstrip and OP 1.[87]

Medical Evacuations

MAJ Bob McWilliams, the CO of the 54th Medical Evacuation Company, recovered the crews of those two UH-1 helicopters in his Dust Off helicopter ambulance and took them to Chu Lai. After refueling there, he returned to Kham Duc and joined MAJ Pat Brady and the other Dust Off crews in evacuating more casualties.[88]

McWilliams wanted to evacuate the wounded men in the southwest bunker on OP1, but Buchwald told him to not try it. Orbiting his helicopter above the hill, McWilliams could hear the pathetic voice of SGT Joseph Simpson on the radio pleading, "Please come get me. I can't stop the bleeding. When are you going to come get me? I can't stop the bleeding." The pitiful tone of that helpless voice, begging to be rescued before he bled to death, has haunted McWilliams's memory of Kham Duc ever since.[89]

That day Brady and his copilot, WO Sewell, evacuated 125 wounded people from Kham Duc—military and civilian, U.S. and Vietnamese—which was a one-day record for Brady. The other Dust Off helicopter ambulances evacuated more than 175 people that day. Their total of more than 300 casualties was also a one-day record for their Dust Off unit.[90] They took them all to the Army 2nd Evacuation Hospital in Chu Lai.

Several Dust Off helicopters, including Brady's, were hit by anti-aircraft machine-gun fire, but were not shot down. Brady later said that in his two years of combat rescue flying in Vietnam—including actions for which he received a Purple Heart, six Distinguished Flying Crosses, the Distinguished Service Cross, and the Medal of Honor—he never saw such heavy enemy fire in daylight.[91]

CWO Rippy had been shot down the previous week in one of the most dangerous helicopter tactics of the war, a low-level hunter-killer flight. Flying his gunship at treetop level, he served as bait to draw fire from hidden enemy troops, while another gunship followed 300 feet above and behind him to return the enemy fire. For Rippy, flying as bait in such extremely high-risk tactics was less memorable than flying at the battle of Kham Duc, the most dramatic combat he ever saw.[92]

OP 1

At 1100 hours, Simpson, Long, and Coen tried to escape from the southwest bunker. Simpson's FM radio could pick up enough fragments of the radio transmissions around the airstrip for him to realize that a mass evacuation was in progress. But as soon as they emerged, NVA fire from the northeast bunker drove them back. After waiting several hours to be rescued, they finally recogniized that if they did not get down to the airstrip soon, they would be abandoned.

Despite his severe wound, Coen volunteered to be the point man and painfully climbed over the berm on the northern perimeter, followed by Simpson and Long. A nearby explosion knocked them all down, wounded Long's leg, and severely wounded Simpson's foot. Seeing that Simpson could not walk, Long took off his pack, put Simpson on his back, and began carrying him down the hill.

Coen suddenly glimpsed the airstrip through the trees and began to scream, fire his rifle wildly, and run down the hill. Long yelled at him to stop, but he vanished into the dense jungle. Whether he was killed by the NVA or died of shock from his wound, Coen was never seen again.[93]

The First C-130 Crash

CPT Warren Orr, the Civic Action officer at the SF headquarters near Danang, was responsible for the civilian refugees around the CIDG camps in I Corps. His assistant, SSG Richard Campbell, had arrived at Kham Duc on May 10. Orr arrived with Schungel's group on the morning of May 12, and together they assembled the village civilians for evacuation.[94]

The pilot of the second C-130 at Kham Duc, MAJ Bernard Bucher, was diverted from his first mission and sent directly there with no briefing on the enemy situation. Approaching the airstrip from the southeast, he received sporadic AK-47 and light machine-gun fire, but was unaware of the more lethal NVA anti-aircraft machine guns on the ridges beyond the northwest end of the airstrip. He stopped near the middle of the airstrip, but did not turn his plane around.

The C-130 was designed to carry ninety-two U.S. troops with their personal equipment, but Orr and Campbell packed 183 Vietnamese civilians into it.[95] Some of the CIDG deserters in civilian clothes also slipped onto the plane. Orr asked 1LT Thompson, the CO of A company 1/46/198, who were still waiting on the tarmac to be evacuated, to get the CIDG deserters out of the plane to make room for more refugees. Thompson told SP4 Fred Cowburn and two other men of his company to force their way onto Bucher's plane and eject the CIDG deserters.[96]

Some of the SF NCOs watching them thought they were fighting with the refugees to get on the plane, and that erroneous impression was propagated in a later published account of the battle.[97] When the rear ramp of the C-130 began to close, Cowburn and the two other men ran up the ramp and jumped off to stay with their company.[98] They did not know it then, but that dutiful action saved their lives.

CPT John Thomasson, the CO of C Company 2/1/196, seeing that Bucher had not turned around and was about to take off toward the northeast, ran alongside the cockpit of the plane, waving his arms and gesturing to Bucher not to take off in that direction. One of the Americal refueling troops on the tarmac, SP4 Wolfgang Richter, also tried with desperate gestures to warn Bucher to turn his plane around.[99]

Whether Bucher did not understand their gestures or chose to ignore them, he insisted on taking off to the northeast. The NVA troops on the northeast ridge overlooking the airstrip had watched the civilians crowd into the C-130, yet as it flew over them they poured their .51 caliber anti-aircraft machine-gun fire into it, ripping gaping holes in its belly and wings.[100] A C-130 pilot orbiting nearby later said he saw more tracer bullets fired at that plane than he had ever seen fired at anything before.[101]

Streaming fuel, hydraulic fluid, and human blood from hundreds of bullet holes, the big plane stalled in mid-air, plunged into the jungle, exploded, and burned. The deaths of those 189 people (183 refugees, five AF crewmen, and one SF officer) was the greatest loss of life from a plane crash in the history of aviation at that time.[102] Bucher was posthumously awarded the Air Force Cross.

The Second CH-47 Crash

A CH-47 helicopter piloted by CPT Charles Stanley and WO Larry Kemp landed on the north end of the airstrip. It was designed to carry thirty-three fully equipped U.S. troops, but fifty men of A Company 1/46/198, including their CO, crowded into it. The overloaded helicopter had too much weight for a vertical take-off, so Stanley had to take off gradually toward the northeast end of the airstrip like a fixed-wing plane.[103]

At about 800 feet the CH-47 was hit by a hail of anti-aircraft machine-gun fire, slightly wounding Stanley and damaging the hydraulic system. Hydraulic fluid sprayed on some of the men in the cargo bay and started a fire. Suddenly, the helicopter plunged 400 feet, lurching and oscillating wildly, tumbling the men inside like dice. According to one of the crewman, CPT Stanley's grip on the cyclic stick froze, and Kemp hit him repeatedly with his fists to gain control of the falling aircraft.[104]

The NVA machine-gun fire intensified. A bullet struck PFC Richard Sands in the head, killing him instantly, and another round hit PFC Larry Carlyle in the foot. The burning Chinook landed hard on its tail, bounced once, and stopped on its wheels with the internal fire spreading rapidly. In the troops' desperate rush to get out, Sands' body was left in the flaming wreck.[105]

A nearby mortar explosion hurled PFC Gerald Gilkey into the air and left him lying unconscious on the airstrip. SP4 William Bledsoe, the medic in the OP 3 squad, saw it happen. Despite the pain of his own serious wounds, he ran 50 yards across the fire-swept airstrip, picked Gilkey up, carried him to safety, and administered life-saving first aid.

For his heroism in saving Gilkey's life at the risk of his own despite his painful wounds; for his treatment of the wounded men in the E/2/1/196 mortar section under attack before and after he was wounded; and for treating a wounded member of his platoon at the risk of his life in a firefight on the way down from OP 3, Bledsoe was awarded the Distinguished Service Cross, the Army's highest award for combat valor.[106] It was the only DSC awarded for the Kham Duc battle.

1LT Thompson, some of the men of his third platoon, and the last of the engineer troops boarded another CH-47 helicopter. Before Thompson could get all his men into it, mortar shells exploded nearby, and the pilot suddenly took off for LZ Ross, leaving behind fifteen men of Thompson's company, including four wounded men. Another CH-47 arrived at LZ Ross later with the remainder of Thompson's company.[107]

WO Larry Kemp, the pilot of the second CH-47 shot down, had never flown a UH-1, but his desire to escape from Kham Duc was so great that he decided to try to fly Rippy's crashed gunship. Most of the instrument panel had been shot away, and its gauges showed zero engine and transmission oil pressure.

He got it started and invited his CH-47 crew to join his escape attempt, but they refused. Rippy had told his operations officer at Chu Lai that he had to abandon his UH-1 at Kham Duc because it was no longer flyable.[93] To Rippy's eternal chagrin, Kemp somehow managed to take it off alone, nurse it through the congested airspace, fly it 24 miles to LZ Ross, and land it safely.[108]

7th Air Force Headquarters

RF-101 and RF-4 photo reconnaissance planes constantly overflew Kham Duc, filming the battle. The film was flown to GEN Momyer's headquarters at Tan Son Nhut airbase, where it was immediately developed, interpreted, and sent to him.[109] Those images and the radio reports from Kham Duc convinced him that the tactical situation there had become critical, and time for the air evacuation was rapidly running out. Despite the loss of seven aircraft that day and two more the previous day, he ordered BG McLaughlin to resume the C-130 landings at all costs.

The Third C-130

LTC Cole and MAJ Bucher did not realize how dangerous the Kham Duc airstrip was before they landed on it, but the next C-130 pilot, LTC William Boyd, was fully aware of what awaited him. He had been warned about the enemy situation by LTC Swain, the A-1E pilot shot down earlier that day. Boyd saw Bucher's C-130 fall, explode, and burn, but despite the extreme danger to himself and his crew, he attempted to land at Kham Duc as ordered.[110]

As he dove for the airstrip, he saw NVA soldiers firing AK-47s and RPD machine guns at his plane and heard the bullets hitting it. As his wheels were about to touch down, a mortar shell exploded 100 feet in front of him, causing him to jerk the plane's nose up and go around again. That action made him even more vulnerable, because the NVA gunners then knew exactly where he was going and riddled his plane with anti-aircraft machine gun and AK-47 bullets.

As soon as he landed and lowered the rear ramp, more than 100 civilians, CIDG troops, and U.S. troops ran to his plane and crowded into it. He immediately turned it around and took off the same way he came in. When he landed at Chu Lai, his C-130 had so many bullet and shrapnel holes that his crew chief painted "Lucky Duc" on the side.[111] For his heroism Boyd was later awarded the Air Force Cross.

The Second C-130 Crash

LTC John Delmore and his co-pilot, CPT Joe Donahue, also saw Bucher crash and were equally aware of the danger awaiting them at Kham Duc. When their plane was 300 feet above the airstrip, it was hit by a hail of anti-aircraft machine-gun bullets that sounded like the blows of a sledgehammer. They ripped 6-inch holes in the fuselage, passed through the cockpit, and exited through the roof, destroying the hydraulic system and setting one engine on fire.

Just before hitting the airstrip Delmore and Donahue managed to get the wheels down. With all four engines running out of control, no brakes, and almost no directional control, the only way they could stop the plane was by forcibly steering it into a dirt bank beside the airstrip. They and their crewmen got out safely and were later evacuated in a Marine CH-46 helicopter.[112]

The SF Camp

Until then, the NVA troops had not directly attacked the eastern perimeter of the SF camp, but the SOG troops in the trench were expecting it. They were ready to face any NVA charge from such a strong defensive position compared to their far more precarious defensive positions in Laos. Purdy, his three NCOs, and his Nung platoon had endured heavy, frequent bombardment at Khe Sanh a few months before and knew they would have the protection of massive airborne firepower, as long as the skies remained clear.

In the early afternoon an unarmed CIDG soldier, the only survivor from OP 2, staggered into the SOG perimeter from the river gulch. Haggard and exhausted from evading NVA troops for hours in the jungle, he said the NVA attackers overran OP 2 so quickly that the American troops were not able to effectively resist them and were all killed. He escaped alone.

More and more of the U.S. reinforcement troops were evacuated, until only the SF A-team, the SOG men, and their loyal indigenous troops were left in the SF camp. By then, it was obvious to the NVA commander that Kham Duc was being abandoned as quickly as possible. It was also obvious that as the number of defenders decreased, the number of U.S. attack aircraft increased, and the NVA casualties produced by those aircraft also increased.

The NVA had learned from their previous disastrous attacks on the airstrip that mass charges across so much flat, open ground in full daylight could not succeed. That afternoon they switched the focus of their attack to the SF camp and massed their assault troops in the heavily vegetated stream gulch on the east side of the SF camp and in the ravine on the south side of it.

The FAC on the east side of the camp, AF LTC Black, saw large numbers of NVA troops moving into those areas and put several CBU and strafing runs on them to try to stop the attacks before they began. The dense vegetation caused the CBU bombs to detonate before they reached the ground, and the NVA troops were too close to the camp to use high-explosive bombs. The planes strafed the area heavily with 20mm automatic cannons firing explosive shells.

Regardless of their mounting casualties, the NVA commander continued to mass more and more troops in the river gulch and the ravine. He seemed determined to capture or kill the remaining defenders in the camp, and he undoubtedly realized that unless his troops could overrun the camp then, the last U.S. troops would soon be gone. He apparently thought that occupying a destroyed and abandoned camp at the cost of so many of his troops would be a hollow victory.

If his objective was to capture the camp, all he had to do was wait for the completion of the ongoing evacuation. Possession of the terrain evidently meant little to him without capturing at least some of the U.S. and indigenous defenders to film as war trophies. He evidently wanted to capture or kill the defenders at any additional cost in NVA casualties more than he wanted the place itself with no extra casualties.

The SOG Trench

At 1530 hours, in a last, suicidal attempt to overrun the camp's eastern perimeter the NVA troops launched a multi-company human-wave charge at it. At that moment, an American officer passing overhead in one of the last evacuation helicopters looked down and saw it. To him they looked like ants pouring out of an ant hole.[113] Some of the SOG men began saying terse goodbyes to each other, knowing that they would stand in that trench and fight the charging hoard to the death.

Windley was sitting stoically on top of the center bunker behind the tripod-mounted .50 caliber machine gun, defiantly wearing his green beret, while everyone else wore a steel helmet. Methodically and expertly pounding out the big rounds, he was cutting down scores of charging NVA troops. The U.S. and indigenous troops were firing their M-60 machine guns non-stop and their M-16 rifles on full automatic, changing ammunition magazines as fast as they could. The grenadiers were pumping out rounds as quickly as they could reload their grenade launchers.

No matter how many NVA troops the defenders and the air strikes killed, more and more of them burst out from the river gulch in a desperate race across the open ground toward the eastern perimeter of the SF camp. Some got close enough to the trench for the SOG defenders to clearly see their faces. The expression of one pathetic NVA soldier engraved itself on McLeroy's memory. Wide-eyed and ashen with terror, he was stumbling forward through a maelstrom of bullets and shrapnel like a doomed robot, as his comrades were falling all around him, knowing the rest of his wretched life was measured in seconds.

Suddenly, a terrifying premonition flashed through McLeroy's mind. At any moment Windley and his .50 caliber machine gun might be knocked off the top of the center bunker. Even if not, all the SOG men would have to stop firing momentarily to reload their weapons, and some of their weapons might jam after so much constant firing. All the attackers needed was a gap in the SOG firing line large enough for them to fire into the trench or throw a hand grenade into it.

Eventually, at least one mortar shell or rocket-propelled grenade would likely explode in the trench or so close to it that it some of the SF troops would be killed or wounded. When they fell—dead or unconscious, bleeding and crying out in pain—the men beside them might stop firing and try to help them. Seeing their SF leaders disabled or killed, some of the indigenous troops might lose the discipline that the presence and example of their SF leaders gave them.

McLeroy envisioned the firing line faltering long enough for some of the fanatical NVA attackers to storm into the trench. The close air support would immediately end, the fight would become point-blank, hand-to-hand chaos, and the attackers would soon overwhelm the defenders with their superior numbers. They would burst into the camp, seizing the camp's mortars, machine guns, recoilless guns, and ammunition. From the protection of the camp's deep trenches and bunkers they would then concentrate their fire on the airstrip.

At that instant something snapped in his mind. His fear, until then barely suppressed, suddenly disappeared, and a wild rage filled him with reckless determination to kill as many of the attackers as he could any way he could before they killed him, as he felt they likely would. Keying his PRC-25 FM radio, he told the FAC overhead, LTC Reese Black, to put an immediate napalm strike on the wire of the SOG perimeter.

Black said he could not put napalm that close to friendly troops, unless it was marked with a smoke grenade. McLeroy yelled to the men nearest him, asking if anyone had a smoke grenade. No one did, but one man said he had a white phosphorous grenade. McLeroy asked him, "Do you want to throw it, or do you want me to throw it?" With no hesitation the young SF NCO climbed out of the trench, boldly stood up on the back side of it, heaved the 2lb, cast iron grenade as far as he could, about 25 yards, and jumped back into the trench.

The grenade began to spurt out a dense cloud of bright-white smoke rising almost straight up. LTC Black anxiously asked McLeroy if he was really sure that he wanted napalm that close. McLeroy vehemently confirmed it, and Black told him to get his men as far down in the trench as possible. McLeroy yelled the order to the troops on his left, Windley yelled it to those on his right, and it was instantly passed up and down the trench.

A quasi-insubordinate young recon NCO standing next to McLeroy was so shocked by what was about to happen that he yelled, "You're crazy! You can't put napalm that close!" McLeroy yelled back at him, "You better get down, 'cause it's coming in right now!" and threw himself face down on the bottom of the deep trench. An A-1E Skyraider piloted by AF CPT Don Dineen flew parallel to the trench and dropped a tumbling napalm canister into the white smoke.

The explosion was instantly followed by a blast wave of superheated air sweeping over the trench, as if the door of a steel mill furnace had been jerked open. The terrifying thought flashed through McLeroy's mind that he was about to burn himself to death with all the men he was responsible for. That instant of terror was followed by the sudden panic of suffocation, as the fire storm sucked the oxygen out of the trench. Seconds later, the searing heat wave passed and oxygen returned to the trench. The NVA troops closest to the trench were cremated in a roaring fire cloud burning at 2,000 degrees Fahrenheit. All that was left of them was smoking, unrecognizable clumps.

It was the first and last ground attack directly on the SF camp. The NVA commander knew then that the closest his troops could ever get to the SF camp was its eastern perimeter, and regardless of how many more troops he sacrificed in mass charges toward it or how close they got to it, they would never capture it. The napalm strike so close to the SOG trench demonstrated that the defenders of that trench would rather burn to death with them than let them take it. He also knew by then that planes carrying napalm were seemingly endless.

The Fifth C-130

At the same time, LTC Franklin Montgomery, despite seeing what happened to Bucher's and Delmore's planes, unhesitatingly landed his C-130 at Kham Duc. As soon as he lowered his rear ramp, some 150 civilians, CIDG troops, and U.S. forces rushed into the cargo bay, knocking the loadmaster down. More than fifty mortar shells and rockets exploded around the plane, but amazingly it was not seriously hit and was able to take off with its overloaded human cargo.[114]

The SF Camp

Only the SF A-team, their few loyal Vietnamese CIDG troops, their Nung bodyguards, and the SOG launch team, the recon teams, and the Hatchet Force platoon with their Nung and Montagnard troops were left in the SF camp. Buchwald radioed Henderson to move all the SF troops to the airstrip and board the next C-130. Overby monitored the transmission, radioed McLeroy in the trench, and told him to prepare to move the SOG troops to the airstrip with the SF team and the camp's remaining CIDG troops.

McLeroy ordered all the machine guns, ammunition, radios, and other equipment that could be useful to the NVA, except personal weapons and ammunition, brought to the center bunker. Two of Purdy's Hatchet Force NCOs rigged the pile for demolition with blocks of C-4 plastic explosive and a time fuse. Overby then radioed McLeroy to move the SOG troops to the airstrip. McLeroy relayed the order, and the men eagerly began to climb out of the trench.

At the same time, Henderson radioed Buchwald and asked him when the last CIDG troops and civilians would be evacuated. Buchwald replied that they had all been evacuated, but Henderson said some had still not been evacuated. Buchwald told him not to worry about it; Henderson replied that worrying about it was a big part of his job. Buchwald said it was a direct order from Sabre Six, the radio name for MG Koster, CG of the American Division.[115]

Schungel and the A-team SF men knew that if they left before all the CIDG troops and civilians did, pandemonium would ensue, and the disgraceful repercussions of an SF team abandoning those people under fire would damage the whole SF CIDG program. Schungel told Buchwald that regardless of the orders of anyone outside his chain of command, and regardless of what the American troops did or did not do, he and his troops would not leave their camp until all the CIDG troops and civilians were gone.[116]

As soon as Overby heard that, he realized that Schungel also wanted the SOG troops to stay until everyone else left. They were already leaving the trench, and the demolition NCOs were about to activate the time fuses on the explosives, when Overby suddenly ran out of the TOC, waving his arms and yelling at McLeroy to hold the SOG troops there.

McLeroy turned around and with all the force of his powerful bass voice bellowed, "Get back in the trench!" Under those circumstances it would have been extremely difficult for any oral command to stop indigenous mercenary troops running for their lives, turn them around, and send them back to the same potentially lethal place they were trying to escape from.

The recon teams and the Hatchet Force platoon had PRC-25 FM radios and knew from monitoring the transmissions that almost all the other defenders had already left. Yet the Nung and Montagnard troops unhesitatingly stopped, turned around, and jumped back into the trench to face the enemy again, knowing they were being left behind to defend the most vulnerable perimeter, while the other defenders escaped. They were willing to stay and face death, as long as their SF leaders stayed with them. Their loyalty, courage, and fighting spirit were why the SF men considered them elite troops.

The Sixth C-130

As soon as Montgomery's C-130 took off, MAJ Billy Mills landed his C-130. When his loadmaster lowered the rear ramp, about 130 people crowded into the cargo bay, including the remaining CIDG and Americal troops. Nelson was about to leave with his troops, when just as the rear ramp of the C-130 was about to close, he apparently thought it would make him look heroic to leave with the last SF men and impulsively ran out of the plane.[117] Protected by an endless parade of planes bombing and strafing, Mills took off to the south and landed at Chu Lai with no serious damage.[118]

Schungel told Overby to take the SOG troops to the ditch on the east side of the airstrip south of the SF camp's front gate and wait there for the next C-130. Overby radioed McLeroy again to move the SOG troops to the airstrip, and McLeroy gave the order a second time. The SOG men left the trench and started running toward the front gate of the camp, while the SF demolition NCOs activated the time fuses.

Near the entrance to the TOC tunnel McLeroy paused, waiting for the last SOG troops to run past him. Overby and the two communication NCOs had soaked the TOC with gasoline to burn everything in it, but Overby did not realize that the volatile gasoline fumes had filled the exit tunnel. When he tossed a burning rag into it, the fumes exploded in his face, hurled him backward, and left him lying unconscious on the ground. All the other SOG troops had run past the TOC entrance before the explosion and did not see it happen.

McLeroy pulled him up, draped Overby's arm over his shoulder, and staggered with him toward the front gate, where he saw Schungel calmly walking toward the gate with his SF troops. Schungel recognized McLeroy from his assignment in Schungel's command the previous year and was surprised to see him. He said, "What are you doing here? I thought you went home." Panting and sweating, with Overby's arm around his neck, McLeroy grunted, "I'm trying to!"

Overby slowly regained full consciousness and groggily continued on his own power to the ditch on the east side of the airstrip, where the last civilians, a few CIDG troops, and the SOG troops were huddled. Eighty-four indigenous troops were in the SOG group: forty-five Nung in the Hatchet platoon, thirty-six Montagnard and South Vietnamese in the recon teams, and the three covert ex-NVA intelligence agents. Thirty-two U.S. SOG men were also there: seven launch site men plus Overby, eighteen men in the recon teams, four men in the Hatchet platoon, and two men with the ex-NVA agents.

The shrieking parade of low-flying jet fighter-bombers and tactical bombers was like the world's largest air show of ground-attack planes. As soon as one swept by, another one followed it in an unbroken series of attacking aircraft forming a moving, exploding wall of steel and fire around the burning airstrip. The shriek of their jet engines was painfully loud, and many of the planes flew so low that the pilots' heads were clearly visible.

The official number of tactical ground-attack aircraft at Kham Duc on May 12, 1968, was less than 150, but the number of sorties flown by those aircraft was more than twice that number. The most authoritative source is the Air Force officer aboard Hillsboro who coordinated all those aircraft, CPT Medley Gatewood. When asked for the number of sorties he coordinated at Kham Duc that day, he replied "probably 350."[119]

The reason for the radical difference between the number of tactical aircraft (not B-52 strategic bombers) there and the number of sorties flown by those aircraft is that after expending their armament, many of them returned to their bases, rearmed, and returned to Kham Duc to continue bombing and strafing in that exceptionally "target rich environment." Each combat departure was one sortie, and during the course of that day, many of the same fighter-bombers and tactical bombers flew two or three sorties to Kham Duc.

None of the people on the ground had ever seen anything like the awesome spectacle they were witnessing. It looked exactly like a war movie, literally life imitating art. With mouths and eyes wide open and many scatological, pornographic, and blasphemous oaths of amazement, the SOG men were repeatedly asking each other if they had ever seen anything like that. It reminded McLeroy of a shark feeding frenzy.

By then, all three camps around the airstrip were blazing. The infernal scene became even more surrealistic when the 500-gallon rubber fuel bladders on the other side of the airstrip began erupting in huge, red fireballs, followed by the deep boom of the exploding demolition charges in the camp. A few minutes later, the thunderous roar of a much larger demolition charge in the camp's ammunition bunker produced a tall, roiling mushroom cloud.

The culmination of the apocalyptic spectacle was the looming approach of a towering monsoon storm cloud with sheet lightning flashing inside its dark interior. It looked more like the staged climax of a disaster movie than a real event. No one who witnessed that awesome sight will ever forget it or the fact that they owe their lives to the combat pilots whose continuous, close fire support allowed the brave crews of the transport aircraft to land and rescue them.

The Seventh C-130

The pilot of the last C-130, AF MAJ James Wallace, was told in his Danang briefing that an estimated 3,000 NVA troops had surrounded Kham Duc. He was familiar with the long airstrip, because he had landed there three weeks before to deliver an engineer bulldozer. Flying toward the burning camp, he could see columns of smoke long before he could see the airstrip. Hillsboro put him in a holding orbit 15 miles south of the camp, where several other C-130s and C-123s were waiting their turn to land.

About every ten minutes a plane would leave the orbit, land, load people, and take off. After about forty minutes, Hillsboro cleared

Wallace to land. On his final approach he saw NVA tracers being fired at his C-130 and F-4 Phantoms dropping napalm within 150 yards of the airstrip. The fires and explosions in and around the SF camp were producing so much smoke that he could not see the other end of the airstrip.

He landed from the southwest, stopped hard near the middle of the airstrip with all four engines roaring, and quickly turned the plane around, while the crew chief lowered the rear ramp. The exploding ammunition dump was throwing burning debris within 30 yards of his plane. Some of the desperate Vietnamese civilians ran under the whirling propellers, and only their small size kept them from being torn to pieces.[120] Many were crying, because they had seen Bucher's C-130 shot down with their family members in it.

A tiny Vietnamese woman who looked nine months pregnant was waddling toward the plane as fast as she could in her little rubber thong sandals, while carrying a small child and leading another by the hand. The one she was leading could not keep up and fell, but her mother did not stop, apparently choosing to save the child in her arms and the one in her womb rather than lose all of them by trying to recover the third one and missing the last evacuation plane.

McLeroy scooped up the child and ran behind the others to the rear ramp of the plane. Before he could hand the terrified child up to the loadmaster, the wind blast from the four huge propellers ripped his sunglasses off his face and hurled them down the airstrip. SFC Greenwood and SSG Windley also saw other small children in danger of being left behind. They each picked up a child, ran to the rear ramp of the plane, and handed it up to the loadmaster.

McLeroy stood by the ramp until the last troops clambered aboard. As the C-130 started to roll forward, he hopped backwards onto the ramp, spun around, and scrambled into the cargo bay, as the loadmaster closed the ramp. The plane lunged forward in a maximum-power take-off, cleared the ridge at the south end of the airstrip, made a low-level left turn along the Dak Se River, and climbed steeply out of Kham Duc's lethal airspace. Five days later McLeroy's Vietnam assignment ended.[121]

The Last CH-47

LTC Schungel, his LLDB counterpart, CPT Henderson, CPT Makowski, the six NCOs who came with Schungel, SSG Campbell, the remaining members of the SF A-team, and LTC Nelson were in the ditch on the east side of the airstrip north of the SF camp. Fifteen minutes after the last C-130 took off, a CH-47 Chinook piloted by WO Larry Busbee on his eleventh flight to Kham Duc from Chu Lai landed and evacuated them without being hit.[122]

The Eighth C-130

A few minutes after the last CH-47 took off, MAJ Van Cleeff's C-130 arrived from Cam Ranh Bay, and the three CCT men got off. Van Cleeff had just arrived in Vietnam the previous day and was unaware of what was happening at Kham Duc. When he saw the buildings on both sides of the airstrip burning and the abandoned 105mm artillery rounds exploding, he took off. As he was gaining altitude, he heard a radio voice say that Kham Duc was now a free-fire zone. He urgently broke into the transmission and announced that he had just left three men there.[123]

The CCT men ran into the burning SF camp, saw no one, then ran across the airstrip into the burning engineer camp, and again saw no one. Freedman tried to use his emergency radio to tell Van Cleeff to return for them, but it was defective. Cowering in a culvert on the west side of the airstrip, the three men mentally prepared themselves to die.

Freedman and Lundie refused to be captured by the NVA and, if they were not killed, they resolved to use their last bullets on themselves. They saw NVA troops moving in the camp and around the airstrip. Some of the enemy troops saw them and began to fire at them. Freedman fired back, silencing an NVA machine gun near the airstrip.[124]

The Second C-123

Several C-130s and C-123s were still orbiting overhead, waiting their turn to land, if needed. BG McLaughlin, whose C-130 was third in line, ordered the next plane in line, a C-123 piloted by LTC Alfred Jeanotte, to land and pick up the CCT men. As soon as Jeanotte touched down, the CCT men in the ditch ran out onto the airstrip, waving their arms, but he immediately took off without slowing down.

One of his crewmen told him he saw the three men running back to the ditch, and Jeanotte announced on the radio that he would land again to pick them up. Then he announced that he did not have enough fuel and had to return to Danang.[125] For his extraordinarily brief heroism in touching down for a few seconds without slowing down to look for the men and immediately taking off without being hit, he received the highest Air Force valor award, the Air Force Cross.

The Third C-123

The next plane in line was a C-123 piloted by LTC Joe Jackson. Unlike most transport pilots, Jackson was a former Korean War fighter pilot and a U-2 high-altitude reconnaissance pilot with the fearlessness required to fly high performance planes on such hazardous missions. He had been orbiting over Kham Duc at 9,000 feet for about an hour, when he was told to try to rescue the three CCT men.

He threw his C-123 into a steep side-slip turn with full flaps down, making it drop like a rock. He landed hard without reversing the two propellers or turning off the auxiliary jet engines on each wing, stood on the brakes, and came to a shuddering stop near the middle of the airstrip. A rocket landed in front of his plane and broke in half without exploding.

As he was turning the plane around, the three CCT men raced out of the ditch again and lunged into its open side door. He immediately began a short, jet-assisted take-off, as mortar shells exploded on the spot where his plane had been a few seconds before. Against all odds, the last aircraft out of Kham Duc took off safely at 1640 hours.[126] For his exceptional gallantry far above and beyond the call of duty as a transport pilot, Jackson was later awarded the Medal of Honor. His co-pilot, MAJ Jesse Campbell, received the Air Force Cross, and his two crewmen received Silver Stars.

For most of the defenders, the battle of Kham Duc was finally over; but not for all. That night Sassenberger, Foreman, and Colonna remained in hiding near the northeast end of the airstrip, and Long and Simpson hid near the bottom of the OP 1 hill. Long repeatedly tried to stop the constant seepage of blood from Simpson's mangled foot, but could not. Through the chill, rainy jungle night, he held SGT Simpson in his arms, helplessly watching him lose consciousness, inexorably bleed out, and quietly die.[127]

Orbiting high above the airstrip in a Cessna O-2, AF CPT Spier, the first and last FAC at Kham Duc, watched the towering monsoon thunderstorm slowly move into the valley. By 1736 hours it had covered the camps and airstrip in darkness and heavy rain, negating future landings and close air support.[128] Despite all the determination and sacrifices of the NVA forces and all the firepower and heroism of the U.S. troops, the fate of everyone on the ground at Kham Duc on May 12 was ultimately determined by the caprice of dark, drifting clouds.

Notes

1   Field Marshal Arthur Wellesley, later Duke of Wellington, on the narrow victory of the English and Prussian armies over Napoleon's French army at the Battle of Waterloo, Belgium, in 1815. Maxwell, Herbert. *Creevey Papers* (London: Murray Publishing House, 1903), p. 236.

2   The leader of the NVA film team at Kham Duc was Nguyen Van Huu, and his cameramen were Le Viet The and Le Kim Nguyen. Message from CDR JTF-FA Honolulu, HI, J2 to SECDEF Washington, D. C., SUBJ/Research and Investigation Team (RIT) Report of Interview of Mr Nguyen Van Huu, 30 June, 1995.

3   Telex messages from Westmoreland to ADM Sharp in Hawaii, GEN Wheeler in Washington, and LTG Goodpaster in Paris, May 12, 1968. Westmoreland Papers, MAC 6210 and 6222, U.S. Army Center for Military History, Fort Lesley J. McNair, Washington, D. C. Telex message from Bromley Smith, NSC, to Walt Rostow, NSC, forwarded to LBJ ranch, May 12, 1968: "Reports from Saigon re Estimate of Enemy Intentions in Kham Duc Area." LBJ Library, Austin, TX, National Security Files (NSF), Vietnam Country File, box 67, folder 2A (5), I Corps and DMZ, 5/68–11/68, documents 110 and 111. In his memoirs LBJ mentions the potentially strategic significance of Kham Duc one day before the start of the Paris negotiations. Johnson, Lyndon. *The Vantage Point* (NY: Holt, Rinehart, and Winston, 1971), p. 508.

4   Due to the problems of inter-service coordination of aircraft at Khe Sanh, in February 1968 Westmoreland proposed making his Deputy CG for Air, AF GEN William Momyer, the single "manager" for all fixed-wing aircraft operating in South Vietnam. Westmoreland's superior in Hawaii, ADM U.S. G. Sharp, approved the plan, but the Marine Corps Commandant strongly objected on the basis that Marine aircraft are needed to support Marine amphibious landings. Nalty, Bernard.

Airpower and the Fight for Khe Sanh (Washington, D.C.: Office of Air Force History, 1973), pp. 74–77. The Commandant's appeal to the Joint Chiefs of Staff resulted in a stalemate. Wheeler, Earl G., "Memorandum for the Secretary of Defense, Subject: Operational Control of III MAF Aviation Assets, Appendix C: Views of the Chief of Staff, U.S. Army and the Chief of Naval Operations on Operational Control of III Marine Amphibious Force Aviation Assets." Without waiting any longer for a decision, on March 8, 1968, Westmoreland named Momyer the Single Manager for Air in Vietnam. Momyer, William. *Air Power in Three Wars* (Maxwell Air Force Base, AL: Air University Press, 1988), p. 323. The Marine Corps appeal was referred to Deputy Secretary of Defense Paul Nitze, who decided in favor of Westmoreland. Nalty, *op. cit.*, p. 80.

5   Littaur, Raphael and Uphoff, Norman (eds). *The Air War in Indochina* (rev. ed.) (Boston, MA: Beacon Press, 1972), pp. 172, 273. The aircraft carriers were the *Ticonderoga* and the *Bon Homme Richard*, each with 70–80 aircraft, and the *Kitty Hawk*, with 85 aircraft. The B-52s were officially controlled by the 3rd Air Division of the Strategic Air Command, but were available to Westmoreland and Momyer on request. Dorr, Robert and Bishop, Chris. *Vietnam Air Warfare* (Edison, NJ: Chartwell Books, 1996), p. 231. Gropman, Alan. *Airpower and the Airlift Evacuation of Kham Duc* (Air War College, Maxwell Air Force Base, AL: USAF Southeast Asia Monograph Series, Volume V, Monograph 7, 1979), p. 30.

6   Interview of Vasquez, Orlando, by McLeroy, Key West, FL, July 1995. Telephonic interview by Sanders, July 14, 2006. 40mm grenades look like large shotgun shells. When fired from an M-79 grenade launcher, they explode on contact and scatter twenty.33 caliber metal balls.

7   Foreman, Wilbert, interview by McLeroy and Cox, Waco, TX, February 1997. Sassenberger, Ron, interview by McLeroy, Key West, FL, July 1995.

8   *Ibid*.

9   Letter from Connolly, John, to McLeroy, January 15, 2000.

10 Statement of Aycock, Robert, A-105 communications NCO, to McLeroy, undated.

11 Ballard, Jack. *Development and Employment of Fixed-Wing Gunships, 1962 to 1972* (Washington, D.C.: Office of Air Force History, United States Air Force, 1982), p. 52.

12 Ballard, *op. cit.*, p. 66.

13 Richardson, Don, "Kham Duc Revisited: A Chronological Study of the Evacuation of Kham Duc, May, 1968", donscott619@aol.com.

14 Smith, Bob, letter to Fred Cowburn, January 6, 1994.

15 Wright, William, interview by McLeroy and Cox, Oklahoma City, OK, April 25, 1997; and by Sanders, Moore, OK, April 25, 2007.

16 "Chronological Order of Events Kham Duc Special Forces Camp", United States Air Force Project Checo, 08–02353, May 12, 1968, hereafter referred to as "Air Force Chronology." For the methodology used in compiling this document for GEN Momyer on May 14, 1968, see Gropman, *op. cit.*, Notes, Chapter III, p. 79.

17 Percoskie, Tony, "Reflections on Kham Duc", *Vietnam Combat*, Harris Publications, September 20, 1989, p. 1.

18 Spier, Wilbert, interview by McLeroy, Indianapolis, IN, November 29, 1995. Statement of Spier, Wilbert, May 29, 1968.

19 "Air Force Chronology," see note 16. Gropman, *op. cit.*, p. 32.

20 Spier statement, *op. cit.*

21 *Ibid*

22 Wright interviews, *op. cit.* Vasquez interview, *op. cit.*

23 Long, Julius, interview by McLeroy, Dublin, VA, November 28, 1995.

24 Buchwald, *op. cit.* Weber, Jeff, telephonic interview by Sanders, July 15, 2007, and interview by Sanders, San Antonio, TX, September 12, 2009.

25 "Award of the Distinguished Service Cross to Bledsoe, William", General Orders Number 4325, September 11, 1968, Headquarters, United States Army, Vietnam.

26 *Ibid*

27 Wright interviews, *op. cit.* Buchwald statement, *op. cit.*

28 *Ibid*

29 A set of three audio cassette tapes in the United States Air Force Historical Research Center at Maxwell Air Force Base, AL, contains Johnson's recording. It also contains the after-action statements (some garbled) by helicopter pilots, a forward air controller, and an air liaison officer.

30 Woodard, Houston, interview by Sanders, San Antonio, TX, September 12, 2009. Duncan, James, statement, undated. Duncan, James, interview by Sanders, San Antonio, TX, September 12, 2009.

31 Gropman, *op. cit.*, pp. 25, 26, 32. Gatewood, Robert, interview by McLeroy. Albuquerque, NM, August 16, 1995. Nalty, Bernard. *Air War Over South Vietnam, 1968–1975* (Washington, D.C.: Air Force History and Museums Program, 2000), p. 111.

32 *Ibid*

33 The two senior FACs were AF LTC Reese Black, senior Air Liaison Officer (ALO) for I Corps, and AF LTC Richard Schuman, senior ALO for the Americal Division. Four AF FACs with the radio name "Jake" worked with the 2nd ARVN Division, and five AF FACs with the radio name "Helix" worked with the Americal Division. The "Jake" FACs were: MAJ Richard Smith, MAJ David Grady, CPT Willard Johnson, and 1LT James Mayton. The "Helix" FACs were: MAJ James Gibler, CPT Jack Plumb, CPT Paul Judge, CPT Phillip Smotherman, and CPT Wilbert Spier. "Kham Duc Action, 11 and 12 May, 1968," Headquarters Americal Division, May 14, 1968.

34 The senior helicopter pilot (in experience) was the aircraft commander and sat in the left seat. The junior helicopter pilot (in experience) sat in the right seat and operated the radios. In this case the pilot and aircraft commander was a warrant officer. The co-pilot was a lieutenant and senior to the pilot in rank, but junior to him in experience.

35 Fitzsimmons, Ed, email to Richardson, *op. cit.*; March 4, 2016. Statement of Blohm, Ron, undated. Swain had diarrhea, and when he bailed out of his burning plane over NVA troops shooting at him, he lost control of his bowels. By the time he got

into the helicopter, his flight suit was soaked with watery feces, and the helicopter crewmen said he stank so badly that they almost threw him out again. Statement of Balmes, Dean (who flew an A-1E at Kham Duc on May 12) at a reunion of the Kham Duc Club, Branson, MO, October 1998.

36 Richardson, *op. cit.*

37 Gropman, *op. cit.*, p. 30. "Grand Slam" is a baseball term for a home run with runners on all three bases, resulting in four scores from one hit. The acronym SLAM officially stood for "seek, locate, annihilate, and monitor." In World War II a 10,000lb. U.S. bomb was called the Grand Slam.

38 Gropman, *op. cit.*, p. 25. Dorr, Robert and Bishop, Chris. *Vietnam Air Warfare* (Edison, NJ: Chartwell Books, 1996), pp. 230–31.

39 Dorr, *op. cit.*, pp. 226–27, 230–31, 235–53. Nalty, Bernard *et al.* *The Air War Over Vietnam*, *op. cit.*, pp. 22, 68, 108, 112, 126, 136, 140, 158. Gunston, Bill. *Aircraft of the Vietnam War* (Wellingborough, Northamptonshire, UK: Patrick Stephens, 1987), pp. 17, 31, 38, 56, 97, 110, 118, 121, 133. U.S. attack aircraft had one of five letter prefixes: F = fighter-bombers; A = tactical bombers; B = strategic bombers; AC = fixed-wing gunships; AH = helicopter gunships. Dorr, *op. cit.* The C-130s came from the 834th Air Division at Tan Son Nhut; the C-123s came from the 311th Air Commando Squadron at Pleiku; the A-1s came from the 6th Air Commando Squadron at Pleiku; the F-4s came from the 8th Tactical Fighter Wing at Ubon, Thailand; the F-100s came from the 31st Tactical Fighter Wing at Tuy Hoa and/ or the 37th Tactical Fighter Wing at Phu Cat; the F-105s came from the 355th Tactical Fighter Wing at Takli, Thailand and/or the 388th Tactical Fighter Wing at Korat, Thailand; the F-5s came from the 522nd ARVN Squadron, part of the 1st ARVN Air Division at Danang and/or Quang Ngai and/or the 3rd ARVN Air Division at Bien Hoa. Ibid., p. 230.

40 Littaur, *op. cit.*, pp. 220–23, 249, 273.

41 *Ibid.*, www.en.wikipedia.org/wiki/Napalm.

42 www.en.wikipedia.org/wiki/Cluster_munition.

43 www.vietnamwar/wikia.com'wiliMk_4/Mk_40_Folding_Fin_Arial_Rocket.

44 Center for Disease Control: cdc.gov/mass casualties/blastinjuryfacts.asp.

45 Truong Nhu Tang. *A Vietcong Memoir* (NY: Harcourt Brace Jovanovich, 1985), pp. 167–71.

46 "After Action Report (Final)," Headquarters, 14th Combat Aviation Battalion, 20 May,1968.

47 The injured man was SP4 Harold Studebaker. The other crewmen were SP4 Ken Oliver and Sp4 Dwayne Bobak. Percoskie, *op. cit.*, p. 2. Sturdevant, Joe, interview by Sanders, San Antonio, TX, September 12, 2009.

48 Sturdevant interview, *op. cit.*

49 Powell, John, interviewed by Cox, Branson, MO, October 1998. Waldo, Daniel, "End of Tour Interview" by Paul Weber, June 18, 1968.

50 Waldo, Daniel, "After Action Report", Company A, 70th Engineer Battalion, May 19, 1968.

51 Hostler, Donald, interview by Paul Weber, June 18, 1968.

52 Warner, Wayne. *One Trip Too Many* (USA: Independent publisher, 2011), pp. 173–78.

53 Statement of Schneider, William, A/1/46/18 LIB, to McLeroy.

54 Cole, Daryl D., "Report of the Incident at Kham Duc, RVN, 12 May 68 Resulting in Battle Damage to Aircraft Nr 55–013", May 16, 1968. Farrar, Walter B., "Comments On The Cole Mission Report After Reading USAF Monograph and Other Documents On Kham Duc", August 1994.

55 Thompson, Bobby, interviews by McLeroy, Fort Knox, KY, November 30, 1995; and by Sanders, San Antonio, TX, October 11, 2008. The original order of extraction is in Schungel, Daniel, "After Action Report, Battle of Kham Duc", Company C, 5th Special Forces Group (Airborne), 1st Special Forces, May 31, 1968.

56 Waldo, Daniel, "After Action Report", Company A, 70th Engineer Battalion, May 19, 1968.

57 Thompson interviews, *op. cit.*

58 Stanton, Shelby. *Green Berets At War* (Novato, CA: Presidio, 1985), p. 165.

59 Cole, *op. cit.* Farrar, *op. cit.*

60 Tavianinni, Gene, telephonic interview by Sanders, June 15, 2008.

61 Schrope, William, email to McLeroy, July 8, 2010. Waldo, *op. cit.*

62 "Air Force Chronology," *op. cit.*, note 15. All the C-130s in Vietnam were temporarily (TDY) assigned to the 834th Air Division at Tan Son Nhut near Saigon and at Cam Ranh Bay south of Nha Trang. Their permanent bases were Naha AFB, Okinawa; Clark AFB, Philippines; Tachikawa AFB, Japan; and Ching Chuan Kang air base, Taiwan. Dorr, *op. cit.*, p. 230.

63 Cole, *op. cit.* Farrar, *op. cit.*

64 Freedman, Mort, email to McLeroy, August 15, 1999. Lundie, James, "Kham Duc, South Vietnam, 12 May 1968", *Combat Controllers Association Newsletter*, undated.

65 Cole, *op. cit.* Thompson interview by Sanders, *op. cit.*

66 Schneider, *op. cit.*

67 Cole, *op. cit.* A maintenance crewman counted 86 bullet and mortar shell fragment holes in the plane.

68 Buchwald, *op. cit.* Thompson interviews, *op. cit.*

69 On May 12, a member of the team was shot three times while running messages from Nelson's TOC to their jeep. One bullet entered his cheek, chipped a front tooth, and exited his mouth. He was quickly evacuated to the Army hospital at Chu Lai in a Dust Off helicopter ambulance and recovered. Merkle, Jerry, telephonic interview by Sanders, July 30, 2009.

70 Bernard, Kenneth, "After Action Report: Kham Duc, Vietnam", May 14, 1968. Pelkey, Christopher, interview by Sanders, Fairfax Station, VA, August 10, 2010. Pelkey, *op. cit.* Pelkey, letter to Mr and Mrs C. J. Pelkey, May 15, 1968. Price, Ron, telephonic interview by Sanders, August 15, 2010. A COFRAM "Firecracker" anti-personnel artillery round contains 60 small grenades in a bomb case that opens in flight. The grenades scatter, partially detonate on impact, bounce up 4 to 6 feet, and explode.

71 Waldo, Daniel, "End of Tour Interview" by Paul Weber, June 18, 1968. Shrimp, Charles, "After Action Report" (2/1/196 LIB), May 14, 1968. Statement of Welte, Ronald, undated. Price, Ron, telephonic interview by Sanders, August 15, 2010. Schrope, Bill, email to McLeroy, July 8, 2010.

72 Schungel, *op. cit.* Jacks, Johnny, telephonic interview by McLeroy, September 2016. The men who arrived with Schungel were SGM Ed Gaydosik, MSG Joseph Lowe, SFC Francis Hinton, SSG Willie Lucas, SGT Johnny Jacks, and SP4 Larry Pound.

73 Jacks, *op. cit.* Statement of Aycock, Robert, telephonic interview by McLeroy, October 1995.

74 Very few conventional Army officers knew of SOG's existence, but most AF FACs were aware of SOG's operations in Laos and Cambodia, because they were supported by AF planes. The FACs supporting SOG's operations often dealt directly with SF operations officers in the SOG launch sites and with SF assistant operations officers or NCOs riding with the FACs during the insertions and extractions of SOG teams, which often involved close air strikes. For that reason LTC Black may have trusted McLeroy's tactical judgment more than he would have trusted the judgment of an unknown lieutenant in a conventional unit.

75 Shelton, Ray, interview by McLeroy, Tyler, TX, May 17, 1997. Mack, John, telephonic interview by Sanders, December 12, 2010. Fogle, James, interview by James Mead, May 16, 1968. Despite the panic of the civilians, Shelton's loadmaster managed to load them and the engineer troops in less than three minutes. Spector, Ronald, "The Evacuation of Kham Duc", *MHQ: The Quarterly Journal of Military History*, Vol. 5, No. 3, Spring 1993, p. 40. "Airlift at Kham Duc", http://BlindBat/khamduc.html.

76 Interview of Phillip Smotherman, Americal Division, Chu Lai, May 29, 1968. Smotherman, Phillip, interview by McLeroy, Oklahoma City, OK, 1997. Gropman, *op. cit.*, p. 17.

77 Gropman, *op. cit.*, p. 17.

78 "After Action Report (Final)," *op. cit.* Gropman, *op. cit.*, pp. 19, 22–23. Marks, Wesley, interview, May 28, 1968. Statement of Wood, Ernest, May 28, 1968. The reported number of people evacuated in helicopters seems greatly overstated, but the accurate number is impossible to determine, because all the reports on the subject differ. For a discussion of the coordinated air effort see Fogle, James, statement, May 16, 1968. Mead, James, statement, May 16, 1968. Sams, Kenneth and Thompson, A. W., "Kham Duc", Hickman AFB, HI, Headquarters, Pacific Air Forces, 8 July, 1968, pp. 22–25. Brownlow, Cecil, "Coordinated Effort Saves Force", *Aviation Week & Space Technology*, Vol. 89, No. 11, September 9, 1968, pp. 92–98.

79 Freedman, Morton, email, *op. cit.* Lundie, *op. cit.* Statement of Gallagher, John, May 17, 1968.

80 Freedman, Morton, statement.

81 *Ibid.* Freedman, email, *op. cit.* Gropman, *op. cit.*, p. 58.

82 Buchwald, statement, *op. cit.* Wright, interviews, *op. cit.*

83 Wright, *op. cit.*

84 Cowburn, Fred, letter to Dick Cowburn, May 14, 1968; Cowburn, Fred, interview by Sanders, San Antonio, TX, October 11, 2008.

85 Rippy, Terry, interview by McLeroy, Durham, NC, April 30, 1997. Statement of Glen Opheim, Rippy's co-pilot, to McLeroy. Statement of Don Richardson, former UH-1 gunship crew chief, to McLeroy, undated.

86 Rippy, interview, *op. cit.* Thomasson, John, statement, undated.

87 Rippy, *op. cit.* Rippy, letter to McLeroy, undated.

88 Email from McWilliams, Robert, to McLeroy, date illegible.

89 *Ibid.*

90 Brady, Patrick, statement to McLeroy. The surnames and ranks of the other Dust Off medical ambulance helicopter pilots who flew at Kham Duc on May 12, 1968 are: CPT Loomis, 1LT Wylie, WO Bell, WO Fox, WO Hall, WO Markowski, WO Schenck, WO Schuster, WO Schwartz, WO Shadrick, and WO Shannahan. Brady, email to McLeroy, June 25, 2013.

91 Brady, *op. cit.* From 1962–73, helicopter ambulances in Vietnam evacuated more than 900,000 wounded soldiers and civilians in nearly 500,000 missions, often under fire, day and night, in all weather. More than 200 helicopter ambulances were shot down, and more than 200 pilots and crewmen were killed in Vietnam. Cook, John. *Rescue Under Fire* (Atglen, PA: Schiffer Military/Aviation History, 1998), pp. 147–48.

92 Rippy, letter, *op. cit.*

93 *Ibid.*

94 Long, *op. cit.*

95 Campbell, Richard, interview by McLeroy, Fort Bragg, NC, November 21, 1995, and by Sanders, Gilbert, AZ, June 9, 2007.

96 *Ibid.* There is no doubt that 183 Vietnamese women and children could fit into a C-130, because on April 29, 1975, at Tan Son Nhut airfield 260 desperate Vietnamese civilians crammed themselves into a C-130. Butler, David. *The Fall of Saigon*, quoted in Langer, Howard. *The Vietnam War* (Westport, CT: Greenwood Press, 2005), p. 284.

97 Cowburn, Fred, letter to Dick Cowburn, May 14, 1968. Cowburn, *op. cit.*, interview by Sanders, San Antonio, TX, October 11, 2008.

98 Stanton, *op. cit.*

99 Cowburn interview, *op. cit.*

100 Thomasson, John, statement, undated. Bollard, Noe, telephonic interview by Sanders, August 25, 2009.

101 SF SFC Richard Gill was watching the plane through binoculars and saw both blood and hydraulic fluid streaming from it. Statement of Gill at a reunion of the Kham Duc Club.

102 Boyd, William, quoted in Sturm, Ted R., "The Lucky Duc", *Airman Magazine*, October 1970. Gropman, *op. cit.*, p. 50.

103 Hobson, Chris. *Vietnam Air Losses* (Hinckley, England: Midland Publishing, 2001), p. 148. Wikipedia.org/wiki/1968_Kham_Duc_C-130_shootdown.

104 Thompson, interviews, *op. cit.* Thompson, Bobby, statement, undated.

105 Shoplock, Dan, interview by Sanders, San Antonio, TX, September 12, 2009.

106 Thompson, interviews, *op. cit.*

107 "Award of the Distinguished Service Cross to Bledsoe, William", Headquarters, United States Army, Vietnam, General Orders Number 4325, September 11, 1968.

108 Thompson, interviews, *op. cit.* Thompson, statement, *op. cit.*

109 Rippy, *op. cit.*

110 The authors did not find documentary evidence for the use of this procedure at Kham Duc, but assume that it must have been used, because of: 1) its availability; 2) Westmoreland's personal concern about the potential effect of the battle at the Paris peace negotiations; 3) Westmoreland's order to Momyer to use every available resource to accomplish the evacuation that day; and 4) Momyer's awareness of the increasing danger that it might not be possible to do so.

111 Gropman, *op. cit.*, pp. 51, 52. Sturm, *op. cit.*, pp. 27, 29.

112 Gropman, *op. cit.*, p. 52.

113 Donahue, Joe, interview by McLeroy, Albuquerque, NM, August 19, 1995; Gropman, *op. cit.*, pp. 52–53. Hobson, *op. cit.*, pp. 148–49.

114 Thompson, interviews, *op. cit.*

115 Gropman, *op. cit.*, p. 53

116 Henderson, Robert, interviews by McLeroy, San Antonio, TX, December 12, 1995, and May 23, 1997, and by Sanders, San Antonio, TX, September 12, 2009.

117 *Ibid.*

118 Buchwald, Donald, letter to McLeroy, undated.

119 Debriefing of MAJ Billy Mills, 773 TAS, Clark AFB, Manila, PI, Americal Interrogation Section, Americal Division, Chu Lai, RVN, May 12, 1968.

120 Interview of Gatewood by McLeroy, Albuquerque, NM, August 16, 1995.

121 Wallace, James L., transcript of telephonic interview by R. L. Bowers at Richards-Gabaur AFB, MO, Project CHECO Oral History 5801, April 3, 1972.

122 *Ibid.*

123 Busbee, Larry, interview by Sanders, San Antonio, TX, September 12, 2009. Evans, Earl, "Larry Busbee's (Pilot of AC/465) Story of Kham Duc as told to Earl Evans", June 20, 1993, www.theboxcar.org.

124 Gropman, *op. cit.*, pp. 58, 59. Gatewood, Robert M., "Memorandum to 834th Air Division Cmdr; Events of May 12, 1968 Operation 'Grand Slam'", May 15, 1968. Tom Newton, Van Cleef's navigator, later reported that Van Cleef and his crew had only been in Vietnam one day of their first tour. Newton, Tom, telephonic interview with Sanders, June 17, 2010.

125 Freedman, email, *op. cit.* Freedman, statement, *op. cit.*

126 Gatewood, memorandum, *op. cit.* Gropman, p. 60.

127 Gropman, *op. cit.*, pp. 60–65. Jackson, Joe, interview, Danang Air Base, May 18, 1968. Schuman, Richard P., "Memorandum from ALO, Americal Division to IDASC: Valor at Kham Duc", undated. The probability of one 122mm rocket landing so close to Jackson's plane is extremely low, since: 1) the NVA would not likely have

brought only one rocket; 2) if they had brought more, they would have used them while U.S. troops were there; 3) no other 122mm rockets were fired during the battle; 4) the 122mm rocket could not be precisely aimed; 5) its minimum range was 1.6 miles; and 6) Jackson's plane was on the ground less than a minute.

128 Spier interview, *op. cit.* Spier, Herbert J., letter to McLeroy, January 18, 2000. Air Force Chronology, *op. cit.*

7

Aftermath

"[We] let them concentrate …, so that they would [be good] targets for airstrikes."

III MARINE AMPHIBIOUS FORCE[1]

Late on the afternoon of May 12, the III MAF headquarters in Danang conducted a hasty press conference to disseminate the official version of the battle. The Marine operations officer, BG Jacob Glick, officially acknowledged that Kham Duc had been deliberately used as passive bait for mass NVA attrition. He stated: "When it appeared that [the] attacking force was … two …regiments, [we] decided to let them concentrate for an attack, so that they would [be good] targets for air strikes."[2]

Glick also acknowledged that Kham Duc could not have been successfully defended with the *pro forma* reinforcement plan of the Americal Division: "You couldn't defend it from the base itself. It would take a tremendous logistics effort and a lot of forces. You'd need fire bases around it."[3] The Americal reinforcement plan did not include "a lot of additional forces," "a tremendous logistics effort," or any fire bases around Kham Duc.

Glick made the nonfactual claim that the evacuation was orderly, systematic, and conducted according to a previously prepared plan. He also said: "We had contingency plans for both Ngoc Tavak and Kham Duc which would allow us to … defend it with the forces there."[4] He seemed unaware of the contradiction of his previous statement that Kham Duc could not be defended from the base itself. He also made the nonfactual statement that only twenty-five friendly troops were killed.[5] He did not mention the thirty-seven U.S. soldiers, airmen, and Marines then missing and unaccounted for at Kham Duc and Ngok Tavak.

Nelson made several knowingly false statements at the III MAF press briefing: "We worked by full moon till midnight to make sure our defensive perimeter was secure and tied together with Special Forces and Engineers [and our] people were well underground."[6] In fact, his troops were not underground; he had no battalion perimeter; none of his companies were "tied together"; none were connected to the SF camp; and he did not "make sure" of anything.

He never left his bunker at any time to inspect his troops and was not even aware that a company of the 1/46/198th LIB was attached to his battalion. He later claimed that his ignorance of their presence was due to radio problems, although none of the other U.S. units at Kham Duc reported radio problems in communicating around the airstrip.[7] For his "heroic leadership" (by the 1968 American Division officer standards) Nelson was awarded a Silver Star, a Purple Heart, and later a promotion to full colonel. Someone altered Buchwald's factual After Action Report to include Nelson's false statements, and Buchwald's accurate, hand-written report disappeared from the official battalion records.[8]

Westmoreland authorized "impact" Silver Stars for all of Nelson's company commanders and staff officers merely for being at Kham Duc on May 12.[9] CG awards of Silver Stars to the members of his command did not require any evidence that the recipient actually did anything heroic enough to deserve the nation's third-highest medal for combat valor. The requirement was only that the recipient made a favorable "impact" on the CG. If necessary, an enhancement of the alleged facts or a totally fictional justification for the award was invented by the experienced wordsmiths on the general's personnel staff.

Westmoreland's indiscriminate shower of Silver Stars did not fall on any of the pilots or crewmen of the Dust Off helicopter ambulances or on any Special Forces officers except LTC Schungel, presumably because they had merely done their duty. None of the SOG troops, who defended the camp's most vulnerable perimeter against the largest ground attack of the battle after most of the reinforcement battalion had been evacuated, were even interviewed for an After Action Report (AAR).

Due to the secrecy of their mission, the 5th SF Group AAR and the Americal Division AAR only listed them by number (erroneously) as "the C&C Detachment."[10]

AF GEN Momyer sent a memo to Westmoreland stating that Kham Duc, not Khe Sanh, was the real test of the new Single Manager for Air system.[11] On May 15, Westmoreland went to LZ Baldy to personally thank the assembled officers of Nelson's battalion for "allowing me to concentrate the enemy and destroy him with airpower,"[12] thus confirming their battalion's role as passive bait for his mass attrition strategy.

No civilian reporter witnessed the battle, and few of them were even aware of Kham Duc's existence until several days after the battle. The only source of public information about it was MACV's brief, official statement. Apparently, Westmoreland's headquarters ordered III MAF and the 5th SF Group to tightly control all publicly disseminated information about it. The only men allowed to talk to reporters were "carefully selected individuals who are aware of the big picture," i.e., those who could be trusted not to deviate from the official talking points.[13]

The MACV press release minimized the battle, and since MACV was the only source of public information on it, it was barely noted by U.S. journalists. They were all focused on the "Mini-Tet" attacks on Saigon, where most of them lived, and on the scheduled start of the peace talks in Paris. *Time* magazine gave the battle two very short paragraphs; *Newsweek* gave it one.[14]

Back at FOB 4, McLeroy stripped off the filthy jungle fatigues he had been sweating in for three days and two nights, took a long, hot, soapy shower, shaved, brushed his teeth, and combed his hair. Then he put on a custom-made white dress shirt, a custom-made white linen suit, a black silk tie, and custom-made black dress shoes, all of which he had bought at relatively little cost in U.S. dollars on an R&R trip to Hong Kong the previous year. When he walked into the FOB 4 bar, one of the NCOs laughingly exclaimed, "It's James Bond!"

A young recon NCO who had been in the trench with McLeroy at Kham Duc courteously invited him to have a drink at his table with the other two Americans on his recon team. He said, "Sir, remember my name, because when you are a colonel commanding a Special Forces

Group, I want to be your sergeant major." It was the highest honor a junior SF officer could ever receive from one of the most elite of all SF warriors at that time, a SOG recon-commando team leader. Ever since that unforgettable day, McLeroy has cherished the memory of it as one of the peak experiences of his life.

Soon after the battle, the American Division held a board of inquiry to determine why the evacuation was so disorganized, why it resulted in so many missing-in-action cases, and why so much equipment was lost.[15] According to some anecdotal accounts a small, unrepresentative minority of the Army troops, evidently thinking it was a leaderless situation of "every man for himself," panicked, deserted their positions, abandoned their weapons, and ran wildly to the nearest aircraft, desperately struggling and pleading to get aboard.[16] That alleged behavior, if factual, was at least partly due to a disgraceful lack of effective leadership by some of their officers and NCOs.

Two of the American Division company commanders testified at the board of inquiry that they saw two other company commanders abandon their troops on the airstrip. They testified that one of those officers completely lost control of his company before abandoning it.[17] A few of the platoon leaders and platoon sergeants may have been guilty of the same cowardly incompetence.

Despite the justifiable condemnations of such behavior, the more important fact is that most of the Army troops and officers at Kham Duc were as disciplined and steady under fire as those of any comparable U.S. unit in Vietnam in 1968. One Marine helicopter pilot praised their orderly behavior, saying: "They were as professional a bunch of soldiers [as] I have ever seen … I wish I could say that about some of the [other] grunts we flew."[18] The behavior of most of the Army men at Kham Duc was both honorable and competent, and a few distinguished themselves by conspicuous displays of exceptional skill and valor.

Total American troop losses at Kham Duc and Ngok Tavak were forty-six men. At, near, or as a direct result of Ngok Tavak, fifteen Marines and two SF men were killed, mortally wounded, or missing. At, near, or as a direct result of Kham Duc, twenty-one Army soldiers, seven Air Force men, and one SF man were killed, mortally wounded, or missing.[19]

The co-authors estimate that approximately 130 of the 333 indigenous allied troops at or near Kham Duc and Ngok Tavak were killed, mortally wounded, or missing.[20] The number of Vietnamese military and civilian casualties at Kham Duc varies in both the primary and secondary sources. Schungel's "After Action Report" lists 272 village civilians at Kham Duc, of whom 89 were rescued and 183 were "KIA/MIA."[21]

Twelve aircraft were shot down at Ngok Tavak and Kham Duc. At or near Ngok Tavak, two CH-46s and one O-1 were lost. At or near Kham Duc, two C-130s, two CH-47s, three UH-1s, one A-1E, and one O-2 were lost. A badly damaged F-4 and A-4 were also rumored to have crashed on the way back to their bases on May 12, and one pilot allegedly did not bail out.[22]

The NVA camera crew from Hanoi could not film the battle due to the constant air attacks. Long after the battle an NVA film crew returned to Kham Duc, shot some obviously staged footage, and spliced it with some unrelated footage in their Hanoi studio to try to make it look as if the NVA forces had just captured Kham Duc. The result was a crude, amateurish, seventeen-minute pastiche titled "Kham Duc Victory." Curiously, it credited only the 21st Regiment of the 2nd NVA Division with the alleged victory and did not mention the 1st VC Regiment, whose troops (almost all NVA) sacrificed their lives at Ngok Tavak and Kham Duc.[23]

The Three Escapees

Early in the morning of May 13, Sassenberger, Foreman, and Colonna cautiously crept out of their hiding place in the jungle below OP 2.[24] They had no compass or map and only knew that they had to walk east toward Chu Lai on the coast. The only way they knew to go east was to walk toward the sun in the morning and away from it in the afternoon. They moved slowly by day, trying to avoid both the NVA troops and the constant bombing around them.

The FAC's target-marking rockets gave them a few seconds' warning of incoming air strikes by tactical bombers. The shriek of the jet engines streaking over them and the randomness of the ear-splitting explosions magnified their feelings of helpless terror. They had no warning of the devastating avalanches of B-52 bombardments nearby. In the earth-shaking thunder, all they could do was fling themselves into the nearest depression, curl their bodies into fetal positions, press their hands against their ears, squeeze their eyes shut, grit their teeth, and curse, pray, or scream.

In one attack the rippling tsunami of shock waves knocked all of them unconscious. On May 14, the bombs fell so close that the shock waves bounced their bodies off the ground, hurled lethal shards of hot metal, rock, and wood over their heads, and threw such geysers of vegetation and dirt into the air that the falling debris almost covered them. When the ordeal finally ended, their ears and noses were bleeding, and they were deafened.[25]

Knowing that their only hope was to be seen from the air before they were seen by the enemy, they avoided the triple-canopy jungle and walked through the thinner vegetation of the more open areas. Foreman's mangled right hand was useless, but his wounds, like those of Sassenberger and Colonna, had stopped bleeding. At night they slept fitfully between the giant roots of the banyan trees, trying in vain to ward off the leeches. They did not know that the slimy, black lumps were eating the dead tissue of their wounds and preventing them from becoming infected.

They continued to push through the thick brush and tall elephant grass in the withering heat. Due to his leg wound Colonna could not keep up with them, and Sassenberger and Foreman took turns half-carrying him, despite their own pain, thirst, hunger, and exhaustion. They had to stop often to rest, and while doing so they sometimes watched monkeys eating. They tried to eat the same kind of vegetation, but it gave them no energy and no relief from their thirst.

By the end of the third day they were dangerously dehydrated. Their lips were cracked, their tongues were swollen, they were suffering from heat exhaustion, and they were so weak that they could barely keep moving. Tortured by the oppressive heat and desperate for water, they licked the dew from leaves and sucked every drop from every tiny rivulet they found, but their raging thirst was never quenched.

By the fourth day they barely felt the pain of their wounds, were starting to hallucinate, and were dangerously close to heat stroke. On the morning of May 16, Sassenberger's bleary eyes saw a deer, but he was afraid to shoot it. He knew the sound might attract NVA troops, and even if not, he knew he could not butcher it. Later he saw a large snake crawling close to him, but it slithered away before he could club it. They would have eaten the snake raw, but their need for water was far greater.

That afternoon, as they were slowly creeping through the jungle on the edge of a steep hillside clearing, they heard a faint, droning sound. Looking up, they saw a small plane in the distance. They left Colonna there and staggered out into the clearing, waving their arms and shouting at the plane. Sassenberger tried to signal it by using his metal cigarette lighter to reflect sunlight on it. Foreman took off his shirt and waved it, hoping that the pilot would see his black skin and know he was an American, but the plane flew on past them.

Foreman decided to make an SOS signal in case it returned. He took the letters, photos, and other pieces of paper from his wallet and told Sassenberger to do the same. They found a large bomb crater in the clearing and anchored the paper with rocks to spell out "SOS" on the sloping wall of the crater. As they anxiously watched, the plane slowly turned and came back toward them. They waved at it frantically, and the pilot moved his wings up and down to show that he had seen them.

The pilot was CPT Willard Johnson, the second AF ALO at Kham Duc. He returned immediately to his Chu Lai headquarters to report the sighting. Another small plane photographing bomb damage also saw them. The pilot photographed their SOS sign and returned to Chu Lai to develop the film.[26] As soon as the sighting was confirmed, the AF 37th Aerospace Rescue and Recovery Squadron in Danang launched two HH-3 helicopters, and the AF 6th Air Commando Squadron at Pleiku scrambled three A-1H Skyraiders to escort them.[27]

Foreman and Sassenberger staggered back to the trees on the edge of the clearing and half-dragged Colonna into the bomb crater with them. While they waited in the sweltering heat of the crater, Foreman saw what he thought was a small stream about 50 yards down the hill. Tortured by thirst, he impulsively decided to go down there in search of water.

About halfway down the slope he heard and saw helicopters circling over the crater above him. With his last burst of adrenaline, he tried to run back up the hillside, but collapsed, so exhausted that he could not stand up. All he could do was sit there and feebly wave at the helicopters.

The three escapees did not realize that they had been observed along their route by NVA troops, who were using them as bait to attract and shoot down the rescue helicopters. As the first two A-1 tactical bombers circled the area at low altitude to draw enemy fire, the NVA troops held their fire, but as soon as the helicopters started to descend, the NVA troops fired at them.

The helicopters climbed to a safe 8,000-foot orbit, and the commander of the A-1s called for reinforcements. Four AF A-1s and four Marine A-4s were diverted to the area and attacked the NVA positions for about an hour. After the A-4s expended all their ordnance, the two A-1s made low passes around the clearing to draw fire.

Receiving none, the A-1 commander cleared the helicopters to descend, but as soon as they did, the surviving NVA troops resumed firing at them. The A-1s continued to bomb and strafe the NVA positions, while one helicopter hovered over the bomb crater and lowered its jungle penetrator seat to Sassenberger. He put Colonna on the seat, but Colonna was too weak to hold onto the cable, so Sassenberger held onto him and the cable as they were winched up.

Foreman, terrified that he had been abandoned again, helplessly watched the helicopter depart without him. A few minutes later, the second helicopter descended and lowered its jungle penetrator near him, but he was too exhausted to reach it. It took the hovering helicopter pilot six minutes to put the dangling device directly into his lap, so Foreman could slowly crawl onto it and be winched up. The AF pararescue NCO gave him some water and cleaned and bandaged his wounded hand. Foreman then collapsed, sobbing from pent-up emotions and exhaustion.[28]

Despite their agonizing, five-day ordeal, the three men had only been able to walk about a mile northeast of the Kham Duc airstrip.[29] They were taken to a Danang hospital to recuperate and prepare for operations to repair their wounds. The terrible memories of their ordeal caused them to suffer from post-traumatic stress disorder (PTSD) for many years.

The Captivity of Julius Long

SP4 Julius Long stayed in hiding beside Simpson's body at the base of the OP 1 hill until the night of May 13.[30] He knew he had to get back to his base at Chu Lai, but had no idea of how far it was. All he knew was that it was on the coast, that the coast was east of Kham Duc, and that the sun comes up in the east. He also knew that if he could see the stars called the Big Dipper at night, he would know where north was, and if he pointed the index finger of his left hand north, his extended thumb would point east.

He started walking into the jungle night. Long was a tough farm boy from the western Virginia mountains and an experienced hunter, who often volunteered to be the point man on patrols. The dark jungle did not terrify him. He knew that with his M-16 rifle, a twenty-round magazine, and two bandoliers of additional ammunition, he could kill any animal in the jungle smaller than an elephant.

For the next two nights he walked cautiously through the jungle darkness without seeing any predators, because the bombing had either killed them or driven them away. In the heat of the day he hid in dense vegetation and slept fitfully among the insects and leeches. The intense heat and constant sweating dehydrated and tortured him with thirst.

On the third day, he found a water-filled bomb crater with the bloated body of an NVA soldier floating in it. Despite his revulsion, his raging thirst forced him to drink the contaminated water. The blood seeping from his open wounds constantly attracted leeches, which he tried in vain to keep off. He continued walking slowly eastward at night, subsisting only on wet leaves, dew, and the small amounts of water he occasionally found in little rivulets.

On May 16, four days after the battle, he was creeping into a small clearing early one morning, when he was surprised by a squad of NVA soldiers hiding in ambush. They pointed their rifles at him, and he knew that he had to surrender or die. If he had known of the five years of horror awaiting him as a prisoner of the VC and NVA, he might have chosen not to surrender.

The NVA soldiers tied his hands behind his back, blindfolded him, and marched him through the rugged mountain and jungle terrain for seven days with only tiny amounts of food. They took him to a camp for South Vietnamese prisoners, where he was the only American, put him in an open-air stockade, and gave him some water and a few bananas. For the next five days, he received only two small bowls of rice daily.

He was bound and blindfolded again and marched through the jungle-covered mountains for nearly three weeks. When he arrived at the second POW camp, he was taken to a bamboo canopy with a table and chairs, where a tall American in an NVA uniform interrogated him. The other POWs warned him that the interrogator was a notorious traitor named Robert Garwood, a former Marine PFC, who had been captured three years earlier. Another POW, a Marine corporal named Earl Weatherman, was thought by the POWs to be a covert informant for Garwood.

Garwood eagerly served the NVA guards as a translator, prisoner interrogator, and prisoner indoctrinator. He lectured the POWs daily on Communist ideology and the Communist version of Vietnamese history. Long saw him slap U.S. POWs and punch them with his fist. All the POWs hated him, and the last request of one dying POW was, "Get Garwood!"[31]

The POWs' diet was mostly rotten red rice that had been stored in filthy containers for years and was so contaminated with weevils and rat feces that it made them vomit and gave them severe dysentery. They all lost control of their bowels, some of them up to a hundred times a day, and their clothes and bodies were constantly soiled with their watery feces. Many men lost more than half their normal body weight and were too weak to stand. They all had to sleep on one lice-infected bamboo pallet, where the helpless men defecated, urinated, and vomited.

They were given no shoes, no mosquito nets, and no blankets for the cold, damp nights. The mosquitoes gave them malaria, and the guards refused to give them quinine for the bone-shaking chills and burning fevers of the ravaging disease, until they were almost dead. The small amounts of quinine they gave them then were too late to help.

The more the camp's POW population grew, the smaller each individual food ration became. During the rainy season months their daily ration of three coffee cups of rotten rice was cut to two cups, and their dysentery combined with malaria made many POWs too weak to eat. The total lack of vitamins in their starvation diet made them vulnerable to scurvy, gingivitis, rickets, beriberi, and bleeding gums, which caused many of them to lose teeth.

In addition to their dysentery, malaria, and starvation, the POWs received extremely rudimentary, if any, first aid treatment for their wounds, which became infected in the camp's ubiquitous filth. Some men died from infected wounds, and other men's limbs were saved from amputation only by the maggots in their wounds eating the dead tissue. Otherwise, the infection would have spread into their bloodstream and caused fatal septic shock.

The POWs were tortured by outbreaks of skin diseases that caused itching pustules. Their need to scratch them was overpowering. When the festering pustules were torn open, they soon became infected, and the infected pus oozed out and spread the disease to other areas of the skin. The hellish, endless torture of itching and scratching was so maddening that many men wanted to die to escape it.[32]

The most admirable POW there was an Army medical doctor named Floyd Kushner. The VC guards refused to give him any medicines for the POWs, apparently because they wanted the POWs to die slow, painful deaths. Even with no medicines Kushner managed to save some of their lives. He saw Long collapse and suspected it was cardiac arrest, but all he could do was pound on Long's chest to try to restart his heart. He pounded so hard that he cracked one of Long's ribs, but he caused his heart to start beating again and saved Long's life.[33]

The men were lightly guarded, because most of them were too sick and weak to escape, but two men on a work detail in the jungle overpowered their guard and ran away. One was soon killed, and the other was wounded and caught. He was shackled to an outdoor bamboo pallet and left there for three months with no protection from the elements. He had to urinate and defecate where he slept, and the other POWs had to feed him and bring him water. His pitiful example for ninety consecutive days and nights eliminated anyone's thoughts of escape.[34]

Long was in the VC camp until early 1971, by which time only twelve of the original twenty-five American POWs in his camp were still alive. One day they were told that they were going to a prison in Hanoi. They were divided into two groups for a ten-day march into Laos, and the six men in Long's group left first. On one of the rugged mountain trails he painfully twisted his ankle, but was forced to keep walking on it, until they reached an NVA "hospital" in the jungle.

Long and another seriously ill POW were left there to recuperate (or die) until the second group from their camp arrived twelve days later. Shackled together in pairs, they walked all day and rode in trucks at night. Long was astounded by the number of NVA regular troops he saw daily coming down the Ho Chi Minh Trail. They often abused the helpless POWs by knocking them down with their rifle butts, and punching and clubbing them when they tried to get up.

After crossing the North Vietnamese border, they were handcuffed and transported in trucks to a railroad station, where they were loaded into boxcars. When they arrived on the outskirts of Hanoi in April 1971, they were taken to a prison called "Plantation Gardens" by its inmates. Their Hanoi prison ration of bread with thin cabbage soup or pumpkin soup was totally inadequate, but far better than the foul rations in their VC jungle prison. At least it was not rotten or contaminated with rat feces and did not make them vomit when they ate it.

The NVA's medical care for the POWs was extremely painful and cruel, but better than their total lack of medical care under the VC. When Long had an appendicitis attack, the doctor cut open his abdomen and removed his appendix with only a local anesthetic. When one of Long's teeth had an abscess, the dentist pulled it out with no anesthetic. Then he pulled out all of Long's other rotten teeth with no anesthetic, leaving him with terribly painful, swollen gums and unable to chew food.[35]

During the eleven-day U.S. B-52 strategic bombing campaign in December 1972, the POWs in the "Plantation Gardens" were handcuffed, blindfolded, loaded into trucks, and transferred to the Hoa Lo prison, the notorious "Hanoi Hilton," in the city center. In March 1973, Long and the other POWs there were finally released and brought back to America. His tortured mind never fully recovered from the hell of nearly five years as a helpless victim of the sadistic Vietnamese Communists. He became an alcoholic recluse and suffered from severe Post Traumatic Stress Disorder the rest of his life.

Return To Kham Duc

For the first year after the battle, photographic analyses from periodic reconnaissance flights in the Kham Duc area showed no sign of any significant enemy activity. In June 1969 MACV's Joint Personnel Recovery Center (JPRC) received information that POWs might be held in the Kham Duc area. The American Division sent a long-range reconnaissance team to investigate, but they found no sign of any POWs or any significant NVA presence there.[36]

Later that year a helicopter carrying a long-range recon team of the 5th SF Group's Project Delta was diverted to an emergency mission, and the pilot had to temporarily leave the SF team on the nearest landing zone, which happened to be Kham Duc. The helicopter received small-arms fire from the surrounding ridges when it took off and again when it returned for the team. While waiting for it, the team noticed heavily used trails and signs of fresh digging around the airstrip, but saw no one.[37]

In 1969, the incredible lack of institutional memory of the 5th SF Group was exemplified by the appallingly ignorant recommendation of a junior "intelligence" officer in its headquarters. He advocated the establishment of a new SF camp at Kham Duc, because he claimed its "ideal location" would "virtually strangle" NVA infiltration from Laos. The absurd implication that one irregular civilian battalion of CIDG conscripts under LLDB leadership could defend Kham Duc from division-size NVA troop units was beyond stupid. His ridiculous analysis shows why the term "military intelligence" sometime seems to be an oxymoron.

In mid-1970, aerial reconnaissance showed that the NVA had resumed road improvement work in the Kham Duc area and had begun to use it as a support base for their infiltrating troops. The Americal Division intelligence analysts thought the NVA might try to make it a major rear services supply and transshipment base. There were also rumors that U.S. prisoners might be held there.[38] In July 1970, the American Division CG, MG Albert Milloy, ordered a U.S./ARVN operation code-named *Elk Canyon* centered on Kham Duc.[39]

The American's 2/1/196 battalion and a battalion of the 2nd ARVN Division, both with attached engineer and artillery units, were airlifted in helicopters to the Kham Duc valley. They placed reinforced companies on hilltop positions around the valley and placed the headquarters of the ARVN troops on the ridge west of the old SF camp, where OP 2 was located during the 1968 battle. The U.S. and ARVN artillery bases east and west of the valley provided fire support for each other.

In the first four days the engineer troops repaired the airstrip, then fixed-wing aircraft brought in tons of supplies. While ARVN units patrolled south and west of the valley, U.S. long-range reconnaissance teams patrolled north and east of it in search of American or ARVN prisoners, but found no signs of any human presence.

Large amounts of U.S. equipment and supplies were discovered in the ruins of the SF camp and airstrip. Left there in the 1968 evacuation, they were still useable in 1970. The NVA troops normally would have collected them soon after the battle, and the fact that those items lay untouched for two years indicates that the NVA were not actively using Kham Duc at that time.

In the pre-dawn darkness of August 5 a sapper platoon supported by RPG and mortar fire penetrated an American Division artillery position. That night, twenty-two sappers and three U.S. soldiers were killed there. Elsewhere, forty-four NVA troops were killed in brief firefights with U.S. and ARVN patrols. On the last day of the operation, a CH-47 helicopter evacuating the last load of American Division troops crashed as it approached LZ Judy, killing thirty-one passengers and crewmen.[40]

The most significant result of the six-week Kham Duc operation was the discovery of the remains of some of the thirty-seven men unaccounted for in the 1968 battle. Troops from the ARVN battalion found human bones on the former OP 2 site, and troops from the American battalion located more bones on the former OP 1 site. The finds were reported to the American headquarters, and a graves registration team led by 1LT

Ronald Lyles was sent to Kham Duc to collect them and search for the remains of the other men left behind there.[41]

The graves registration team obtained a large aerial photo of the area, reviewed all the documentation of the battle, excavated parts of the OP 1 and OP 2 sites, found more bones, and sent them to the Army mortuary in Saigon for forensic examination. They were identified as those of SSG Johnny Carter, PFC Antonio Guzman, PFC Randall Lloyd, PFC Harry Sisk, and SP4 Richard Bowers. The remains were prepared for burial and returned to their next of kin.[42]

Thirty-two men left behind at Kham Duc and Ngok Tavak were still unaccounted for at the end of the war. For more than ten years after the withdrawal of U.S. forces the Communist government refused to allow any U.S. excavation. In 1988, American and Vietnamese teams finally began joint operations to locate and recover their missing personnel. In 1992, the U.S. Joint Task Force – Full Accounting (JTFFA) established an office in Hanoi. The JTFFA was later renamed the Joint POW/MIA Command (JPAC).[43]

In 1993, the JTFFA located the site where the C-130 with 183 Vietnamese refugees and six Americans was shot down. In 1994, a JTFFA team collected some 6,000 bone fragments there and sent them to the Army's Central Identification Laboratory in Hawaii (CILHI) for forensic examination. In 2007, the remains of the five Air Force crewmen and one Special Forces officer who died in that crash were identified and interred in a military funeral at Arlington National Cemetery.[44]

Many of the families of the missing men suffered emotionally for years because of the remote but haunting possibility that their loved ones might still be alive as POWs. Some veterans of the two battles also suffered survivors' guilt during those years from their uncertainty of the fate of their missing comrades. The first to begin a personal quest for the recovery of the remains of the Marines at Ngok Tavak was Tim Brown, a former corporal in the Marine platoon, who was medically evacuated shortly before the battle.

He and a few other members of Vietnam Veterans of America spent more than ten years in repeated attempts to pressure the U.S. government to excavate the site and search for the remains of the eleven Marines and one SF sergeant left there in 1968. In 1994, they persuaded some members of the Vietnamese government to cooperate with future excavations for the remains of both U.S. and Vietnamese casualties.

In 1995, Brown and a few veterans of the battle, including two retired NVA officers and the Australian CO of the SF and Marine troops there, went to Ngok Tavak and held a brief memorial ceremony. In 1996, Brown's VVA group returned to Vietnam and met with a high-ranking Vietnamese officer in Hanoi, who for the first time expressed official government support for their project.[45]

Meanwhile, a group of family members of some of the men unaccounted for at Kham Duc were pressuring the U.S. government to excavate the former OP 1 and OP 2 sites. The most active ones were Mrs Laverne Ransbottom, the mother of 2LT Frederick Ransbottom; Bill Skivington, the father of PFC William Skivington; and Vicky Gannon and Dovie Huffman, the sisters of PFC Danny Widner.[46]

In 1984, Bill Wright, an OP 1 survivor, who lived not far from Mrs Ransbottom in the Oklahoma City area, contacted her and learned of the network of families of the missing men at Kham Duc. Through her he also re-established contact with Julius Long, the former POW from OP 1. He then began an intensive search for all the information on the battle he could find.

From his online research and his and Long's personal recollections, he deduced what he thought was the most likely locations of some of the remains on OPs 1 and 2. He presented his findings to the VVA's POW/MIA committee, and in 1998 they arranged for him to brief a BG, the Deputy Assistant Secretary of Defense for POW/Missing Personnel Affairs, at the Pentagon. The VVA requested that Wright be sent with a JTFFA team to excavate the Kham Duc OP sites, and the request was granted.

In June of that year, Wright and McLeroy accompanied a JTFFA team to Kham Duc to excavate the two OP sites, but no remains were found at either. In September 1998, the JTFFA excavated Ngok Tavak and recovered some skeletal and dental remains, which they sent to the Central Identification Laboratory in Hawaii (CILHI) for analysis. In 1999 the JTFFA conducted another excavation at Ngok Tavak and found a few personal items, but no remains.

Eventually, five sets of remains were matched with DNA evidence from relatives, and in 2005 the matches were confirmed by three independent forensic experts.[47] The remains of seven others were identified by a combination of circumstantial evidence and laboratory tests. On October 7, 2005, they were interred together in a formal military ceremony at Arlington National Cemetery.[48] Tim Brown's long, grim quest to recover the remains of his former Marine comrades at Ngok Tavak was finally accomplished.

At the same time, the JTFFA was systematically collecting all available data on the Kham Duc battle in the hope of finding clues to the location of more remains of missing men. Laverne Ransbottom, Vicky Gannon, and Dovie Huffman exerted constant political pressure on their Congressmen and Senators, demanding that the Pentagon send the JTFFA back to Kham Duc for a more thorough and extensive excavation. They suspected that the Pentagon militocracy had given up on the extremely expensive project and decided to terminate it.[49]

Their lobbying efforts, assisted by the VVA and their Congressional representatives, were eventually successful. In early 2006, a JPAC team returned to Kham Duc to conduct the most thorough possible excavation of the OP 2 hilltop. In addition to numerous artifacts, some human remains were found that were thought to be American. They were sent to the CILHI laboratory in Hawaii and given first priority for forensic analysis.

Laverne Ransbottom, Vicky Gannon, Dovie Huffman, and the Skivington family were elated that their years of dogged, often adversarial, sometimes bitter relations with the Pentagon had at last been vindicated. The remains of 2LT Fred Ransbottom and PFC William Skivington were identified, and their families were invited to a formal repatriation ceremony at CILHI.[50]

No traces of the other missing men, including Danny Widner, the brother of Vicky Gannon and the late Dovie Huffman, were found, but Vicky Gannon shared vicariously in the emotional closure of her extended family. At least she had the certain knowledge that literally no stone and no cubic inch of dirt had been left unturned in conducting the most thorough possible search for any evidence to confirm the death of her beloved brother.

At CILHI the artifacts from the excavation site were displayed for the family members. When Laverne Ransbottom saw her son's high school class ring, she impulsively picked it up and kissed it.[51] That tangible symbol of his fate seemed to finally give her the emotional closure she had faithfully sought ever since she lost him on that bitter Mother's Day nearly forty years before.

Notes

1   Anonymous, untitled, undated part-paraphrase and part-quotation of statements to reporters by Marine BG Jacob Glick, May 12, 1968, at III MAF headquarters, Danang, microfilm designation 02CH/29/2/4& Sup.; Alfred F. Simpson Historical Research Center (AFSHRC), Maxwell AFB, AL. Sams, Kenneth and Thompson, A. W., "Kham Duc Project CHECO (Contemporary Historical Examination of Current Operations) Report," Headquarters, Pacific Air Forces (PACAF), Hickam AFB, HI, July 8, 1968, pp. 5–6, cited in Gropman, Alan. *Airpower and the Air Evacuation of Kham Duc* (Maxwell AFB, AL: USAF Southeast Asia Monograph Series, Volume V, Monograph 7, Air University, 1976), p. 75.

2   Glick, *op. cit.*

3   *Ibid.*

4   *Ibid.*

5   *Ibid.*

6   Sams and Thompson, *op. cit.*

7   Nelson, letter to Hardy Bogue, February 5, 1993.

8   Statement of Buchwald, Donald.

9   Impact Award List, Commanding General, Americal Division, USARV Form 157-R, Item 16 (undated).

10 Schungel, Daniel, "After Action Report Battle of Kham Duc," Company C, 5th Special Forces Group, May 31, 1968. Chung, Donald, "Summary of Operation Golden Valley," Headquarters, Americal Division, May 16, 1968.

11 Letter from Momyer to Westmoreland, May 15, 1968, quoted in Nalty, Bernard. *Air Power and the Fight for Khe Sanh* (Washington, D.C.: Office of Air Force History, 1973), pp. 80, 116.

12 Thomasson's statement to McLeroy, May 9, 1997, and Westmoreland's telephonic statement to McLeroy confirming Thomasson's statement, July 13, 1997.

13   Sidle [no first name, no date, probably May 12, 1968] message from III MAF to IFFV and 5th Special Forces Group.

14 *Newsweek*, May 27, 1968, p. 18. *Time*, May 24, 1968, p. 35.

15 Parson Nels, Headquarters, Americal Division, Special Orders No. 136, Investigation Board, May 15, 1968. Headquarters, 2nd Battalion, 1st Infantry, Board of Inquiry, Missing Persons, May 27, 1968. Statement of Thompson, Bobby, CO of A/1/46/198,

to McLeroy, October 6, 1995. Statement of Thomasson, John, CO of C/2/1/196, to McLeroy, May 9, 1997.

16 Informal, unconfirmed statements of various former American troops, SF troops, helicopter crewmen, and fixed wing crewmen regarding actions they allegedly witnessed on the Kham Duc airstrip on May 12.

17 Nels, *op. cit.* Thompson and Thomasson, statements, *op. cit.*

18 McGinley, Bernie, email to Bill Schneider, July 6, 2010.

19 The 29 U.S. KIA/MIAs at, near, or as a direct result of the Kham Duc battle were (in rank, then alphabetical order): Air Force (7)—MAJ Bernard Bucher, MAJ John McElroy, CPT Griffen Scarborough, 1LT Omar Jones, 1LT Stephan Moreland, SSG Frank Helper, and Airman 2nd Class George Long. Infantry (20)—2LT Frederick Ransbottom, SSG Johnnie Carter, SGT Edward Pigg, SGT Joseph Simpson, SP5 Harry Sisk, SP5 John Stuller, SP4 Richard Bowers, SP4 Antonio Guzman, SP4 Juan Jiminez, SP4 Maurice Moore, SP4 Imlay Widdison, PFC Robert Bennett, PFC Harry Coen, PFC Andrew Craven, PFC Randall Lloyd, PFC Robert Salmela, PFC Richard Sands, PFC William Skivington, PFC Danny Widner, and PFC Roy Williams. Artillery (1)—SSG Pearl Bush. Special Forces (1)—CPT Warren Orr. The 17 U.S. KIA/MIAs at, near, or as a direct result of the Ngok Tavak battle (in rank, then alphabetical order) were: Marines (15)—1LT Horace Fleming, SSG Thomas Schriver, LCPL Joseph Cook, LCPL Thomas Fritsch, LCPL Raymond Heyne, LCPL Bruce Lindsey, LCPL Donald Mitchell, LCPL James Sargent, PFC Thomas Blackman, PFC Paul Czerwonka, PFC Barry Hempel, CPL Gerald King, PFC Robert Lopez, PFC William McGonigle, and PFC Verle Skidmore. Special Forces (2)—SGT Glenn Miller and SP4 Thomas Perry.

20 Documentary evidence for the number of allied indigenous troops killed or missing at Kham Duc and Ngok Tavak varies in the following four sources: 1) Chung, Donald, "Summary of Operation Golden Valley," Headquarters Americal Division, 16 May, 1968; 2) Schungel, Daniel F., "After Action Report Battle of Kham Duc," Company C, 5th Special Group (Airborne), 31 May, 1968; 3) "Kham Duc Withdrawal" [undated]; 4) "Casualties: Attack On Kham Duc SF Camp and Ngok Tavak Forward Operating Base" [undated].

21 According to a retired AF three-star LTG, who as a captain flew two F-100 sorties at Kham Duc, one A-4 and one F-4 allegedly were so badly damaged there that they crashed on the way back to their bases, and only one pilot bailed out. Oral statement of AF LTG (ret.) Harley Hughes to McLeroy, Washington, D.C., October, 1999.

22 Gropman, *op. cit.*, p. 29.

23 Message from Joint Staff, Washington, D.C., to RUEKJCS/White House National Security Council Washington, D.C.//USDP: ISA/DPMO//, *et al.*, Oral History Program (OHP97–016) Report and Evaluation: http://lcweb2.loc.gov/frd/pow.html. Dr Huynh Van Thanh, October 20, 1997 (date of interview August 5, 1997) in JTFFA Miscellaneous Prisoner of War files, Reel 471, pp. 210–12. A copy of the film was obtained by the JTFFA and sent to Mrs Ransbottom, the mother of 2LT Frederick Ransbottom. McLeroy later viewed it with a Vietnamese translator.

24 Interview of Sassenberger by McLeroy, Key West, FL, June 25, 1995. Interview of Foreman by McLeroy and Sharon Cox, Waco, TX, February 1, 1996. Statement by Accused or Suspect Person, John C. Colonna, Chu Lai, RVN, July 10, 1968. Statement by Accused or Suspect Person, Wilbert Foremen [sic], Fort Hood, TX, July 27, 1968. Looney (no first name), telex message III MAF COC to Americal TOC Interrogation Report: Preliminary Debriefing of SGT Sassenberger, SP4 Wilbert Foreman, and SP4 John C. Colonna, May 18, 1968.

25 *cf.* Truong Nhu Tang. *A Vietcong Memoir* (NY: Harcourt Brace, 1985), pp. 167–70.

26 "Jolly Greens, A-1Hs Pull Daring Rescue," *Seventh Air Force News*, June 12, 1968.

27 *Ibid.*

28 *Ibid.* Foreman, interview, *op. cit.*

29 Bearden, Winston, "Daily Staff Journal or Duty Officer's Log", 196th Infantry Brigade, May 15, 1968.

30 Interview of Julius Long by McLeroy, Dublin, VA, August 5, 1997. Agent Report (Julius W. Long, Jr), 109th MI Group, April 2, 1973, in JTFFA Miscellaneous Prisoner of War files, Reel 471, pp. 210–12, 222.

31 Anton, Frank. *Why Didn't You Get Me Out* (Arlington, TX: Summit Publishing Group, 1997), chapter 7.

32 Kushner, Hal, "A Very Personal Story of Vietnam," Speech to Reunion of 1/9th Cav, 1st Air Cavalry Division, undated. Anton, *op. cit.*

33 Long, interview, *op. cit.*

34 *Ibid*

35 *Ibid.*

36 Veith, George J. *Code Name Bright Light* (NY: Free Press, 1998), p. 240. Interview of MG Albert E. Milloy by Sanders; Henderson, NV, June 19, 2006.

37 Taylor, Donald, "The Huey", projectdelta.net.

38 Milloy, interview, *op. cit.* Sanders was present in the Americal Division TOC, when the intelligence was received regarding NVA operations near Kham Duc, including use of the area as a POW camp.

39 Milloy, interview, *op. cit.* Sanders was present in the Americal Division TOC, when the 1968 battle was reviewed in detail and the operation plan to reoccupy Kham Duc was developed.

40 After Action Report Elk Canyon I, Headquarters, 2nd Battalion, 1st Infantry, 196th Brigade (undated), attached maps and charts dated September 19, 1970. Neville, Thomas, "Kham Duc Revisited", *Americal Magazine*, Fall, 1970. Griffen, Ronald, "Night Sweats At Kham Duc", *Vietnam* magazine, June 2009, pp. 32–37. "GI Helo Downed: Toll High," *Stars and Stripes*, August 28, 1970. The loss was almost half of all the U.S. KIAs in Vietnam during the previous week and was publicly noted as such by the U.S. Secretary of Defense, Melvin Laird.

41 Malachowski, Eugene and Kennedy, Craig, "Statement of Recovery, July 19, 1970." "Search and Recovery Operation, Kham Duc, August 29, 1970," Company A, 23rd Supply and Transportation Battalion, Americal Division. Lyles, Ronald,

"Memorandum to Captain Rawlings or Chief Warrant Officer Kennedy, Kham Duc (Operation Elk Canyon) July–August, 1970," undated. Neep, Wesley A., "Summary of Search, Recovery and Identification of Remains Recovered from Kham Duc, October 26, 1970".

42 Lyles, *op. cit.*

43 In 1987, President Reagan sent retired GEN John Vessey to Hanoi as his Special POW Emissary. Vietnamese cooperation with U.S. efforts to locate and repatriate the remains of missing military personnel was the result of GEN Vessey's diplomatic efforts in Hanoi. In 2003, the JTFFA was combined with the U.S. Army's Central Identification Laboratory in Hawaii (CILHI) to become the Joint POW/MIA Accounting Command (JPAC) with a world-wide mission to search for, recover, and identify missing U.S. personnel from World War II to the present.

44 http://dailynightlymsnbc.msn.com/archive/2008/12/18/1718754.aspx.

45 Brown, Tim, letter to Bill Schneider, June 24, 1994. Brown, Tim, letter to Keith Gary Flanagan, Casualty Resolution Supervisor, Detachment 2, JTFFA, U.S. MIA Office, Hanoi, SRV, March 2, 1995.

46 Interview of Laverne Ransbottom by Sanders, Edmond, OK, April 21, 2007. Interview of Vickie Gannon by Sanders, San Antonio, TX, September 12, 2009. Oral statements of Bill Wright to McLeroy during their 1998 trip to Kham Duc with the JTFFA team.

47 They were the remains of CPL Gerald King, LCPL Joseph Cook, LCPL Raymond Heyne, LCPL Wayne Mitchell, and LCPL Thomas Fritsch.

48 Circumstantial evidence and laboratory tests identified with high probability the remains of SF SGT Glenn Miller and six Marines: LCPL James Sargent, PFC Thomas Blackman, PFC Paul Czerwonka, PFC Barry Hempel, PFC Robert Lopez, and PFC William McGonigle.

49 Sanders' interviews of Ransbottom and Gannon, *op. cit.*

50 *Ibid.*

51 *Ibid.*

8

Analysis

"… tactical success is not necessarily strategic success, and tactical failure is not necessarily strategic failure."

HARRY SUMMERS[1]

The key fact of the battle of Kham Duc is that it was a massive, hastily improvised air ambush of two reinforced NVA regiments by virtually unlimited numbers of combat aircraft attacking in ideal weather for visual flight. The attackers were vastly more numerous than the defenders, but the inflexible NVA attack plan did not envision the possibility of such an unlikely concentration of air power in such unlikely weather at such an unlikely time and place. The air counterattack was enabled by the ability of AF GEN William Momyer, Westmoreland's new Single Manager for Air, to rapidly concentrate almost 150 aircraft in about 350 attack sorties at the height of the battle.

The Clausewitzian concept of combat "friction" refers to unforeseen complications that can cause serious and sometimes fatal tactical problems in otherwise sound operational plans.[2] At Kham Duc both adversaries suffered unexpected tactical friction, but the attackers suffered from it far more than the defenders. For the NVA there were three sources of such friction.

First, the NVA leaders apparently assumed that they could delay their main attack until the arrival of the secondary weather effects of the southwest monsoon in Laos. They knew the camp's only effective defense was continuous, close air support, which required visual target identification, and they knew the usual low cloud ceiling over Kham

Duc in May would negate that air support. They did not seem to have considered the unlikely possibility that the sky over Kham Duc in early May would be clear for three consecutive days during their attack.

Second, they did not expect the command of almost all the aircraft in Vietnam to be centralized and focused on the defense of Kham Duc during their attack. That possibility was even more unlikely during the NVA's "Mini-Tet" campaign in May 1968, when VC and NVA forces were attacking 118 other targets much more tactically important than Kham Duc.

Third, the NVA planners seem to have assumed that Westmoreland would aggressively defend the camp with massive reinforcements, as he did at Khe Sanh earlier that year and at Dak To the previous year. They apparently thought that his aversion to retreating from any terrain under attack would prevent his doing so at Kham Duc.

It evidently did not occur to them that he had the option of evacuating the defenders and abandoning the camp. When they saw that happening, they knew they could not wait any longer for the cloud cover to return and had to launch their main attack then or never. By fanatically continuing to attack *en masse* under a clear sky with a virtual air armada above them, they actually facilitated Westmoreland's operational strategy of mass attrition tactics.

There were also three sources of real or potential tactical friction for the U.S. forces. The first was the American Division's unrealistic reinforcement plan based on the initial deployment of only one battalion. The permanent defense of Kham Duc would have required three reinforced infantry battalions, each with an attached artillery battery and engineer company. They would also have needed fortified, company-size, mutually supporting positions on the high ground around the SF camp and airstrip with external, protected artillery support.

Even a force that size could not have defended an isolated camp so close to the Laotian border against a well-commanded, multi-regimental NVA attack without constant, close air support. To provide that air support in Kham Duc's unpredictable May weather, TACAN and GCA navigation systems would have to be previously installed in protected concrete bunkers. Even so, the American Division could not have provided such a defense and have accomplished its primary strategic mission of protecting the populated lowland areas in southern I Corps.

Second, there was no centralized command authority for the U.S. ground and air forces at Kham Duc. A joint-services air operation of such complexity and magnitude had never even been planned, much less rehearsed, with the crews of all the Air Force, Army, Navy, and Marine attack planes, transport planes, FAC planes, attack helicopters, and transport helicopters.

Third, the two Americal battalion commanders either neglected to ask or refused to ask the resident SF commander for his relatively well-informed estimate of the enemy situation. Because of that failure they did not realize that mere squads could never defend the little hilltop outposts against such an overwhelming NVA force in a surprise attack at night.

The converse of tactical friction can be called tactical synergistic serendipity. Synergism is a combined effect greater than the sum of its parts, and serendipity is the fortuitous discovery of positive things. Tactical synergistic serendipity is the spontaneous, cooperative improvisation of practical solutions to tactical problems that result in a combined tactical effect greater than the sum of its parts.

Despite many potentially disastrous operational problems, the defense of Kham Duc and the evacuation of almost all its defenders was a model of the tactical synergistic serendipity with which U.S. combat forces have historically excelled.[3] With a three-day window of clear flying weather and virtually unlimited air support, the spontaneous cooperation of more than 100 attack and transport aircraft made the rapidly improvised mass evacuation almost totally successful.

The battle of Kham Duc-Ngok Tavak, like any set-piece battle, can be analyzed with the nine classic "principles of war" derived from the writings of the 19th-Century Prussian General, Carl von Clausewitz. They are called: the Objective, the Offensive, Mass, Economy of Force, Maneuver, Unity of Command, Security, Surprise, and Simplicity.[4]

The first principle, the Objective, means that every major military operation should be directed toward a clearly defined and potentially decisive military objective. The NVA leader apparently had two strategic and potentially decisive objectives: 1) to kill or capture the camp's defenders and make a propaganda film of them; and 2) to time the attack to just before the start of the Paris peace talks for maximum propaganda effect and negotiating leverage. The NVA objective had great strategic potential, but was not tactically achieved. The U.S. objective was merely tactical: to cause maximum attrition in the attacking force, while evacuating the defenders. The U.S. objective had no strategic potential, but was tactically achieved.

The second principle, the Offensive, means a commander should seize and maintain the tactical initiative so as to control the pace and course of the battle and exploit enemy weaknesses. The NVA initially seized the offensive by planning and executing the attack on their terms. The U.S. forces had no realistic prior plan to defend the camp or systematically evacuate it. The American tactics were reactive, improvised, and weather-dependent, yet tactically effective for GEN Westmoreland's mass attrition "strategy-of-tactics."

The third principle, Mass, means that maximum combat power should be concentrated at the times and places most likely to lead to a decisive victory. The NVA forces had enough troop and firepower mass to overwhelm the camp under normal conditions. On the night of May 10/11 they could have attacked the hilltop OPs, the SF camp, the engineer camp, and the Americal positions around the airstrip simultaneously. The American ground forces were greatly outnumbered, but the U.S. combined air forces massed a decisive concentration of superior firepower at the critical period of the battle.

The fourth principle, Economy of Force, is the reciprocal of Mass. It means minimum combat power should be used for secondary objectives, so that maximum combat power (mass) can be used to accomplish the primary objectives. Most of the available U.S. ground forces in I Corps were withheld to accomplish the strategic American objective of defending the key terrain in the most densely populated areas. Minimum U.S. ground forces combined with maximum air forces produced maximum NVA casualties with minimum U.S. and allied casualties.

The fifth principle, Maneuver (flexibility), is a prerequisite for the effective application of the principles of Economy of Force and Mass. It means a commander should maintain the flexibility to concentrate or disperse his forces so as to place and keep the enemy at a tactical disadvantage. The ground maneuverability of the NVA forces was excellent, but the flexible air maneuverability of the combined air forces was far more tactically effective.

The sixth principle, Unity of Command, means a single commander should be given the authority to coordinate all allied forces toward common tactical goals. If the allied forces share tactically compatible objectives and methods, however, their improvised cooperation can often achieve a Unity of Action that temporarily replaces the need for unity of command.

The U.S. ground forces were initially endangered by a lack of tactical unity of command, and the NVA forces were far superior in their application of the first aspect of the principle: the coordination of all forces to achieve a common tactical objective. The combined U.S. air forces were greatly superior in the implied second aspect of the principle, however, the coordination of maximum combat power on the main enemy forces,

Although the lack of unity of command was potentially disastrous for the U.S. ground forces, the superior unity of command of the U.S. air forces more than compensated for that lack. The new, centralized control of virtually all the American aircraft operating in Vietnam enabled the U.S. air commander to rapidly concentrate almost unprecedented numbers of aircraft over Kham Duc. This flexible unity of action in the air was far more tactically effective than the inflexible NVA unity of command on the ground.

The seventh principle, Security, means that the enemy should not be allowed to obtain any unexpected tactical advantage. The NVA never had any tactical advantage in their repeated attacks on May 12, because they could not control the abnormally clear weather window or the massive air counterattack it enabled.

The U.S. forces were aware of the NVA advantages of greatly superior numbers and proximity to their Laotian sanctuaries and supply lines. The NVA were aware of the U.S. disadvantages of inferior numbers in a vulnerable location with normally adverse weather for sustained, close, visual air support.

The eighth principle, Surprise, is the reciprocal of Security. It means that an attacking force should choose times, places, and means of combat for which the enemy is least prepared. The senior leaders of both adversaries were not surprised by the obviously developing, set-piece battle, but some of their troops were tactically surprised. The U.S. troops at Ngok Tavak and on the hilltop outposts around Kham Duc were surprised by the timing of the night attacks. The NVA forces were surprised by the abnormally clear skies for three consecutive days and the arrival of virtually unlimited air firepower over Kham Duc at the height of the battle.

The ninth principle, Simplicity, means that leaders should make their tactical plans as simple as possible and communicate them as clearly and concisely as possible to minimize confusion. The simple American plan was to passively lure large numbers of NVA troops to an isolated area and destroy them with concentrated air firepower, while evacuating the defenders. The combined U.S. air forces executed that simple plan with devastating effectiveness.

The apparent NVA plan was far more complex. It was to build up their forces around Kham Duc, announce their growing presence by shooting at the arriving and departing aircraft, demonstrate their intention by attacking Ngok Tavak, and thus lure major U.S. reinforcements. They realistically expected the secondary weather effects of the southwest monsoon to negate close, visual air support, which would have allowed them to overwhelm the camp's isolated defenders.

They apparently hoped that a film of the battle that made Kham Duc look like a U.S. Dien Bien Phu would strengthen their negotiating position in Paris and intensify domestic pressure on the U.S. government to end the war on favorable terms for North Vietnam. When their critical assumptions about the weather and its effect on American close, visual air support proved mistaken, they either could not or would not alter their inflexible attack plan.

In summary, the NVA applied only one of the nine principles of war more effectively than the U.S. forces did: the Offensive. The U.S. forces applied seven of the nine principles more effectively than the NVA did:

Objective, Mass, Economy of Force, Maneuver, Unity of Command, Surprise, and Simplicity. The ninth principle, Security (i.e., protection of critical information), was neither tactically nor strategically relevant for either adversary.

An anthology of counterfactual historical speculation titled "What If?" is based on the premise that some metaphorical "roads not taken" belong on the "historical map."[5] No allegation of empirical fact can be validly based on a nonfactual assumption, of course, so the following scenario is merely an intuitively probabilistic one based on rational inference from ten realistic propositions.

First, shortly after the last troops were evacuated, a thunderstorm covered the valley. If it had arrived earlier and lasted all day, which often happened there in May, it would have negated visibility of the ground from the air. With no visual target identification, there could have been no close, visual air support. Even with radar-guided bombing, high-explosive bombs could only be used at distances from friendly troops greater than the lethal zone of the bombs.

Second, one of the main VC/NVA assault tactics called "grab them by their belts" was to push their attacking troops so close to the American positions that U.S. artillery and bombs could not be used without a high risk of hitting their own troops.[6] Instead of attacking the Americal Division companies around the airstrip in daylight, several NVA battalions could have concentrated a successful night attack against the lightly defended perimeters of the SF camp.

On the night of May 10, they could have charged the SF camp *en masse* and overrun one or more of its perimeters with their sheer weight of numbers. They could then have killed or captured the few SF men, the relatively few indigenous SOG troops, and the unreliable, if not actively treacherous, camp CIDG troops.

Third, if the NVA troops had captured the SF camp and its 4.2inch mortar, 106mm recoilless rifles, 81mm mortars, 60mm mortars, .50 caliber machine guns, and .30 caliber machine guns, they could have used those weapons from the protection of the camp's deep trenches and fortified bunkers to attack the exposed U.S. positions around the airstrip. With the support of their mortars, heavy machine guns, and recoilless rifles in the surrounding hills, they could have destroyed the engineer troops and the Americal enclaves around the airstrip.

Fourth, the film crew that accompanied the two NVA regiments would have shot lurid footage of the gloating conquerors and the dead and captured U.S. and indigenous defenders. That footage would have been rushed to Hanoi for editing and splicing to make Kham Duc look as much as possible like Dien Bien Phu. The film would have been given to the major media representatives in Paris to cover the start of peace negotiations between the American and North Vietnamese delegations.

Fifth, after the Tet battles three months before, the three American television networks were openly adversarial to "LBJ's war." They would have broadcast a sensational film of "The Fall of Kham Duc" even more dramatically and repeatedly than they did their deceptive footage of the Khe Sanh battle. At that time most of the print media shared the television media's unrealistically negative view of the U.S. military's combat performance in Vietnam.[7] The inevitable comparison of Kham Duc to Dien Bien Phu would have seemed to validate the claims of Hanoi and its American supporters that the U.S. military was losing the combat in the Vietnam War.

Sixth, LBJ's manic-depressive mood swings in his attitude toward the North Vietnamese Politburo alternated between hopeful optimism and angry belligerence.[8] From 1965–68, he ordered eight partial bombing halts in futile attempts to persuade the DRV leaders to negotiate an "honorable" peace settlement. Each time that they refused, his mood became more bellicose. In May 1968, they responded to his April bombing halt in North Vietnam with nationwide attacks in South Vietnam, which infuriated him.

Seventh, LBJ undoubtedly would have seen a film making the U.S. defeat at Kham Duc look like the humiliating French defeat at Dien Bien Phu as an outrageous personal and national insult. He was determined not to be the first U.S. President to lose a war, and he had always been hypersensitive to potential criticism for being weak on national defense, which was synonymous with militant anti-Communism. He had come to believe that his advisors, most of whom were then urging him to capitulate in Paris, were blind to the clear and present danger of international Communism,[9] the basis of all American Cold War foreign policy.

Eighth, the only appropriate and immediately available military response was an unrestricted, sustained, strategic bombing campaign of the key targets in North Vietnam. For years the Joint Chiefs of Staff had been urging LBJ to accept their plans for such a bombing campaign against those targets, and he could have implemented that plan at any time merely by authorizing it.[10]

Ninth, the strategic bombing operation that should have been approved in mid-1965 was the same plan that Nixon finally authorized in December 1972. Eleven days after the start of the first truly strategic air campaign of the war, North Vietnam was virtually defenseless against renewed U.S. air attacks.[11] The Politburo urgently requested a resumption of the negotiations, and a month later American participation in the war ended on terms acceptable to Nixon (although not to the South Vietnamese government or the U.S. Joint Chiefs of Staff).

Tenth, it is reasonable to conclude, therefore, that if the transitional monsoon weather at Kham Duc had made the visual identification of ground targets impossible on May 12, 1968, the most likely result would have been the death or capture of all the U.S. and allied defenders. A film of that defeat by the waiting NVA camera crew would have been edited to make Kham Duc look like an American Dien Bien Phu, and the film would have been widely distributed and broadcast.

At that critical moment in the war, it almost certainly would have caused LBJ to react radically either by capitulating or by authorizing the unrestricted, sustained, strategic bombing campaign against Hanoi and Haiphong that the Joint Chiefs of Staff had been urging since 1965 and that Nixon authorized in December 1972. Under such conditions, his hyper-machismo and militant anti-Communist ideology most likely would have made him choose the latter option.

If he had capitulated then, the war would have ended four years sooner on less favorable terms for the Republic of Viet Nam than those in 1973. If he had strategically escalated the air war directly against North Vietnam then, the war could have ended four years sooner on much better terms for the survival of the Republic of Viet Nam than those in 1973.

Notes

1   Summers, Harry, Jr. *On Strategy* (Novato, CA: Presidio Press, 1982), p. 90.
2   *Ibid.*, p. 33.
3   Doubler, Michael. *Closing With the Enemy* (Lawrence, KS: University Press of Kansas, 1994), pp. 1–64.
4   Summers, *op. cit.*, pp. 196–206. Clausewitz never wrote any "principles of war." The nine classic "principles" attributed to him were derived by Col. J. F. C. Fuller, a distinguished British officer, from Clausewitz's partially completed and posthumously published book titled *On War*. Fuller first published them in 1925 in his book titled *The Foundations of the Science of War*.
5   Cowley, Robert (ed.). *What If* (NY: Putnam, 1999).
6   *cf.* Wilkins, Warren. *Grab Their Belts To Fight Them* (Annapolis, MD: Naval Institute Press, 2011). If radar bombing had been available at Kham Duc, the same margin of safety that was required at Khe Sanh would have been required there. At Khe Sanh, B-52 bombing was limited to 1,000 meters from the defensive perimeter, and tactical bombing was limited to 500 meters from it. Nalty, Bernard. *Air Power and the Fight For Khe Sanh* (Washington, D.C.: Office of Air Force History, 1973), pp. 66, 86. In their attack on the eastern perimeter of the SF camp on May 12, many NVA troops got much closer than those minimum safety distances.
7   Kennedy, William. *The Military and the Media* (Westport, CT: Praeger, 1993), pp. 87–125.
8   Hershman, Jablow. *Power Beyond Reason* (Fort Lee, NJ: Barricade Books, 2002), pp. 12–20.
9   *Ibid.*
10 Sharp, U. S. G. *Strategy for Defeat* (Novato, CA: Presidio, 1978), Appendix C, p. 278.
11 Davidson, *op. cit.*, pp. 726–29. Phillip; *Vietnam At War* (Oxford University Press, 1991); pp. 726–729.

9

Conclusion

"You will kill ten of ours and we will kill one of yours, but ... it is you who will tire."

HO CHI MINH[1]

Kham Duc could have been, and very nearly was, both a tactical and a strategic disaster for the U.S. forces. A rapid and practically unlimited concentration of attack aircraft combined with a rare, three-day window of clear flying weather in a transitional monsoon month made it a major tactical disaster for most of the attackers, but not for most of the defenders.

Westmoreland approved the evacuation plan the night before the main NVA attack, because he agreed with GEN Abrams and LTG Cushman that one anachronistic little SF trip-wire border camp was not worth diverting the major troop and logistics resources necessary to defend it from a permanent NVA threat in a tactically unfavorable area.[2] After it had served as passive bait for mass NVA attrition, its voluntary forfeiture as surplus military real estate was considered a good trade for Westmoreland's "tactical strategy" of mass enemy attrition.

For U.S. forces the battle of Kham Duc was a classic Pyrrhic victory:[3] a tactical success due to unlimited airpower, a lucky weather window, and incompetent NVA leadership. Yet it was part of an eventual strategic failure due to President Johnson's ignorance of the main American enemy, the DRV Politburo, and their three-stage strategy for military hegemony in Indochina. The strategic failure was also due to his irrational fear of direct Chinese intervention in the war. He refused to take the strategic advice of his senior military experts, the Joint Chiefs of Staff, to end the war quickly and conventionally with a massive air and land campaign against the NVA in the DRV, Laos, and Cambodia.[4]

From 1964–68, the offensive, total war, long-term Indochina strategy of the resolute DRV Politburo was superior to the defensive, limited war, short-term South Vietnam strategy of the vacillating U.S. Commander-In-Chief. The DRV leaders were determined to fight a total war for hegemony in Southeast Asia and were willing to pay any human and economic price to win it. They began it unconventionally with Mao's three-phase, long-term, rural attrition strategy, but like Mao, they always planned to win it conventionally in the third phase of that strategy.

The DRV Politburo leaders knew that the key to a long-term, strategic attrition victory over the tactically superior U.S. military forces was simply surviving to buy enough time. They knew that they could never defeat the U.S. military's capacity to indefinitely continue a low-intensity counterinsurgency war. But they always believed they eventually could defeat the American political will to indefinitely continue a high-intensity, semi-conventional war that the U.S. military was never allowed to decisively win.

In 1968, the NVA learned that they could never win battles like Khe Sanh and Kham Duc tactically, but they also learned that they did not have to win such battles tactically, because they had six strategic advantages: 1) a constant supply of Soviet bloc and Chinese war materiel; 2) politically protected ports in North Vietnam; 3) politically protected supply routes and base areas in Laos and Cambodia; 4) no fear of a U.S. strategic expansion of the war after 1968; 5) no fear of domestic opposition in their tyrannical police state; and 6) a callous willingness to continue incurring enormous casualties with increasingly younger troops for no permanent military gain.

With those six strategic advantages they dared to gamble that regardless of the human and economic cost to them, and regardless of the tactical dominance of the U.S. military in all the major battles, their ability to prolong the war militarily would eventually be greater than the U.S. President's ability to prolong it politically. The NVA were willing to continue losing battles like Kham Duc and Khe Sanh tactically at a cost that would have been unsustainable, if they had been forced to fight such battles at times and places controlled by the U.S. forces.

The NVA could outlast the U.S. forces politically only because they did not have to fight such battles simultaneously in Laos, Cambodia, and North Vietnam. They could always retreat to their political sanctuaries in those countries to resupply their ravaged combat units with more and newer Soviet weapons and more young and expendable NVA troops, while preparing to fight and retreat again, whenever and wherever they chose.

For seven years from 1965–72, U.S. combat forces in South Vietnam took every major enemy position they were ordered to take, defended every major friendly position they were ordered to defend, won all the big battles, and killed more than ten times as many enemy troops as they lost. Unlike the NVA, however, they did not fight a seven-year strategic war for Indochina. They fought a one-year tactical war for South Vietnam seven times, won it tactically every year for seven years, and were withdrawn because of American domestic politics.

The DRV Politburo clung fanatically to their belief that eventually the U.S. Congress would no longer permit the American military to continue winning such strategically meaningless tactical battles at an increasingly unsustainable political cost. As predicted, Congress finally rejected the apparently endless partial escalations and de-escalations, withdrew U.S. military forces from South Vietnam, cut off essential military supplies to it, and prohibited U.S. combat air support for its forces. The modern, conventional, Soviet-equipped North Vietnamese Army then invaded South Vietnam again and quickly conquered it with no need for any VC guerrillas and no concern for any village "hearts and minds."

All the large battles in South Vietnam were U.S. tactical victories due to American combat superiority, yet strategic failures due to President Johnson's narcissistic, militarily incompetent micro-management of the U.S. forces in Southeast Asia from mid-1965–69.[5] The Politburo finally won their American War in America by political default because of their superior resolve and superior grand strategy, not in South Vietnam with superior tactics or superior forces.

At the start of the First Indochina War in 1946, Ho Chi Minh predicted to the French: "You will kill ten of ours and we will kill one of yours, but in the end it is you who will tire." Both of his predictions proved equally true in the Second Indochina War: the first for the U.S. military, the second for the U.S. Congress. The paradoxical battle of Kham Duc—a short-term U.S. tactical success, yet part of a long-term strategic failure—was no exception to that tragic fact.

Notes

1 N. Khac Huyen. *Vision Accomplished?* (NY: Collier-Macmillan, 1971), p. 155.
2 Westmoreland, William. *A Soldier Reports* (NY: Doubleday, 1976), p. 360.
3 A Pyrrhic victory is a short-term tactical victory so militarily or politically costly that it can lead to a long-term strategic defeat.
4 An example of a brief but strategically successful air campaign against North Vietnam is Nixon's December, 1972 authorization of constant, unrestricted B-52 bombing of all critical targets around Hanoi combined with simultaneous aerial mining of North Vietnamese harbors.
5 In February 1965 President Eisenhower, a former 5-star general, advised LBJ to decisively "hit the head of the snake" [in North Vietnam.] On February 10, 1965 Johnson confessed to his Vice President, Humphrey, and later to Mrs. Johnson: "I am not temperamentally equipped to be Commander-In-Chief. I'm too sentimental to give the orders" [to strategically attack and defeat North Vietnam, where the war originated and was controlled.] Beschloss, Michael; *Presidents of War;* Crown; NY; 2018; p. 525. He was also too egomaniacal to let his senior military professionals give the necessary orders to win the war against the North Vietnamese Politburo directly and quickly, which could have been done at any time from 1965 to 1969.

Appendix

Origins

In June 1940, France surrendered to the invading German Army, and in September the Japanese troops in southern China entered Tonkin (northern Vietnam). In August 1941, the Japanese Army, using the French puppet government as a political front, extended their control over the rest of Vietnam: Annam (central Vietnam) and Cochin China (southern Vietnam).

One of the first concerns of the occupying Japanese army was the vulnerability to sea or air interdiction of the only highway and railroad along the eastern coastline of the South China Sea. They feared that any blockage of that strategic terrain would slow or prevent the movement of their troops between northern and southern Vietnam, effectively cutting their forces in half.

To counter that potential threat, the Japanese ordered the French Governor General, Admiral Jean Decoux, to extend QL (national road) 14 north from Kontum through the Central Highlands to the coastal highway south of Danang. Decoux, appointed by the pro-Nazi Vichy regime in France, cooperated enthusiastically with Germany's ally, Japan. From late 1941 to mid-1945, more roads and bridges were built in Vietnam than in the previous fifteen years.[1]

By late 1941, the extension of QL 14 north from Kontum had reached the village of Dak Gle 17 miles south of Kham Duc (see map in Chapter V).[2] Pressured by the Japanese Army, the French engineers likely completed the new road to Kham Duc by early 1942 at the latest. When completed, it ran by the west side of Kham Duc, then northwest to intersect QL 1 near the coast south of Danang.

In the Kham Duc valley the French engineers widened the road to make a small, dirt airstrip. In good weather for visual flying, small planes based there could patrol the new road to the south and bring in supplies. They also built a large, concrete building on a hill overlooking the airstrip. It was originally the administrative headquarters for the small militia outposts that maintained and guarded QL 14 south of Kham Duc.

In World War II the building was occasionally used as a hunting lodge by the titular Vietnamese emperor, Bao Dai, and his entourage. The legend that Ngo Dinh Diem, the first President of the Republic of Viet Nam, built it as his hunting lodge (also called his "palace" in some versions of the legend) confuses him with Bao Dai or Diem's brother, Ngo Dinh Nhu, both of whom were avid big game hunters. Diem was a devout Catholic, but was also deeply influenced by the Confucianism of his Mandarin class and its spiritual veneration of wild nature. Because of that belief, he opposed killing animals for sport.[3]

From late 1946 to around 1950, the large building was likely a regional headquarters for French mechanized units. By 1950, Viet Minh sabotage and ambushes made the remote parts of QL 14 unusable, and the French abandoned them. The Viet Minh destroyed most of the French buildings, including the large one at Kham Duc. Only its concrete foundations remained.

In 1955, repairs began on QL 14, and in late 1959 the road was reopened to Kham Duc.[4] President Ngo Dinh Diem went there once by car, but not merely to pray and meditate on its natural beauty. In 1960 and 1962 he narrowly survived attempted *coups d'état* and thereafter lived in constant fear of another coup attempt.[5] In 1961, he had the dirt airstrip at Kham Duc lengthened and paved and stationed an infantry battalion there to guard it.

Allegedly, his emergency escape plan in another coup attempt was to fly to Kham Duc in a private plane, refuel there, fly to Vientiane in Laos, and seek asylum in the French embassy.[6] In November 1963, he and his brother were assassinated in a third, successful coup before he could activate his alleged escape plan.

The first U.S. Army Special Forces troops arrived at Kham Duc in September 1963. SF 1LT Wayne Long and five SF NCOs from Fort Bragg, North Carolina, brought two companies of South Vietnamese mercenaries recruited and paid by the CIA station in Danang. Their secret mission was to enter eastern Laos clandestinely on foot and interdict some of the NVA troops constantly infiltrating into South Vietnam on the Ho Chi Minh Trail in nearby Laos. It was the first U.S. cross-border ground operation of the war, and it was planned and controlled by the CIA.

Before arriving at Kham Duc, Long and half of his twelve-man SF team trained their mercenary troops for five weeks in infantry weapons and six weeks in jungle patrolling tactics. In addition to 240 Vietnamese, they had eight Nung bodyguards, fifteen Montagnard scouts, and a twelve-man LLDB (Vietnamese Special Forces) team. The Vietnamese 1LT in command of the LLDB team was the nominal commander of the force, but he accepted Long's *de facto* command, as he undoubtedly was ordered to do by his ARVN commander.

The only residents at Kham Duc at that time were half of an ARVN artillery battery and an ARVN infantry platoon, a total of seventy-five Vietnamese soldiers. Three of their 105mm howitzers were there, and the other two were at Ngok Tavak with another infantry platoon. The artillery CO was not informed of Long's mission, but also accepted Long's leadership.

The rustic structures on each side of the airstrip had been occupied by the parent battalion of the ARVN artillery and infantry troops. The ARVN battalion was withdrawn shortly before Long's arrival, and its five howitzers and two infantry platoons were left at Kham Duc and Ngok Tavak, presumably at the CIA's request. Long housed his 280 troops in the ARVN barracks.

Long and his NCOs used the ARVN artillery fire base at Ngok Tavak as a FOB for training patrols south of Kham Duc. Groups of twenty to fifty mercenary troops with two U.S. SF men were flown in Marine CH-34 helicopters to infiltration points on the Vietnam side of the nearby Laotian border. From there they walked 6–9 miles into Laos and spent up to fourteen days ambushing trails and attacking NVA targets of opportunity. Then they walked back into South Vietnam and met the Marine helicopters at pre-arranged pickup sites.

At first, the NVA were highly vulnerable to the unexpected attacks, because neither the French nor the ARVN forces had ever patrolled in that remote area before. On almost every patrol Long's men initiated the attacks, killed NVA infiltrators, and captured weapons and ammunition. In four months of combat patrolling Long lost only five troops in an ambush.

On one patrol persistent low clouds and rain prevented the helicopters from landing and forced Long and his men to wait in the cold rain with no food for two days. They finally had to walk back to Kham Duc, carrying their wounded. The cold rain and wind made some of their lowland troops hypothermic. Long and his men had to struggle up and down the steep, muddy, jungle-covered slopes for nearly three days to cover 6 miles back to the SF camp. On another patrol the weather again kept the helicopters from meeting them. They ran out of food, and when they finally walked back to Kham Duc four days later, Long had lost 23lb.[7]

In February 1964, Long's SF half-team and mercenary force under CIA control were replaced by a full SF A-team with an indigenous company of Civilian Irregular Defense Group (CIDG) troops under U.S. Army control. The SF team enlarged and fortified the camp. One of the SF NCOs, SFC William Jackson, was accidentally killed on a local patrol, and the camp was unofficially called Camp Jackson in his memory.[8]

Five miles south of the Kham Duc SF camp on a low ridge on the west side of the Dak Se River were the ruins of a small earthen fort called Ngok Tavak.[9] Apparently, no records exist of when or why it was built there, but some answers can be reasonably inferred from other facts.

First, it could not have been built before late 1941, the earliest date that the construction of QL 14 could have reached that area. Second, it could not have been manned by any French military unit from mid-1941 to mid-1945, because during World War II the Japanese Army interned all the French military forces in Indochina in their garrisons.[10] Third, contrary to legend, it was never a Foreign Legion post.

In the First Indochina War (1946–54) only about 20,000 Legionnaires were stationed in Indochina. They were too few to defend Tonkin, Annam, and Cochin China simultaneously, and most of them were needed in Tonkin, where all the big battles were fought. The Legion's mechanized groups were limited to the few usable roads, which did not include the remote sections of QL 14 around Ngok Tavak.

The only Legionnaires in Annam were those guarding the French coastal enclaves around Hue, Danang, and Nha Trang and the coastal highway and railroad connecting them.[11] Unlike the Japanese, the French had no strategic interests in the remote Central Highlands and no need to station scarce Legionnaires at an anachronistic and indefensible little outpost like Ngok Tavak.

Fourth, it was not a real fort and was not designed to resist any modern military force. It had no fortified overhead cover, and its shallow trenches and low earthen berms were surrounded by higher hills. It could not be reliably supported by air due to frequent low clouds and ground fog, and the nearest reinforcements were at Kham Duc.

In adverse weather for visual flight the fastest way for those reinforcements to get to Ngok Tavak was on QL 14. Even if they survived that ambush gauntlet, without constant, close air support they would be equally isolated and vulnerable to enemy fire from the surrounding hills. The sustained fire of heavy mortars and recoilless rifles alone would eventually breach the earthen berms and kill the exposed defenders.

Ngok Tavak can only have been a French colonial constabulary (rural militia police) post built during the Japanese occupation to protect the new road (QL 14) from potential Montagnard attacks. There had been two previous Montagnard revolts against French encroachments into their territories: one from 1931–33, and another from 1936–38, ending only three years before the new road entered the Jeh territory.[12]

During World War II, constabulary outposts along QL 14 like Ngok Tavak were manned by Rhade, Bahnar, Jarai, and Sedang Montagnard militia troops commanded by French colonial officers.[13] From 1946–54, the potential Montagnard threat to QL 14 was eclipsed by the larger and more lethal Viet Minh threat. The French withdrew their scarce highland forces to defend the towns of Kontum, Pleiku, and Ban Me Thuot and abandoned the little militia outposts on the remote sections of QL 14, including Ngok Tavak.

U.S. Army Special Forces

The formation of the Special Forces (SF), popularly known as Green Berets, began indirectly in 1940, when British Prime Minister Winston Churchill created an unconventional warfare (UW) unit called the Special

Operations Executive (SOE). It trained small teams of language-qualified volunteers—military and civilian, British and foreign—to conduct covert and clandestine UW against German forces in enemy-occupied nations during World War II.

SOE teams were clandestinely infiltrated into those areas to organize covert escape and evasion networks for downed airmen and train covert underground and auxiliary agents for espionage, sabotage, subversion, assassination, and target reconnaissance. SOE teams equipped, trained, and led indigenous guerrillas in ambushing, sniping, and raiding vulnerable enemy troop units and damaging transportation, communication, and logistics facilities with explosives.

In 1941, William Stephenson, a Canadian confidant of both Churchill and President Roosevelt, persuaded FDR to establish a similar U.S. organization to work with the SOE in Europe. FDR authorized one of his own confidants, William Donovan, a World War I Medal of Honor recipient, to create the top-secret Office of Strategic Services (OSS). In 1942, it began its UW operations in enemy-occupied areas of the European Theater and later in the Far East Theater.

The three main OSS subdivisions were secret intelligence (SI), special operations (SO), and operational groups (OG). The small SO teams, like those of the SOE, were foreign language-qualified, military and civilian volunteers trained to conduct various types of UW in enemy areas. The OG teams were larger, paramilitary units that equipped, trained, and led indigenous forces in both short-term commando raids and long-term guerrilla warfare in enemy areas.

After World War II, the OSS was disbanded, and in 1947 its former SI and SO activities were assigned to the recently created Central Intelligence Agency (CIA). After the Korean War, the Army Ranger units were deactivated, and their special missions were not assigned to any other unit. In 1952, COL Aaron Bank and a few other former OSS officers in the Psychological Operations Section of the Pentagon's Special Warfare Division persuaded the Department of the Army to create a secret Army unit to perform the UW missions of the OSS OGs.

The creation of the Army Special Forces was part of the U.S. response to the Cold War threats of a Soviet invasion of Western Europe and a

Chinese invasion of Southeast Asia. The original SF mission was to assist U.S. and/or allied conventional forces by conducting UW operations against conventional Soviet or Chinese Communist forces in enemy-occupied areas. Until 1964, all SF activities in Vietnam were controlled by the CIA station at the U.S. embassy.

The SF were not designed to replace the Ranger companies of the conventional Infantry, but its diverse UW skills included Ranger tactics and techniques, and many veterans of the World War II and Korean War Airborne and Ranger units volunteered for it. The first SF mission in the Republic of Viet Nam in 1957 was Ranger training. Two SF officers and ten NCOs trained fifty-eight Army of the Republic of Viet Nam commandos in Ranger techniques and tactics.

Those trainees were the nucleus of a new paramilitary unit that later became the Luc-Luong Dac-Biet, the South Vietnamese version of Special Forces. In 1958 and 1959, other SF teams trained LLDB teams and ARVN Ranger companies. In 1960, SF instructors established three Ranger training centers in South Vietnam, and in 1961 and 1962, SF teams assisted in the training of sixty ARVN Ranger companies.

The second SF mission in South Vietnam was counterinsurgency (CI). It was the U.S. response to the Cold War strategy of Nikita Khrushchev, Stalin's successor in the USSR. In January 1961, he publicly announced the USSR's policy of providing military and economic support for all insurgent (i.e., Communist-controlled) "wars of liberation" in Third World countries.

President Kennedy, in his inaugural address that same month, indirectly announced the new U.S. policy of providing military and economic support to friendly Third World nations fighting Communist insurgencies. He authorized CI programs to provide military and economic aid to the RVN.

Because insurgents use many of the UW tactics in which the SF specialized, and because the Kennedy brothers were enamored of the Special Forces, SF were chosen as the appropriate U.S. military unit to conduct CI operations. The new UW units created in the Navy (SEALs and Riverine Forces) and Air Force (Air Commandos) were mainly combat forces, not CI forces. The SF teams were the only UW unit with both missions.

The Truong Son mountain range and its highland plateaus were originally inhabited by eighteen major groups of some thirty indigenous tribes called Montagnards (mountain people) in French. Compared to the culture of the lowland ethnic Vietnamese they were economically, politically, and technologically disadvantaged. Most lowland Vietnamese despised the primitive little dark-skinned tribesmen with unintelligible languages, and most Montagnards hated and feared the arrogant, often exploitative ethnic Vietnamese.

The few ARVN troops in the Central Highlands could not defend the Montagnards from Communist Viet Cong attacks, and they did not trust the Montagnards' loyalty enough to give them weapons to defend themselves. The U.S. advisors to the RVN knew that with no anti-Communist forces in that area, the VC would increasingly use it for infiltration, guerrilla bases, food sources, recruits, and forced laborers.

In an attempt to resist those VC activities and develop the Montagnards' paramilitary potential, the Saigon CIA station organized the Civilian Irregular Defense Group. Twelve-man SF teams were assigned to CIDG camps in the highlands to help the Montagnards with various self-defense and "area development" projects, later called "civic action" projects.

The main activities of the SF teams were equipping and training the CIDG troops to protect their villages from local VC attacks and organizing practical projects to improve the villagers' basic standard of living. CIDG troops led by SF teams armed with surplus World War II weapons could defend their villages against small bands of VC terrorists and local guerrillas.

By 1964, however, large, regular North Vietnamese Army units were infiltrating into South Vietnam to train, augment, and lead increasingly large, combined VC/NVA units. VC squads of five to ten troops became VC/NVA platoons of twenty to thirty troops. VC platoons became VC/NVA companies of eighty to a hundred troops; VC companies became VC/NVA battalions of 400–500 troops. The small-scale, guerrilla tactics of local VC squads and platoons became the mobile, semi-conventional tactics of VC/NVA companies and battalions.

The CIDG camps were not fortified to withstand attacks by such forces, and the CIDG forces were not trained or equipped to defend their villages and camps against them. The CIA realized that local CIDG patrols to protect their villages from local VC guerrilla bands were inadequate in the face of the rapidly growing VC/NVA threat in the border regions.

As the infiltration of NVA troops increased, the SF mission in the Central Highlands evolved from village defense and local civic action to border surveillance and interdiction. For several reasons it was an impossible mission for the SF teams and CIDG troops to accomplish. First, the SF teams were not allowed to command the CIDG troops and could only "advise" their LLDB counterparts, who were the official commanders of the CIDG camps.

Second, a few LLDB teams were skilled, motivated, honest, and brave professional soldiers, but most were corrupt, cowardly, unqualified, and unmotivated political appointees. In the vast, jungle-covered Truong Son mountain range between South Vietnam and Laos it was not difficult for the infiltrating NVA troops to avoid the isolated CIDG camps, and most LLDB commanders in those camps were equally eager to avoid the NVA infiltrators.

Third, the LLDB teams were lowland ethnic Vietnamese, whose appearance, language, and culture were radically different from those of the CIDG Montagnards. The contempt of most LLDB teams for Montagnards as racially inferior savages and the tribesmen's bitter resentment of their exploitation by the lowland ethnic Vietnamese caused mutual mistrust and hostility.

Fourth, in some remote mountain areas there were not enough Montagnards to recruit for the CIDG border camps, and in other areas the local Montagnards were too primitive and elusive to be organized even as irregular soldiers. To fill the void, ethnic Vietnamese prisoners in city jails were sent under guard to serve as CIDG border troops in the mountains. They were more like low security prisoners than combat soldiers willing and able to fight infiltrating NVA troops.

Fifth, some of the CIDG troops were covert VC infiltrators. They collected intelligence on the camp defenses, passed that information on to VC agents outside the camp, and initiated attacks on the camps from the inside. VC intimidation often prevented local villagers from giving the CIDG camps warning of VC attacks from their observations of VC preparations.

Sixth, even in areas with enough Montagnards to recruit, they had critical problems as border interdiction troops. Their tribal culture, rudimentary military training, World War II surplus weapons, and poor LLDB leadership were inferior to the military culture, training, leadership, and weapons of the NVA troops infiltrating into South Vietnam. With notable exceptions, the combat performance of CIDG troops against NVA units was conspicuously weak.

The SF headquarters in each of South Vietnam's four Corps Tactical Zones (CTZs) had special indigenous companies called Mobile Strike Forces (MSF). The four "Mike" Forces operated only in their CTZ. In I Corps in 1968 they were mainly Nung and Montagnard troops commanded by SF officers and NCOs plus a few attached Australian officers and warrant officers.

The Nung were a dark-skinned, lowland tribe originally from Guangxi province in southern China. They spoke Cantonese as a second language, but were neither racially nor ethnically Chinese. Their original language belonged to the Tai linguistic group, which included related languages of other Montagnard tribes.

In World War II, many Nung clans migrated to the northeast border with Tonkin (in northern Vietnam) to escape Japanese troops in southern China. In the Chinese civil war (1946–49) some Nung troops fought with the anti-Communist Nationalist forces, and after the Communist victory, some Nung clans migrated into northern Vietnam.

In the First Indochina War (1946–54) some Nung troops fought with the French forces; others fought with the Viet Minh. After the Viet Minh victory in Tonkin in 1954, some Nung clans migrated still farther south into central Vietnam (Annam) and southern Vietnam (Cochin China). Many settled in Cholon, Saigon's twin city of ethnic Chinese.[14]

The South Vietnamese Army did not regard ethnic minorities like the Nung loyal enough to be regular ARVN soldiers, but the U.S. Special Forces teams recruited them as mercenaries in elite SF indigenous units. The Green Berets admired the proud warrior tradition and exceptional toughness, courage, and loyalty of most Nung soldiers. The combat quality of the Nung troops in the SF Mike Force companies was usually far superior to the Montagnard and Vietnamese troops in most CIDG companies, and the Mike Force troops were much better paid and equipped.

The original Mike Force mission was to provide emergency reinforcement troops for SF camps under attack by local VC forces. It was soon expanded to include semi-conventional infantry operations against regular main-force VC and NVA units, for which the Mike Force troops were not trained or equipped. As the length and lethality of the war increased, Nung casualties mounted, and many Nung veterans were killed or disabled.

Some of the younger Nung troops who replaced them did not share the warrior tradition of their elders. After 1967, nominally Nung Mike Force companies included Chinese street toughs from Cholon, who claimed to be Nung, but lacked the traditional warrior pride and fighting spirit of the older Nung soldiers.[15]

Ho Chi Minh Trail

The Truong Son Strategic Supply Route, better known as the Ho Chi Minh Trail, was begun in May 1959. It was vital for the supply of war materiel and replacement troops to the Viet Cong and North Vietnamese Army forces in South Vietnam. Because of its strategic importance the NVA made eastern Laos and Cambodia virtual extensions of North Vietnam.

Aided by Russian and Chinese technicians, NVA engineers improved and expanded old animal trails, Montagnard paths, and stream beds in the Truong Son range into dirt roads suitable for Soviet trucks. River fords were hidden as underwater bridges built just below the surface of the water. Roads and paths were wound around trees to enhance their concealment from the air. Open areas in the tree canopy were camouflaged by interlacing tree tops or connecting them with trellises interwoven with living plants and vines.

The result was a complex, interconnected, 12,000-mile network of roads, paths, bridges, caves, bypasses, and tunnels. The Trail's widest east-west axis was 30 miles, and its longest north-south axis from the DRV to the delta of South Vietnam was 3,500 miles. After traversing three mountain passes from North Vietnam into Laos, the Trail was divided into eleven regions, five large base areas, five main roads, twenty-nine branch roads, and many frequently changed shortcuts and bypasses.

In addition to sanctuary bases for the VC and NVA troop units recovering from or preparing for combat in South Vietnam, fifteen large logistics headquarters called *binh trams* were spaced along the Trail. They were commanded by NVA colonels with up to 2,000 troops in anti-aircraft, transportation, engineer, logistics, and infantry battalions. Men and women served as route guides, cooks, nurses, porters, mechanics, maintenance workers, and construction workers. Anti-aircraft and infantry battalions guarded each sector of the trail and the roads from it into South Vietnam.

Crude bivouac facilities called "communication liaison stations" were spaced about one day's march between the *binh trams* to provide basic food, shelter, medical aid, and route guides for transient NVA troops. From 1959–75, an estimated 300,000 Laotian men, women, and children were used as forced laborers to repair sections of the Trail and augment the scarce NVA food supplies with the produce of their small, subsistence farms.

The route guides only knew the Trail sections halfway to the next bivouac stations north and south of theirs. They met the route guide escorting NVA troops from the station north of theirs halfway between those stations and took the NVA troops to their own station for the night. The next day they took the NVA troops halfway to the station south of theirs, where they were met by a route guide from that station.

U.S. intelligence analysts identified base areas as places where large numbers of NVA troops could always be found. The first headquarters of the 559th Transportation Division was in Vinh, North Vietnam, and its main logistics center was at Base Area (BA) 604 near Tchepone, Laos (see map in photo section).

Troops and supplies from North Vietnam were unloaded at BA 604 and distributed to base areas farther south. BA 604 sent most of its supplies to BA 611, where they were distributed among the base stations south of it. BA 614 east of Chevane in Laos sent its allocations to South Vietnam on an extension of Road 165 from Chevane to QL 14.

In October 1968, a second Trail headquarters was established in southern Laos near the junction of Roads 92 and 922. It controlled an infantry division, three anti-aircraft regiments, two engineering regiments, thirty-five engineering battalions, twenty-three anti-aircraft battalions, eighteen transportation battalions, and two pipeline battalions.

An estimated 50,000 NVA troops guarded, maintained, and extended the Trail network, and an estimated 10,000 NVA anti-aircraft guns were hidden along the Trail. Most of them were around BA 604 near the junction of Roads 9 and 92 east of Tchepone and near BA 611. The U.S. Air Force, which conducted most of the attacks on the Laotian Trail, lost more planes at those two places than anywhere else in Laos.

Some 8,000 trucks traveled sections of the Trail network in relays at an average speed of 5–8 miles an hour, depending on road conditions. The drivers only traveled 15–20 miles back and forth on one stretch of road. Like the trail guides, they only knew the road halfway to the next way stations north and south of theirs. Driving back and forth on the same road every night and overcast day, they learned that section of road and the terrain on each side of it in detail.

On overcast and rainy days and nights, when there was less chance of air attacks, up to 100 trucks traveled in convoys with their lights on. Many trucks had radios to warn them of incoming air attacks and inform them of current road conditions. Fuel and lubricants for up to twenty-five trucks were stored in camouflaged truck parks hidden 3 miles off the main roads. At each way station the cargo of each truck was unloaded and transferred to another truck.

NVA monitoring stations at intervals along the roads collected current data on road conditions and the number of trucks passing through in each time period. The data was sent to traffic controllers on each section of the Trail, so that emergency route changes and repairs could be made as quickly as possible. Most road repair work was done at night, and each *binh tram* had two or three bulldozers for that purpose.

Damaged or destroyed trucks were replaced by others from the nearest way station to the north. That station replaced those trucks with trucks from the next way station to its north, and so on back to Haiphong harbor in North Vietnam, where new trucks and repair parts constantly arrived by ship from Russia and the Soviet bloc nations.

During daylight hours most transient NVA troops walked from one way station to another on trails at safe distances from the roads. The average infiltrating unit was a battalion moving at between 1 and 3 miles per hour, depending on the terrain. Preceded by route guides, they walked in platoon or company groups spaced about 100 yards apart. They did not fire at passing aircraft, but quickly moved off the trail and stood still or lay down. Several times a day they changed their camouflage foliage to match the foliage they were passing through.

The CIA estimated that between 1966 and 1971 the NVA sent 630,000 troops, 400,000 weapons, 50,000 tons of ammunition, and 100,000 tons of food into South Vietnam on the Trail network. In 1968, the CIA estimated that the NVA needed to send 8,000 troops and 100 tons of ammunition and weapons to South Vietnam every month to replace their huge losses in the nationwide battles that year.

Every year more and younger draftees from North Vietnam and more and newer military supplies from the USSR and China were sent down the Trail network into South Vietnam. Regardless of how often and how heavily the Trail was bombed, and regardless of the human cost of constantly repairing it, the NVA continued relentlessly to do so year after year.

An estimated 20 percent of the infiltrating NVA troops died on the Trail, but only 2 percent of those deaths were caused by U.S. air attacks. Ninety-eight percent of the NVA deaths on the Trail were from disease, malnutrition, exhaustion, accidents, or prolonged exposure to the cold, rainy weather.

Seventy-nine large military cemeteries are located along the Trail, including one covering 40 acres with more than 10,000 sets of remains. They are grim evidence of the human cost to the NVA of building, maintaining, extending, and defending the Trail network from the start of the NVA invasion of the Republic of Viet Nam in 1959 to the NVA's final conquest in 1975.[16]

SOG OP 35

In January 1961, President Kennedy ordered the CIA to begin unconventional warfare operations against North Vietnam. Because of the Cuban invasion fiasco in April of that year, he ordered all CIA paramilitary and UW programs transferred to the Pentagon. In early 1964, the Pentagon created the Studies and Observations Group (SOG) as a joint-services unit with a cross-border UW mission in Southeast Asia.

SOG was modeled on the Office of Strategic Services in World War II, when the OSS was the UW tip of a conventional military spear. Behind that UW tip was a large, regular Army with an offensive strategy for a decisive military victory against the main enemy, the German Army. Unlike the OSS, SOG had no conventional spear behind its UW tip and no conventional strategy for a decisive military victory against its main enemy, the North Vietnamese Army.

SOG was neither an Army nor a CIA operation. Neither Westmoreland nor Abrams, the MACV commanders from 1964–72, included it in their operational planning, because they did not command it and were not allowed to regularly operate in Laos or Cambodia. SOG was commanded by the SACSA officer (Special Assistant for Counterinsurgency and Special Activities) in the Office of the Chairman of the Joint Chiefs of Staff in the Pentagon. It was formally a component unit of the Military Assistance Command, Vietnam (MACV) under the cover name of Studies and Observations Group.

The cross-border missions of Operation 35 (Op 35), SOG's "Ground Studies" branch, were its main activity in terms of the number of men and aircraft committed to it and the number of NVA casualties produced by it. Op 35 had three covert forward operating bases (FOBs) in three of the four CTZ of South Vietnam. FOB 4 in I Corps was on a beach in the Marble Mountain area of the Tien Sha Peninsula east of Danang, near where the headquarters of the overt 5th SF Group in I Corps was also located.

Most Op 35 troops were Army SF men, but some Air Force and a few Navy and Marine troops also served in SOG. The Army troops were given cover assignments to the overt 5th SF Group and wore green berets, but their top-secret mission required them to live apart from other SF troops. Ironically, SOG's cross-border missions were not a secret to the NVA. They were only a secret to the U.S. media, the U.S. public, and most of the non-SF troops in Vietnam.

Most SOG recon-commando teams had three SF men and four to nine carefully selected and trained indigenous mercenaries, usually Montagnards or Nung. Op 35 also had some ethnic Vietnamese and

Cambodian teams, but different language groups were not intermixed on the same team. Op 35 also had American-led indigenous platoons and companies called Hatchet Forces that made occasional incursions into Laos and Cambodia to raid and ambush NVA targets. Most Hatchet Force troops in I Corps were Nung, and in 1968 most of their operations were on the Vietnam side of the border.

Op 35 combat actions were a classic example of the principle of war called economy of force, and as tactical force multipliers they were exceptionally effective. Op 35's recon teams had several missions, but the main one was to locate NVA troop units, bases, convoys, and supply depots on the Ho Chi Minh Trail network in Laos and Cambodia and direct air strikes against them.

In 1968, they usually did not have to search for NVA troops, because on almost every mission they encountered large numbers of them. The NVA sacrificed thousands of troops in fanatical efforts to kill or capture the SOG recon teams. No matter how many NVA troops the SOG teams killed and how much NVA war materiel they destroyed, the NVA promptly replaced their human and materiel losses.

Few U.S. ground combat actions in the war were as hazardous as SOG's cross-border missions. Some 12,000 SF men served in South Vietnam, but only 2,000 of them served in SOG. Those 2,000 suffered more than half of all SF fatalities and 85 percent of SF missing-in-action cases in the war. In 1968, the number of Purple Heart medals awarded to Op 35 recon men was more than the total authorized U.S. troop strength of the three SOG recon companies.

By 1968, Op 35 no longer had enough volunteers to replace its increasing losses and conduct its growing number of missions. Men from the 1st SF Group on Okinawa, the 10th SF Group in Germany, and the 7th SF Group at Fort Bragg were assigned to Op 35, whether or not they wanted that notoriously dangerous assignment.

That year twenty-nine helicopters carrying SOG troops were shot down: fifty-six U.S. SOG men were killed, 214 were wounded, and twenty-seven were missing (presumed dead). The same year 133 indigenous SOG troops were killed, 481 were wounded, and fifty-five were missing (presumed dead). During the war twelve entire SOG recon teams disappeared after insertion and were never heard from again. Forty-nine U.S. SOG troops and some of the pilots and air crews supporting them are still unaccounted for. In total, 163 Amerian SOG men were killed, and eighty were missing (presumed dead).

Repeat volunteers for Op 35 recon teams were the most elite of all SF men, and the motivation of such men was as special as their missions. The challenge and pride of gambling their lives against far greater odds and repeatedly winning by skillfully evading their enemies, killing them, and surviving to do it again and again was emotionally addictive to some.

Despite the likely fatal consequences of repeatedly taking such risks, a life on the razor' edge as a prestigious member of a small band of truly elite warriors with much more freedom than that of almost any other soldiers was far more valuable to them than a longer and more normal life. Their motto was, "You have never truly lived, until you have almost died," and its implication seemed to be, "The more you have almost died, the more you have truly lived."

Of the eighteen SF Medal of Honor recipients for actions in the Vietnam War, nine were in SOG. In the seventy-man recon company at FOB 4 (CCN), two men received the Medal of Honor and three received the Distinguished Service Cross. In the sixty-man recon company at FOB 2 (CCC), five men received the Medal of Honor and one received the DSC, which made it proportionally the most highly decorated American unit in the Vietnam War. When SOG's top-secret history was finally declassified, the exceptional valor of its covert warriors was revealed, and SOG was awarded a Presidential Unit Citation, the highest U.S. valor award for a military unit.[17]

Notes

1   Fall, Bernard. *The Two Viet-Nams* (2nd ed.) (NY: Praeger, 1967), pp. 41–49. Decoux's motive for his enthusiastic cooperation with the Japanese occupation forces in building new infrastructure projects in Vietnam was the same as that of the fictional COL Nicholson in the novel *The Bridge on the River Kwai*. The author of that novel, Pierre Boulle, served on Decoux's staff, and the fictional characteristics of Boulle's COL Nicholson were based on the actual characteristics of ADM Decoux. Fall, *op. cit.*, p. 49.

2   Smith, Gordon. *The Blood Hunters* (Chicago, IL: Moody Press, 1942), p. 123. Smith was a missionary linguist, and he and his wife, Laura, were the first Protestant missionaries to the Montagnard tribes in South Vietnam. They lived in Vietnam and traveled extensively in the Truong Son range for twenty years, studying the tribal languages and attempting to convert the Montagnards to Christianity.

3   Statements of Uynh Dang, former ARVN LTC and LLDB intelligence officer, in answer to written questions by McLeroy translated into Vietnamese by Lan Thanh Le, former LLDB officer, March 10, 1998, and translated into English by William Laurie, August 19, 2009.

4   *Ibid.* Smith, Mrs Gordon. *Victory In Viet Nam* (Grand Rapids, MI: Zondervan, 1965), p. 151.

5   Bowman, John. *The Vietnam War: An Almanac* (NY: Bison Books, 1985), pp. 49, 55.

6   Emails from Wayne Long, retired U.S. Army SF colonel, to McLeroy in August 1999 regarding statements made to Long by Tucker Gougelmann, the CIA officer who controlled Long's secret mission at Kham Duc in 1963.

7   Long, *op. cit.*

8   Steve Sherman's archive of U.S. Army Special Forces personnel and units in SE Asia (Houston, TX: Radix Press), Sherman1@flash.net.

9   See topographical map in Chapter VI.

10 Fall, Bernard. *Viet-Nam Witness* (NY: Praeger, 1966), p. 87.

11 Porch, Douglas. *The French Foreign Legion* (NY: HarperCollins, 1991), pp. 537, 547.

12 Smith, Harvey *et al. Area Handbook for South Vietnam* (Washington, D.C.: U.S. Government Printing Office, 1967), p. 76.

13 At Dak Gle, a constabulary post on QL 14 in 1941, the French colonial officer in charge told Gordon Smith, *op. cit.*, that the Jeh were wretchedly poor and dangerously untrustworthy. Smith noted that the Montagnard troops were from the Rhade, Jarai, Sedang, and Bahnar tribes. Smith, Gordon, *op. cit.*, pp. 120–24.

14 Schrock, Joann *et al. Minority Groups In The Republic of Vietnam* (Washington, D.C.: Department of the Army Pamphlet No. 550–105, Headquarters, Department of the Army, 1966), pp. 309–16, 320–36, 351, 355–56, 362, 365, 376, 1131–55. Smith, Harvey, *op. cit.* pp. 59–60.

15 The information on the Army Special Forces is from the following sources: Kelly, Francis. *U.S. Army Special Forces, 1961–1971* (Washington, D.C.: Department of the Army, 1985), pp. 4–24, 39–41, 44–57, 59–63. Simpson, Charles. *Inside the Green Berets* (Novato, CA: Presidio, 1983), pp. 95–112, 121–84, 199–216. Stanton, Shelby. *Green Berets at War* (Novato, CA: Presidio, 1985), pp. 35–213, 232–54. Rottman, Gordon. *Green Berets in Vietnam, 1957–73* (Oxford, UK: Osprey, 2002). It is also partly based on McLeroy's training and experience as an SF officer serving with CIDG and LLDB troops during his five-month assignment in 1967 on SF team A-104 at Ha Thanh, Quang Ngai Province, I Corps.

16 The information on the Ho Chi Minh Trail is from the following sources: Doyle, Edward *et al. The Vietnam Experience: The North* (Boston, MA: Boston Publishing,

1986), pp. 32–33, 46, 62. Hanyok, Robert. *Spartans in Darkness* (n.p. prob. Fort Meade, MD: Center for Cryptologic History, National Security Agency, 2002), pp. 94–100. Prados, John. *The Blood Road* (NY: John Wily, 1999), pp. 10–16, 25–29, 84–86, 112–13, 188, 194, 256, 269, 312–15.

17 The information on SOG Op 35 is from the following sources: Plaster, John. *SOG: A Photo History of the Secret Wars* (Boulder, CO: Paladin Press, 2000), pp. 29–67. Plaster, John. *Secret Commandos* (NY: Simon & Schuster, 2004), pp. 23–42, 110–11. Plaster, John. *SOG: The Secret Wars of America's Commandos in Vietnam* (NY: Simon & Schuster, 1997), pp. 41–42, 50, 255. Shultz, Richard. *The Secret War Against Hanoi* (NY: HarperCollins, 1999), pp. 223–52. Gillespie, Robert. *Black Ops, Vietnam* (Annapolis, MD: Naval Institute Press, 2011), pp. 142–50. Rottman, Gordon. *US MACV-SOG Reconnaissance Team In Vietnam* (Oxford, UK: Osprey, 2011). It is also partly based on McLeroy's experience as the Officer-In-Charge (OIC) of FOB 4's launch site at Kham Duc for three months in 1968. In the second quarter of 1968, FOB 3 at Khe Sanh was closed. FOB 4 near Danang was designated Command and Control North (CCN). FOB 2 near Kontum was designated Command and Control Center (CCC). FOB 1 at Phu Bai was transferred to CCN, and an FOB designated Command and Control South (CCS) was opened at Ban Me Thuot. A comprehensive collection of primary source documents related to SOG is on a CD-ROM titled *MACV Studies and Observations Group Documentation Study and Command Histories*, edited and published by Steve Sherman, Sherman1@flash.net (Houston, TX: Radix Press).

Glossary

A

AAR—After Action Report
ABCCC—Airborne Battlefield Command and Control Center (Air Force C-130 cargo plane)
ABN—airborne = a military parachute unit or parachute-qualified soldier
A-camp—a rural fortification for an SF A-team, an LLDB A-team, and CIDG troops
AF—U.S. Air Force (USAF)
AHC—Assault Helicopter Company
AHSC—Assault Helicopter Support Company
Air Force Cross—the highest U.S. Air Force award for combat valor, second to the Medal of Honor
ALCC—Airlift Control Center
Americal—23rd Infantry Division, U.S. Army
AO—area of operations
ARVN—Army of the Republic of Viet Nam (= South Vietnam)
A-Team—SF Operational Detachment A
Axis nations—Germany, Japan, and Italy in World War II

B

Bac Si—Vietnamese for medical doctor
Battery (Btry)—six artillery guns and related crewmen
BG—brigadier general (1 star)
Bn—battalion = three or more companies
Brigade—three or more battalions within a division or as an independent unit

C

CA/PO—civic action/psychological operations officer
CBU—cluster bomb unit; bomb that opens while falling and scatters smaller bomblets
CCT—Combat Control Team (AF ground-based air controllers)
CG—commanding general
CI—counterinsurgency
CIA—Central Intelligence Agency

CIDG—Civilian Irregular Defense Group
Claymore—a directional surface mine packed with C-4 explosive and 700 steel balls
CO—commanding officer
COL—colonel (06)
Company—three or more platoons
Concertina wire—coiled, expandable, looped steel wire with razor-like blades
CONEX—(Container Express) an 8ft × 8ft × 20ft steel cargo box with a door
Corps—two or more divisions
CPL—corporal (E-4)
CPT—captain (03)
C-Team—SF headquarters for each CTZ
CTZ—Corps Tactical Zone (I, II, III, IV) = military regions of South Vietnam

D

Division—two or more brigades
DMZ—Demilitarized Zone between North and South Vietnam
DRV—Democratic Republic of Viet Nam (= North Vietnam)
DSC—Distinguished Service Cross; highest U.S. Army award for valor, second to Medal of Honor
Dust Off—radio code name for Army helicopter ambulances

E

EM—enlisted man/men (lower rank than sergeant)

F

FAC—Forward Air Controller (AF)
1LT—first lieutenant (02)
FSB—Fire Support Base = artillery base
FOB—Forward Operating Base
French Indochina—Laos, Cambodia, Tonkin (northern Vietnam), Annam (central Vietnam), and Cochin China (southern Vietnam)

G

GEN—general; highest-ranking U.S. Army, Air Force, and Marine officer = 4 stars
GCA—ground control approach
Grenade—hand-held explosive device (fragmentation, smoke, thermite, tear gas, etc)

I

I (eye) Corps—First Corps Tactical Zone = the five northern provinces of South Vietnam
I (eye) DASC—I Corps Direct Air Support Center

K

KIA—killed in action (KHA = killed in hostile action)

L

LAW—light anti-tank rocket
LBE—load-bearing equipment = web gear (canvas or nylon belt and suspenders with attached pouches)
LCPL—lance corporal (Marine E-3)
LIB—light infantry brigade
LLDB—Luc-Luong Dac-Biet (South Vietnamese SF)
LRRP—long-range reconnaissance patrol (of Brigade, Division, or Corps headquarters)
LTC—lieutenant colonel (05)
LTG—lieutenant general (3 stars)
LZ—landing zone

M

MACV—Military Assistance Command, Vietnam
MAF—Marine Amphibious Force (= Army Corps)
MAJ—major (04)
MG—major general (2 stars)
MSG—master sergeant (E-8)
MIA—missing in action
Mike Force—Mobile Strike Force = SF-led, indigenous light infantry company
Mini-gun—7.62mm fast-firing machine gun with six rotating barrels
MOH—Medal of Honor = the highest U.S. decoration for combat valor, awarded by the President in the name of Congress

N

Napalm—fire bomb made of a jellied gasoline compound
Navy Cross—the highest U.S. Navy and Marine award for combat valor, second to MOH
NCO—non-commissioned officer (= sergeant)
Nung—tribal minority group in Vietnam
NVA—North Vietnamese Army (= PAVN)

O

OIC—officer-in-charge
OP—observation post
Op 35—SOG Operation 35 ("Ground Studies")

P

PAVN—People's Army of Vietnam (= NVA)
PFC—private first class (E-3)
Platoon—three or more squads
POW—prisoner of war
Proletarian—Marxist term for an urban wage worker
PVT—private (E-1)

Q

QL—*Quoc Lo* (Vietnamese) = National Road

R

Regiment—three to five battalions

S

Sapper—NVA or VC demolitionist commando
SF—U.S. Army Special Forces (aka Green Berets)
SFC—sergeant first class (E-7)
SFG—Special Forces Group (1st, 5th, 7th, 8th, 10th, etc.)
SGM—sergeant major (E-9)
SGT—sergeant (E-5)
Slick—a lightly armed UH-1 transport helicopter
2LT—second lieutenant (O-1)
SOG—Studies and Observations Group = Special Operations Group
SOP—standard operating procedures
Sortie—the departure of a military aircraft on a combat mission
SP4—specialist fourth class (E-4)
SP5—specialist fifth class (E-5)
Spooky—AC-47 fixed-wing, side-firing gunship plane with 3 Miniguns and flares
Squad—four to twelve troops
SSGT—staff sergeant (E-6)

T

Tanglefoot—barbed wire strung in a web pattern near the ground to cause stumbling
Tarmac—aircraft turn-around or parking area near an airstrip
Thermite grenade—incendiary device producing 4,000 degrees F. heat by an internal
    chemical reaction
III MAF—Third Marine Amphibious Force

TOC—Tactical Operations Center
Tracers—glowing bullets with colored phosphorous tips
TSGT—technical sergeant = AF E-7 NCO (equivalent to Army SFC)

U

USMC—U.S. Marine Corps
UW—unconventional warfare

V

VC—Viet Cong (South Vietnamese Communist soldier, terrorist, or unit)
Viet Minh—Vietnamese anti-French forces in the First Indochina War (1946–54)
VPA—Vietnam People's Army (= PAVN = NVA)

W

Web gear—canvas or nylon belt and suspenders with attached pouches (= LBE)
WIA—wounded in action (= WHA—wounded in hostile action)
WO—warrant officer (WO1, WO2, WO3, WO4)

X

XO—executive officer.

Sources

PRIMARY

ARCHIVAL

The primary source documents are in the archives of the United States Army and the United States Air Force. One key document is in the LBJ Library at the University of Texas at Austin.

U.S. Army

The Army documents are in the National Archives II at College Park, MD (NA II); the U.S. Army Center of Military History at Fort Lesley McNair in Washington, DC (CMH); and the U.S. Army Military History Institute at Carlisle Barracks, PA (MHI). The records of the 5th Special Forces Group and the 23rd Division (Americal) are also in NA II. The primary source Army documents are:

1. After Action Report: Battle of Kham Duc, Co C, 5th Special Forces Group, 31 May 68, and Annex A: After Action Report: Ngok Tavak FOB, 16 May 68.
2. After Action Report (Final), Headquarters, 14th Combat Aviation Battalion, May 20, 1968.
3. After Action Report Elk Canyon I, Headquarters, 2nd Battalion, 1st Infantry, 196th Brigade (undated; attached maps and charts dated September 19, 1970).
4. After Action Report Kham Duc, Vietnam, A Btry., 3/82 Artillery; Bernard, Kenneth; May 14, 1968.
5. After Action Report Kham Duc, Vietnam, HHC 2/1 Infantry, May 14, 1968.
6. After Action Report: Operation Santa Barbara, Upgrading KHAM DUC Air Field, 24 July 68 (including interview of Capt. Daniel Waldo, Jr., CO of A Company, 70th Engineer Battalion, 937th Engineer Group, 18th Engineer Brigade), Pleiku, 18 June 68.
7. Agent Report (Julius W. Long, Jr.), 109th MI Group, April 2, 1973.

8. Airborne Radio Relay Schedule for Kham Duc, Americal Division G-3, May 11, 1968.

9. Analysis of Area Operations, Company C, 5th Special Forces Group (Airborne), 1st Special Forces, July 2, 1969.

10. Area Analysis Study of Kham Duc, Office of Senior Intelligence Advisor, Advisory Team 2, (Jan-May, 1969).

11. Assessment of Enemy Activity in Vicinity of Detachment A-105 (Kham Duc), Hqs. 5th Special Forces Group, (no date, probably March, 1968).

12. Attack at KHAM DUC, RVN, May 1968, Director of Operations, ODCSOPS, to Department of the Army Review of the Preliminary Investigation into the My Lai Incident (Peers Inquiry), February 10, 1970.

13. Award of the Distinguished Service Cross, Bledsoe, William H., US 53841757, Specialist Four, United States Army, General Orders Number 4325, Headquarters, U.S. Army Vietnam, September 11, 1968.

14. Back Channel to MG LC Shea, OPS IA Director DA (handwritten memorandum) from COL Ladd, Jonathan (undated).

15. Board of Inquiry, Missing Persons, Headquarters, 2nd Battalion, 1st Infantry, May 27, 1968.

16. Board of Inquiry, Missing Persons, Headquarters, United States Army, Vietnam to Chief, Casualty Division, TAGO, DA, Washington, D.C., May 27, 1968.

17. Camp Information Sheet [Kham Duc], undated. Change to OPLAN 1–68 GOLDEN VALLEY (Relief/Reinforcement of CIDG Camps), May 4, 1968.

18. Combat Action Report (Operation Carentan II), June 4, 1968.

19. Combat Action Report (RCS AVDF-GC 1) 2/1 Infantry, 196th Brigade, Americal Division, June 4, 1968.

20. Combat Support After Action Interview/Report, Upgrading KHAM DUC Air field (Operation Santa Barbara), July 24, 1968.

21. Daily Staff Journal, Americal Div TOC, May 10, 11, 1968.

22. Daily Staff Journal, Period Covered From 0001 Hours 10 May 8 68 to 2400 Hours 10 May 68, Company C, 5th Special Forces Group (Airborne), 1st Special Forces.

23. Daily Staff Journal, 196th Infantry Brigade, May 15, 1968.

24. Daily Staff Journal, 198th Infantry Brigade, April 1, 1968.

25. 5th Special Forces Group Comparative Studies and Enemy Reconnaissance Reports, Hqs. United States Army Combat Developments Command, Ft. Belvoir, VA, 21 May 69.

26. Impact Award List, Commanding General, Americal Division, USARV Form 157-R (undated).

27. Incident at Kham Duc, Message from CO, 5th SFGA, Danang to CO 5th SFGA, Nha Trang, CG III MAF, Danang, Attn: G-3, June 13, 1967.

28. Intelligence Estimate (Kham Duc), Hqs. 5th SFGA, 18 March 68.

29. Intelligence Estimate Update (Kham Duc), Hqs. 5th SFGA, 28 April 68.
30. INTSUM #131–68, Headquarters, Americal Division, May 11, 1968.
31. Investigation Board, Headquarters, Americal Division, Special Orders Number 136, May 15, 1968.
32. Kham Duc Action, Headquarters, Americal Division, May 11 and 12, 1968.
33. Lang Vei—Kham Duc Comparative Study, Hqs. 5th Special Forces Group, 20 July 1968.
34. MACV, Westmoreland Messages, CMH.
35. Memorandum from Lyles, Ronald to Captain Rawlings or Chief Warrant Officer Kennedy, Kham Duc (Operation Elk Canyon), July–August 1970 (undated).
36. Memorandum for the Secretary of Defense, Subject: Operational Control of III MAF Aviation Assets, dated 19 April, 1968.
37. Monthly Operational Report, 1–31 May 1968, 5th Special Forces Group, June 15, 1968.
38. Monthly Operational Summary for Month of January, 1968, Kham Duc, January 31, 1968.
39. Monthly Operational Summary for Month of February, 1968, Kham Duc, February 28, 1968.
40. Monthly Operational Summary for Month of March, 1968, Kham Duc, March 31, 1968.
41. Monthly Operational Summary for Month of April, 1968, Kham Duc, April 30, 1968.
42. Morning Report, Co B 2d Bn 1st Inf, 196th Bde, Record of Personnel Actions, May 14, 1968.
43. Operational Report and Lessons Learned, May–July 1968, Americal Division.
44. Operational Report—Lessons Learned For Quarterly Period Ending 31 July 1968, 5th Special Forces Group.
45. Operational Report, 70th Engineer Battalion (Combat) (Army), April 30, 1968, RCS CSFOR-65.
46. Operational Report, 70th Engineer Battalion (Combat) (Army), July 31, 1968, RCS CSFOR-65.
47. Order of Battle Summary 1 March Thru 31 March 1968, Combined Intelligence Center Vietnam (Headquarters, Armed Forces of R.V.N. Office of Joint General Staff—J-2 and Headquarters, U.S. Military Assistance Command Vietnam Office of Assistant Chief of Staff J-2).
48. Periodic Intelligence Report 14–20 July 68, III MAF PERINTREP 29–68.
49. Quarterly Evaluation Jan–Mar 68, Headquarters United States Military Assistance Command Vietnam.
50. Special Study: Kham Duc, Detachment B, 1st Military Intelligence Bn., 14 March 1968.

51. Statement by Accused or Suspect Person, John C. Colonna, July 10, 1968.
52. Statement by Accused or Suspect Person, Wilbert Foreman, July 27, 1968.
53. Statement of Anderson, Jack, May 29, 1968.
54. Statement of Bays, Lee (undated).
55. Statement of Bernhardt, Eugene (undated).
56. Statement of Blohm, Ron (undated).
57. Statement of Buchwald, Donald (undated).
58. Statement of Buchwald, Donald, November 7, 1978.
59. Statement of Duncan, James (undated).
60. Statement of Gibler, James, May 18, 1968.
61. Statement of Karnasiewicz, Raymond (undated).
62. Statement of Makowski, Eugene (undated).
63. Statement of Nelson, Robert (undated).
64. Statement of Pelkey, Christopher (undated).
65. Statement of Recovery, Company A, 23rd Supply & Transport Battalion, Americal Division, Search and Recovery Operation Kham Duc, August 29, 1970.
66. Statement of Schneider, William (undated).
67. Statement of Schungel, Daniel (undated).
68. Statement of Spier, Herbert, May 29, 1968.
69. Statement of Tavianinni, Gene (undated).
70. Statement of Thomasson, John (undated).
71. Statement of Thompson, Bobby (undated).
72. Statement of Wood, Ernest, May 28, 1968.
73. Summary, Operation Golden Valley, Hqs. Americal Division, 16 May 68.
74. Telex Message, Commanding Officer, Company C, 5th Special Forces Group to Commanding Officer, Company B, 5th Special Forces Group, February 16, 1968.
75. Telex Message, Commanding Officer, Company C, 5th Special Forces Group to Commanding Officer, Company B, 5th Special Forces Group, March 1, 1968.
76. Telex Messages (Periodic) (Flash) Company C, 5th Special Forces Group, Danang to Commanding Officer, 5th Special Forces Group, May 12, 1968.
77. Telex Messages MAC 6210, 6222 and 6264, from GEN Westmoreland COMUSMACV to ADM Sharp CINCPAC, copies to GEN Wheeler Chairman, JCS and LTG Goodpaster, May 12 and 13, 1968.
78. Telex Message MAC 7462, from General Abrams DEPCOMUSMACV to LTG Cushman, CG III MAF, June 6, 1968.
79. Telex Message MSG 230143Z, Operation Pierce Valley, from Ramsey, Lloyd, to LTG Nickerson, June 11, 1969.
80. Telex Message, Schungel, Daniel to Ladd, Jonathan, attached by Ladd to Telex Message to Shea, L. C., Director, I&CA ODCSOPS DA, May 22, 1968.

81. Telex Message VTA 918HMZVVV, CG, Americal Division, CHL RVN to CO A Det C Company, 5th SF Group, Danang, Kham Duc Operations, May 14, 1968.

82. USMACV Command History, 1968; History Branch, Office of the Secretary, Joint Staff, MACV; Vol. I, Chapter III—The Enemy; Vol. II, Chapter VII—Intelligence; Chapter X—Research and Development.

U.S. Air Force

The primary source Air Force documents are in the United States Air Force (formerly Albert F. Simpson) Historical Research Center at Maxwell Air Force Base, Alabama. A collection of primary sources are in an undated compilation titled "The Battle of Kham Duc, An Air Force View" edited by Barry Spink, Air Force Historical Research Agency, Maxwell AFB, AL. It is based on Project CHECO (Contemporary Historical Examination of Current Operations) Report, "Kham Duc, Special Report, 10–14 May 1968" by Kenneth Sams and A.W. Thompson, Directorate of Tactical Evaluation, CHECO Division, 7th AF, Pacific Air Forces, Hickam Air Force Base, Hawaii. A microfilm series titled "Kham Duc" contains interviews and documents from various Air Force sources. A set of three audio cassette tapes contains statements (some garbled) by some helicopter pilots, a forward air controller, and an AF air liaison officer during the battle.

83. Chronological Order of Events, Kham Duc Special Forces Camp, May 12, 1968, Project CHECO 08–02353, AFR 212–6, 210–3, AFM 210–1, No. 0283835, (undated).

84. Dissemination of Threat Information on Kham Duc Special Forces Camp (including Extracts From Documents Indicating a Threat to Kham Duc Special Forces Camp), Air Force Project Corona Harvest, AFR 212–6, 210–3, 210–1, No. 0283883, May 13, 1968.

85. Kham Duc, Project CHECO Report, July 8, 1968.

86. Memorandum to 834 Air Division Cmdr, Events of 12 May 1968—Operation "Grand Slam," May 15, 1968.

87. Memorandum to IDASC, Valor at Kham Duc, (undated).

88. Report of the Incident at Kham Duc, RVN, 12 May 1968, Resulting in Battle Damage to Aircraft Nr 55–013, May 16, 1968.

89. 7th AF Log, Chronological Order of Events, Kham Duc Special Forces Camp, 12 May 68.

90. Statement of Farrar, Walter, August, 1994.

91. Statement of Freedman, Mort (undated).

92. Statement of Gallagher, John, May 17, 1968.

93. Statement of Spier, Herbert, May 29, 1968.

94. Tactical Aerodrome Directory South Vietnam, 7651st Aeronautical Chart and Information Squadron, February 15, 1968.

95. Tactical Air Command, Air Warfare, SEA Briefing, (undated), vietnam@ttu.edu, Kham Duc, Item No. 1768010005.

96. Tape recording, Johnson, Willard C., May 11–12, 1968, Project CHECO Reports.

U.S. Marine Corps

The primary source records of the Marine artillery battery at Ngok Tavak are in NA II. The Command Chronologies, 1967–1968 and the Oral History Tapes are in the Marine Corps Historical Center, Archives Section, Washington, D.C. Navy Yard. The relevant documents are:

97. Operation Plan 303–67; 1st Marine Division, Da Nang, Republic of Viet Nam, 6 September, 1967.

98. FMF-Pac MarOpsV [sic], Jan–Dec 68.

99. III MAF ComdCs [sic], Jan–Dec 68.

100. 3d MarDiv ComdCs [sic], Jan–Dec. 68.

101. 11th Mar ComdCs [sic], Jan–Dec 68.

102. Meritorious Unit Commendation (Recommendation), Headquarters, 2nd Battalion, 13th Marines, 1st Marine Division (Rein) FMF.

103. Statement of Glick, J. E., May 12, 1968.

104. Statement of Marks, Wesley (undated).

105. Target Data Sheet, Kham Duc Special Forces Camp, III Marine Amphibious Force, June 13, 1966.

106. Telex Message (Top Secret – Eyes Only) from Nickerson, Herman, LTG CG III MAF to COMUSMACV, Outgoing Messages, Item No. 1201005076, May 14, 1969.

107. Telex Message, Interrogation Report, III MAF COC to MACV COC J-2, May 18, 1968.

108. III MAF OP Golden Valley, 12 May 68, Interview: LT. Col. Richard Schuman, ALO, Americal Division, Chu Lai, 28 May 68.

109. III MAF PERINTREP (PIR) 29–68.

Central Intelligence Agency

110. "Communist Reactions to Certain U.S. Courses of Action," Central Intelligence Agency, February 6, 1967.

111. "Hanoi's Negotiating Position and Concept of Negotiations," IM 0587/68, Central Intelligence Agency, May 6, 1968.

112. "Hanoi's Paris Initiative and the Possibility of a New Communist Military Offensive," Memorandum SC No. 08360/68, Directorate of Intelligence, Central Intelligence Agency, May 3, 1968.

113. "Speculation on Hanoi's Motives," Office of National Estimates, Memorandum for the Director: ONE memo for DCI, Central Intelligence Agency, April 8, 1968.

CINCPAC

114. Report on the War in Vietnam, Section I: Report on Air and Naval Campaigns Against North Vietnam, Pacific Command-Wide Support of the War June 1964–1968 (including North Vietnam Target Element Summary 1967), 1968.

115. "Remarks by CINCPAC at a Briefing for the Secretary of Defense, the Undersecretary of State and Others in Saigon on 5 July, 1967," reprinted in Sharp, U. S. G. *Strategy for Defeat* Novato, CA: Presidio Press, 1978), pp. 285–92.

Department of Defense

116. Administrative Message from Commander, Joint Task Force Full Accounting to Secretary of Defense, USDP: RSA, Interview of Requested Source, Nguyen Huy Chong, December 13, 1993.

117. Administrative Message from Commander, Joint Task Force Full Accounting to Secretary of Defense, Washington, D.C., USDP: ISA/DPMO, Oral History Program (OHP 970014) Report and Evaluation: Mr. Van Cong Bich, October 2, 1997.

118. Circumstances of Loss, Case 1167, Joint Task Force-Full Accounting (undated).

119. Current Status and Analysis, OP2 ZC98864 09309, Joint POW/MIA Accounting Command, (undated).

120. Kham Duc Unaccounted for Status, Joint Task Force-Full Accounting, July 28, 1992.

121. Memorandum from Joint Staff, Washington, D.C. to RUEAHOF/CDRPERSCOM Alexandria, VA, *et al.*, Evaluation of SRV Oral History Interview, Mr. Van Cong Bich, January 14, 1994, JTFFA Casualty Files, Reel 530, pages 130–32.

122. Message, Joint Staff, Washington, D.C. to RUEKJCS/White House National Security Council, Washington, D.C.//USDP: ISA/DPMO//, *et al.*, Oral History Program (OHP 97–016) Report and Evaluation: Dr. Huynh Van Thanh, October 20, 1997 (date of interview August 5, 1997), JTFFA Miscellaneous Prisoner of War Files, Reel 471, pages 210–12.

123. Memorandum for the Secretary of Defense from Joint Chiefs of Staff; Subject: Operational Control of III MAF Aviation Assets; Appendix B: Views of the Commandant of the Marine Corps on Operational Control of III Marine Amphibious Force Aviation Assets; Appendix C: Views of the Chief of Staff, US Army and the Chief of Naval Operations on Operational Control of III Marine Amphibious Force Aviation Assets; April 19, 1968.

124. Research and Investigation Team (RIT) Report of Interview of Mr. Nguyen Van Huu, Joint Task Force-Full Accounting, Narrative Message to SECDEF, Washington, D.C., June 30, 1995.

125. Statement of John Vessey to House Subcommittee on Asian and Pacific Affairs, July 17, 1991.

126. Summary of Search, Recovery and Identification of Remains Recovered from Kham Duc, US DAC, October 26, 1970.

U.S. State Department

"Aggression From the North: The Record of North Viet-Nam's Campaign To Conquer South Viet-Nam," Department of State Publication 7839, U.S. Government Printing Office, Washington, D.C., 1965.

"Working Paper On The North Vietnamese Role In The War in South Vietnam," U.S. Department of State, May, 1968.

INTERVIEWS BY AUTHORS

U.S. Army

1. Baker, Wayne; 2. Bollard, Noe; 3. Brady, Patrick; 4. Brigewitch, Roy; 5. Buchwald, Donald; 6. Busbee, Larry; 7. Clark, Henry; 8. Cook, Gregory; 9. Cowburn, Fred; 10. Davis, Glen; 11. Dieterich, Virgil; 12. Foreman, Wilbert; 13. Fuller, Elbert; 14. Kerns, Tony; 15. Kochick, Steve; 16. Lee, Tim; 17. Long, Julius; 18. Mays, Karal; 19. Means, Robert; 20. Merkle, Jerry; 21. Milloy, Albert E.; 22. Newell, Richard; 23. Opheim, Glen; 24. Paranoski, Thomas; 25. Pelkey, Christopher; 26. Percoskie, Anthony; 27. Pickens, Homer; 28. Powell, John; 29. Price, Ron; 30. Rippy, Terry; 31. Sassenberger, Ron; 32. Sauer, Gerhard; 33. Schmitz, Jon; 34. Schneider, William; 35. Schooler Gary; 36. Schrope, William; 37. Shoplock, Daniel; 38.

Singlaub, John; 39. Sturdevant, Joe; 40. Tavianinni, Gene; 41. Thomasson, John; 42. Thompson, Bobby; 43. Vazquez, Orlando; 44. Waldo, Daniel; 45. Weber, Jeff; 46. Wright, William.

Army Special Forces

1. Aycock, Robert; 2. Bernhardt, Eugene; 3. Campbell, Richard; 4. Deleshaw, Jack; 5. Duncan, James; 6. Gartner, Wolfgang; 7. Gill, Richard; 8. Greenwood, Kenneth; 9. Henderson, Robert; 10. Jacks, Johnny; 11. Jones, L. B.; 12. Long, Wayne; 13. Lumpkins, John; 14. Makowski, Eugene; 15. Matheney, Jack; 16. Monaghan, Robert; 17. Overby, Lauren; 18. Purdy, Lee; 19. Strange, Robert; 20. Swicegood, Willie; 21. Windley, M. C.; 22. Woodard, Houston.

U.S. Air Force

1. Dineen, Donald; 2. Donahue, Joseph; 3. Farrar, Walter; 4. Freedman, Morton; 5. Gatewood, Medley; 6. Gibler, James; 7. Hughes, Harley; 8. Lawhun, Milford; 9. Mack, John; 10. Newton, Tom; 11 Schuman, Richard; 12. Shelton, Raymond; 13. Smotherman, Phillip; 14. Spier, Herb.

U.S. Marine Corps

1. Adams, Robert; 2. Bays, Robert; 3. Brown, Tim; 4. Flater, Rhett; 5. Garlitz, James; 6. Marshaka, Robert; 7. Schunck, Henry; 8. Whisman, Gene.

U.S. Military Assistance Command Vietnam (MACV)

Goodpaster, Andrew; Pickens, Homer; Westmoreland, William.

United States Embassy, Vietnam

Deeter, Bill.

Kham Duc Veterans' Relatives

Ransbottom, Laverne; Gannon, Vicki.

INTERVIEWS BY OTHERS

U.S. Military

1. Black, Reece; 2. Boyd, William; 3. Buchwald, Donald; 4. Connolly, John; 5. Ells, Albert; 6. Everts, Peter; 7. Fogle, James; 8. Gallagher, John; 9. Hostler, Donald; 10. Jackson, Joe; 11. Lopes, Ronald; 12. Marks, Wesley; 13. Mead, John; 14. Metz, Hampton M.; 15. Schuman, Richard; 16. Smith, Richard J.; 17. Smotherman, Phillip B.; 18. Spiers, Herbert; 19. Summerman, S. T.; 20. Waldo, Daniel; 21. Wallace, James L.; 22. Wood, Ernest.

People's Army of Vietnam

127. Pham Thanh Du, BG (ret.), Operations Officer of the 2nd PAVN Division and Commander of its 1st Regiment at Kham Duc, April 21 and July 1, 1998 by a military team of the U.S. Joint Task Force-Full Accounting (JTFFA) in Danang, SRV. His comments in Vietnamese with English oral translation were videotaped by Harry Albert on the 1995 VVA trip to Kham Duc and Ngok Tavak.

128. Van Cong Bich, COL (ret.), Political Officer of the 1st and 21st Regiments, 2nd PAVN Division, on November 11, 1993 and August 5, 1997 by a U.S. military team of the JTFFA in Danang, SRV.

129. Dan Ngoc Mai, MAJ (ret.), Commander of the 1st Battalion, 1st Regiment, 2nd PAVN Division at Ngok Tavak by a U.S. military team of the JTFFA on April 21 and July 2, 1999 in Danang, SRV. His comments in Vietnamese with English translation were videotaped by Harry Albert on the 1995 VVA trip to Kham Duc and Ngok Tavak.

ELECTRONIC MAIL

1. Brady, Patrick to Sanders, May 4, 2010; 2. Buchwald, Donald to McLeroy, August 15, 2000; Ibid., August 20, 2000; 4. Ibid., August 28, 2000; 5. Ibid., August 30, 2000; 6. Ibid., September 27, 2000; 7. Ibid., February 8, 2001; 8. Uynh Dang to McLeroy, August 19, 2009; 9. Fitzsimmons, Ed to Scott, Don, March 4, 2016; 10. Freedman, Mort to McLeroy, August 15, 1999; 11. Fuller, Bert to McLeroy, January 15, 2000; 12. Kushner, Hal (speech) copy to McLeroy, February 2, 2000; 13. Lawhun, Milford to McLeroy, May 2, 2000; 14. Rose, Greg to Sanders, June 28, 2009; 15. Sanders, A. C. to Schneider, William, February 25, 2003; 16. Sanders, Walter M. to McLeroy, January 17, 2000; 17. Whisman, Gene to Sanders, June 28, 2009; 18. White, John to McLeroy, November 18, 1999.

LETTERS

1. Brown, Tim to Bill Schneider (copy in Kham Duc Newsletter, June 24, 1994); 2. Brown, Tim to Flanagan, Casualty Resolution Supervisor, Detachment 2 JFF–FA, U.S. MIA Office, Hanoi, SRV, March 2, 1995; 3. Buchwald, Carole to McLeroy (undated); 4. Buchwald, Donald to Hardy Bogue, November 13, 1992; 5. Ibid., February 5, 1993; 6. Buchwald, Donald to McLeroy, November 18, 1997; 7. Ibid. (undated); 8. Buchwald, Donald to E. E. Fuller, December 10, 1999; 9. Ibid., January 5, 2000; 10. Buchwald, Donald to McLeroy, January 24, 1998; 11. Ibid., January 11, 1999; 12. Ibid., November 15, 1999; 13. Ibid., November 17, 1999; 14. Ibid., January 2, 2000; 15. Ibid., undated; 16. Ibid., undated; 17. Connolly, John to McLeroy, November 5, 1998; 18. Ibid., January 15, 2000; 19. Cowburn, Fred to Cowburn, Dick, May 14, 1968; 20. Deleshaw, Jack to Schneider, William, undated; 21. Distascio, Dominic (addressee unknown, undated); 22. Hughes, Harley to McLeroy (undated); 23. Jones, Robert L., Deputy Assistant Secretary of Defense (Prisoner of War/Missing Personnel Office), to J. A. Sternburg, Acting Executive Director, Vietnam Veterans of America, March 24, 1999; 24. Means, Bob to Janousek, Richard (undated); 25. Nelson, Robert to Bogue, Hardy, October 24, 1992; 26. Paranoski, Thomas (addressee unknown, undated); 27. Pelkey, Christopher to Pelkey, C. J., May 15, 1968; 28. Phan, Ky Ba to McLeroy, January 6, 1998; 29. Rippy, Terry to McLeroy, (undated); 30. Rossen, William to McLeroy, August 11, 1999; 31. Ibid., September 4, 1999; 32. Ibid., October 9, 1999; 33. Ibid., November 2, 1999; 34. Ibid., November 27, 1999; 35. Schneider, Bill to May, Tony, September 16, 1986; 36. Shoplock, Daniel to Sanders, June 14, 2007; 37. Smith, Bob to Cowburn, Fred, January 6, 1994; 38. Spiers, Herbert to McLeroy, January 18, 2000; 39. Stanfel, C. A. to Coen, Harry B., June 12, 1969; 40. Turner, Claude to Gatewood, Robert, May 15, 1968; 41. Westasis, Dominic M. to McLeroy, June 14, 1999; 42. White, John to McLeroy, November 6, 1995.

OTHER DOCUMENTS

130. "Agreement on the Cessation of Hostilities in Vietnam, July 20, 1954," reprinted in U.S. Congress, Senate, Committee on Foreign Relations, 90th Congress, 1st

Session, *Background Information Relation to Southeast Asia and Vietnam,* 3rd Revised Edition, U.S. Government Printing Office, Washington, D.C., 1967.

131. "Geneva Conference Final Declaration," reprinted in Gravel, Mike. *The Pentagon Papers: The Defense Department History of US Decision Making on Vietnam, Vol. I* (Boston, MA: Beacon Press, 1973).

132. Telex message from Bromley Smith, NSC, to Walt Rostow, NSC, forwarded to LBJ ranch, May 12, 1968, "Reports from Saigon re Estimate of Enemy Intentions in Kham Duc Area".

133. Note to GEN Andrew Goodpaster from McLeroy summarizing their telephone conversations regarding President Johnson, Ambassador Harriman, the Paris Peace Talks, and Kham Duc, signed by GEN Goodpaster to confirm his agreement and returned to McLeroy.

134. Richardson, Don. "Kham Duc Revisited: A Chronological Study of the Evacuation of Kham Duc," donscott619@aol.com. Richardson's chronological document compilation is a unique, unpublished primary source.

SECONDARY

BOOKS

Ahern, Thomas L. *Vietnam Declassified* (Lexington, KY: The University Press of Kentucky, 2002).

Ang, Cheng Guan. *Ending the Vietnam War* (New York: RoutledgeCurzon, 2004).

_____. *The Vietnamese War From the Other Side* (New York: RoutledgeCurzon, 2002).

Anonymous. *The Marines in Vietnam 1954–1973* (Washington, D.C.: History and Museums Division, Headquarters, U.S. Marine Corps; U.S. Government Printing Office, 1974).

Anonymous. *U.S. Army Field Manual 7–11: Rifle Company Infantry, Airborne and Mechanized* (Washington, D.C.: Headquarters, Department of the Army, 1965).

Anonymous. *U.S. Army Field Manual 23–82: 106mm Recoilless Rifle* (Washington, D.C.: Headquarters, Department of the Army, 1965).

Anonymous. *U.S. Army Special Forces A-Team Vietnam Combat Manual* (Boulder, CO: Paladin Press, 1988).

Anton, Frank. *Why Didn't You Get Me Out* (San Antonio, TX: Summit Publishing, 1997).

Appy, Christian G. *Patriots* (New York: Viking Penguin, 2003).

Ayensu, Edward (ed.). *Jungles* (New York: Crown Publishers, NY, 1980).

Ballard, Jack. *Development and Employment of Fixed-Wing Gunships, 1962–1972* (Washington, D.C.: Office of Air Force History, 1992).

Bamford, James. *Body of Secrets: Anatomy of the Ultra-Secret National Security Agency* (New York: Anchor Books, 2002).

Bao Ninh. *The Sorrow of War: A Novel of North Vietnam* (New York: Riverhead Books, 1993).

Barrett, David M. *Lyndon B. Johnson's Vietnam Papers* (College Station, TX: Texas A&M University Press, 1997).

_____. *Uncertain Warriors* (Lawrence, KS: University Press of Kansas, 1993).

Berger, Carl (ed.). *The United States Air Force in Southeast Asia, 1961–1973* (Washington, D.C.: Office of Air Force History, 1984).

Berman, Larry. *No Peace, No Honor* (New York: The Free Press, 2001).

Berry, Clifton F., Jr. *The Illustrated History of the Vietnam War: Chargers* (New York: Bantam Books, [no date]).

Bonds, Ray. *The Vietnam War* (New York: Smithmark Publishers, 1996).

Bowers, Ray. *The United States Air Force In Southeast Asia: Tactical Airlift* (Washington, D.C.: Office of Air Force History, 1983).

Bowman, John S. (ed.). *The World Almanac of the Vietnam War* (New York: World Almanac, 1985).

Brady, Patrick. *Dead Men Flying* (Washington D.C.: WND Books, 2012).

Braestrup, Peter. *Big Story* (Novato, CA: Presidio Press, 1994).

Brown, Ashley (ed.). *The Green Berets* (New York: Villard Books, 1986).

Bui Tin. *From Enemy To Friend* (Annapolis, MD: Naval Institute Press, 2002).

_____. *Following Ho Chi Minh* (Honolulu, HI: University of Hawaii Press, 1995).

Campbell, Tom. *The Old Man's Trail* (Annapolis, MD: Naval Institute Press, 2002).

Carlock, Chuck. *Firebirds* (New York: Bantam Books, 1995).

Catino, Martin Scott. *The Aggressors* (Indianapolis, IN: Dog Ear Publishing, 2010).

Chanoff, David and Van Toai, Doan. *Portrait of the Enemy* (New York: Random House, 1986).

_____. *Vietnam: A Portrait of its People at War* (rev.) (London: I. B. Tauris, 2001).

Chen, King C. *Vietnam and China, 1938–1954*; (Princeton, NJ: Princeton University Press, 1969).

Chinnery, Philip D. *Air Commando* (New York: St Martin's Press, 1994).

Chuong, Nguyen Huy. *Su Doan 2, Tap 1 (Second Division, Volume I)* (Da Nang, Socialist Republic of Viet Nam: Da Nang Publishing House, 1989), excerpts translated by Merle Pribbenow.

Clodfelter, Mark. *The Limits of Air Power* (New York: The Free Press, 1989).

Colby, William with McCargar, James. *Lost Victory* (Chicago, IL: Contemporary Books, 1989).

Collins, John. *Military Geography for Professionals and the Public* (Washington, D.C.: Brassey's, 1998).

Colvin, John. *Volcano Under the Snow* (London: Quartet Books, 1996).

Conboy, Ken and Bowra, Ken. *The NVA and Viet Cong* (London: Osprey, 1991).

Crosby, David. *A Guide To Airborne Weapons* (Charleston, SC: Nautical and Aviation Publishing, 2002).

Curry, Cecil B. *Victory At Any Cost* (Washington, D.C.: Brassey's, 1997).

Dallek, Robert. *Flawed Giant* (New York: Oxford University Press, 1998).

Davidson, Phillip. *Secrets of the Vietnam War* (Novato, CA: Presidio Press, 1990).

_____. *Vietnam At War* (Novato, CA: Presidio Press, 1991).

Davies, Bruce. *The Battle at Ngok Tavak* (Crows Nest, NSW, Australia: Allen & Unwin, 2008).

Davis, Larry: *Gunships* (Carrollton, TX: Squadron/Signal Publications, 1982).

Delezen, John: *Red Plateau* [n.p.] (Corps Productions, Ernie Spencer, 2005).

Doleman, Edgar C. Jr *et al.* *Tools of War* (Boston, MA: Boston Publishing, 1984).

Dorr, Robert and Bishop, Chris. *Vietnam Air Warfare* (Edison, NJ: Hartwell Books, 1996).

Doubler, Michael. *Closing With the Enemy* (Lawrence, KS: University Press of Kansas, 1994).

Doyle, Edward *et al.* *The Vietnam Experience: The North* (Boston, MA: Boston Publishing, 1986).

Duiker, William. *The Communist Road to Power in Vietnam* (Boulder, CO: Westview, 1996).

_____. *Ho Chi Minh* (New York: Hyperion, 2000).

_____. *Sacred War* (New York: McGraw-Hill, 1995).

Dunn, Peter M. *The First Vietnam War* (London: C. Hurst, 1985).

Drury, Richard. *My Secret War* (New York: St Martin's Press, 1986).

Emering, Edward J. *Weapons and Field Gear of the North Vietnamese Army and Viet Cong* (Atglen, PA: Schiffer Military/Aviation History, 1998).

Ebert, James. *A Life In A Year* (Novato, CA: Presidio Press, 1993).

Ezell, Edward: *The Illustrated History of Personal Firepower* (New York: Bantam Books, [no date]).

Fall, Bernard. *Anatomy of a Crisis* (Garden City, NY: Doubleday, 1969).

_____. *Hell In a Very Small Place* (Philadelphia, PA: J. B. Lippincott, 1967).

_____. *Street Without Joy* (New York: Schocken Books, 1967).

_____. *The Two Viet-Nams (2nd rev. ed.)* (New York: Praeger, 1967).

_____. *Viet-Nam Witness* (New York: Praeger, 1966).

Fallaci, Oriana. *Interview With History* (Boston, MA: Houghton Mifflin, 1976).

Flanagan, John. *Vietnam Above the Treetops* (New York: Dell, 1992).

Forster, Randy E. M. *Vietnam Firebases 1965–73* (Oxford, UK: Osprey, 2007).

Frankum, Ronald B. *Like Rolling Thunder* (Lanham, MD: Rowman & Littlefield, 2005).

Frost, Frank. *Australia's War in Vietnam* (Sydney: Allen & Unwin, 1987).

Fulbright, J. W. (Chairman, Committee on Foreign Relations, Unites States Senate). *Background Information Relating to Southeast Asia and Vietnam* (5th Revised Edition) (Washington, D.C.: U.S. Government Printing Office, 1969).

Fuller, John. *Air Weather Service Support to the United States Army* (Scott Air Force Base, IL: Military Airlift Command, 1979).

Gettleman, Marvin E. (ed.). *Vietnam* (Greenwich, NY: Fawcett, 1965).

Giap, Vo Nguyen. *Big Victory, Great Task* (New York: Praeger, 1968).

_____. *Dien Bien Phu* (Ha Noi, Socialist Republic of Viet Nam: Foreign Languages Publishing House, 1964).

_____. *How We Won the War* (Philadelphia, PA: Recon Publications, 1976).

_____. *People's War People's Army* (Honolulu, HI: University Press of the Pacific, 2001).

Gilbert, Ed. *The U.S. Marine Corps in the Vietnam War* (Oxford, UK: Osprey, 2006).

Gillespie, Robert. *Black Ops, Vietnam* (Annapolis, MD: Naval Institute Press, 2011).

Gravel, Mike. *The Pentagon Papers* (Boston, MA: Beacon Press, 1971).

Gropman, Alan. *Airpower and the Airlift Evacuation of Kham Duc* (Maxwell Air Force Base, AL: Air War College Press, USAF Southeast Asia Monograph 7, Volume V, 1979).

Gunston, Bill. *Aircraft of the Vietnam War* (Wellingborough, UK: Patrick Stephens, 1987).

Haas, Michael. *Apollo's Warriors* (Maxwell Air Force Base, AL: Air University Press, 1997).

Hammell, Eric. *Khe Sanh* (New York: Crown Publishing, 1989).

Hammer, Ellen. *The Struggle For Indochina* (Stanford, CA: Stanford University Press, 1966).

Hammond, William. *The Military and the Media 1962–1968* (Washington, D.C.: U.S. Army Center for Military History, 1988).

_____. *Reporting Vietnam* (Lawrence, KS: University Press of Kansas, 1998).

Hanyok, Robert. *Spartans in Darkness* (Washington, D.C.: National Security Agency, Center for Cryptologic History, 2002).

Harrison, Marshall. *A Lonely Kind of War* (New York: Pocket Books, 1989).

Harvey, Frank. *Air War: Vietnam* (New York: Bantam Books, 1967).

Hershman, Jablow. *Power Beyond Reason* (Fort Lee, NJ: Barricade Books, 2002).

Hickey, Gerald. *Free In the Forest* (New Haven, CT: Yale University Press, 1982).

_____. *Sons of the Mountains* (New Haven, CT: Yale University Press, 1982).

Hobson, Chris. *Vietnam Air Losses* (Hinckley, UK: Midland Publishing, 2001).

Holmes, Richard. *Acts of War* (New York: The Free Press, 1985).

Humphries, James. *Through The Valley* (Boulder, CO: Lynne Rienner Publishing, 1999).

Infantry Magazine (eds); *A Distant Challenge* (Nashville, TN: Battery Press, 1983).

Jackson, Robert (ed.). *The Encyclopedia of Aircraft* (New York: Barnes & Noble, 2004).

Johnson, Lyndon. *The Vantage Point* (New York: Holt Rinehart and Winston, 1971).

Just, Ward. *Reporting Vietnam* (New York: The Library of America, 1998).

Keegan, John and Holmes, Richard. *Soldiers* (New York: Viking Penguin, 1986).

Kelly, Francis. *U.S. Army Special Forces* (Washington, D.C.: Department of the Army, 1985).

Kelley, Michael P. *Where We Were In Vietnam* (Central Point, OR: Hellgate Press, 2002).

Kimball, Jeffrey. *Nixon's Vietnam War* (Lawrence, KS: University Press of Kansas, 1998).

Kindsvatter, Peter. *American Soldiers* (Lawrence, KS: University Press of Kansas, 2003).

Kinnard, Douglas. *The War Managers* (Hanover, NH: University Press of New England, 1977).

Kennedy, William. *The Military and the Media* (Westport, CT: Praeger, 1993).

Kissinger, Henry. *Ending the Vietnam War* (New York: Simon & Schuster; 2003).

Kolb, Richard (ed.). *Brutal Battles Of Vietnam* (Kansas City, MO; Veterans of Foreign Wars, 2017).

Kort, Michael. *The Vietnam War Reexamined* (Cambridge, UK: Cambridge University Press, 2018).

Lanning, Michael Lee and Craig, Dan. *Inside the VC and the NVA* (New York: Ballantine, 1992).

Lavalle, A. J. C. (ed.). *Airpower and the 1972 Spring Invasion* (Washington, D.C.: Office of Air Force History, 1976/1985).

Leepson, Marc (ed.). *Webster's New World Dictionary of the Vietnam War* (New York: Simon & Schuster, 1999).

Lehrack, Otto. *Road of 10,000 Pains* (Minneapolis, MS: Zenith Press, 2010).

Lien-Hang T. Nguyen. *Hanoi's War* (Chapel Hill, NC: University of North Carolina Press, 2012).

Littauer, Raphael and Uphoff, Norman (eds). *The Air War in Indochina* (rev. ed.) (Boston, MA: Beacon Press, 1972).

MacDonald, Peter. *Giap* (New York: Norton, 1993).

Mao Tse-tung. *On Guerrilla Warfare* (Samuel Griffith, trans.) (New York: Praeger, 1961).

Matthews, Lloyd and Brown, Dale. *Assessing the Vietnam War* (New York: Pergamon-Brassey, 1987).

McCarthy, James *et al.* *Linebacker II* (Maxwell Air Force Base, AL: Air War College Monograph 8, USAF Southeast Asia Monograph Series, Vol. VI, 1979).

McNeill, Ian. *The Team* (Canberra, Australia: The Australian War Memorial, 1984).

Mersky, Peter B. and Polmar, Norman. *The Naval Air War in Vietnam* (Annapolis, MD: Nautical and Aviation Publishing, 1981).

Michel, Marshall L. *The Eleven Days of Christmas* (San Francisco, CA: Encounter Books, 2002).

Moise, Edwin. *The A to Z of the Vietnam War* (Lanham, MD: Scarecrow Press, 2005).

Momyer, William W. *Airpower in Three Wars* (Washington, D.C.: U.S. Government Printing Office, 1978).

Moore, John N. and Turner, Robert F. (eds). *The Real Lessons of the Vietnam War* (Durham, NC: Carolina Academic Press, 2002).

Morris, Jim. *War Story* (Boulder, CO: Sycamore Islands Books, 1979).

Mrozek, Donald. *Air Power and the Ground War in Vietnam* (Maxwell Air Force Base, AL: Air University Press, 1988).

Nalty, Bernard. *Air Power and the Fight For Khe Sanh* (Washington, D.C.: Office of Air Force History, 1973).

_____. *Air War over South Vietnam* (Washington, D.C.: Air Force History and Museums Program, United States Air Force, [no date]).

_____ et al. An Illustrated Guide to the Air War Over Vietnam (New York: Prentice Hall, 1981).

Nguyen Tien Hung and Schecter, Jerrold L. *The Palace File* (New York: Harper & Row, 1986).

Oberdorfer, Don. *TET!* (Garden City, NY: Doubleday, 1971).

Olson, Gregory Allen (ed.). *Landmark Speeches on the Vietnam War* (College Station, TX: Texas A&M University Press, 2010).

Palmer, Dave Richard. *Summons of the Trumpet* (San Rafael, CA: Presidio Press, 1978).

Pearson, Willard. *The War In The Northern Provinces, 1966–1968* (Washington, D.C.: Department of the Army, 1991).

Phillips, William R. *Night of the Silver Stars* (Annapolis, MD: Naval Institute Press, 1997).

Pike, Douglas. *PAVN* (New York: Da Capo, 1986).

_____. *Viet Cong* (Cambridge, MA: M.I.T. Press, 1966).

_____. *Vietnam and the Soviet Union* Boulder, CO: Westview Press, 1987).

Pimlott, John. *Vietnam: The Decisive Battles* (New York: Macmillan, 1990).

Pisor, Robert. *The End of the Line* (New York: Norton, 1982).

Plaster, John: *SOG* (New York: Simon & Schuster, 1997).

_____. *Secret Commandos* (New York: Simon & Schuster, 2004).

_____. *SOG: A Photo History of the Secret Wars* (Boulder, CO: Paladin, 2000).

Porch, Douglas. *The French Foreign Legion* (New York: HarperCollins, 1991).

Prados, John. *The Blood Road* (New York: John Wiley, 1999).

_____ and Stubbe, Ray W. *Valley of Decision* (Boston, MA: Houghton Mifflin, 1991).

Pretty, R.T. and Archer, D.H.R. (eds). *Jane's Weapon Systems 1971–72* (London: Sampson Low Marston, [no date]).

Pribbenow, Merle (trans.). *Victory In Vietnam* (Lawrence, KS: The Military History Institute of Vietnam, People's Army Publishing House, The University Press of Kansas, 2002).

Prokosch, Eric. *The Technology of Killing* (London: Zed Books, 1995).

Ripley, Dillon. *The Land and Wildlife of Tropical Asia* (New York: Time-Life Books, 1975).

Robbins, James. *This Time We Win* (New York: Encounter Books, 2010).

Robinson, Anthony (ed.). *Weapons of the Vietnam War* (Greenwich, CT: Bison Books, 1983).

Rosser-Owen, David. *Vietnam Weapons Handbook* (Wellingborough, Northants, UK: Patrick Stephens, 1986).

Rottman, Gordon. *Green Berets in Vietnam: 1957–73* (Oxford, UK: Osprey, 2002).

_____. *Mobile Strike Forces in Vietnam: 1966–70* (Oxford, UK: Osprey, 2007).

_____. *North Vietnamese Army Soldier 1958–75* (Oxford, UK: Osprey, 2009).

_____. *Special Forces Camps in Vietnam: 1961–70* (Oxford, UK: Osprey, 2005).

_____. *US Army Infantryman in Vietnam: 1965–73* (Oxford, UK: Osprey, 2005).

_____. *US MACV-SOG Reconnaissance Team in Vietnam* (Oxford, UK: Osprey, 2011).

_____. *Viet Cong Fighter* (Oxford, UK: Osprey, 2007).

Roy, Jules. *The Battle of Dienbienphu* (New York: Harper & Row, 1963).

Schandler, Herbert. *Lyndon Johnson and Vietnam* (Princeton, NJ: Princeton University Press, 1983).

Schell, Jonathan. *The Real War* (New York: Da Capo, 2000).

Schlight, John. *The War in South Vietnam* (Washington, D.C.: Office of Air Force History, 1999).

Schrock, Joann L. *et al. Minority Groups in the Republic of Vietnam* (Washington, D.C.: Department of the Army Pamphlet No. 550–105, 1966).

Sharp, U. S. G. *Strategy for Defeat* (Novato, CA: Presidio Press, 1978).

_____ and Westmoreland, William C. *Report on the War in Vietnam* (Washington, D.C.: U.S. Government Printing Office, 1968).

Schulimson, Jack *et al. U.S. Marines In Vietnam: The Defining Year, 1968* (Washington, D.C.: History and Museums Division, Headquarters, U.S. Marine Corps, 1997).

Shultz, Richard. *The Secret War Against Hanoi* (New York: HarperCollins, 1999).

Simpson, Charles M. III. *Inside the Green Berets* (Novato, CA: Presidio Press 1983).

Simpson, Howard R. *Dien Bien Phu* Washington, D.C.: Brassey's, 1994).

Singlaub, John with McConnell, Malcolm. *Hazardous Duty* (New York: Summit Books, 1991).

Smith, Gordon Hedderly. *The Blood Hunters*; Chicago, IL; Moody Press; 1942.

Smith, Harvey *et al. Area Handbook for South Vietnam* (Washington, D.C.: DA Pam No. 550–55, U.S. Government Printing Office, 1967).

_____. *Area Handbook for North Vietnam* (Washington, D.C.: DA Pam No. 550–57, U.S. Government Printing Office, 1967).

Smith, Mrs Gordon. *Farther Into the Night* (Grand Rapids, MI: Zondervan Publishing, 1956).

_____. *Gongs In the Night* (Grand Rapids, MI: Zondervan Publishing, 1943).

_____. *Victory in Viet Nam* (Grand Rapids, MI: Zondervan Publishing, 1965).

Smith, John T. *The Linebacker Raids* (London: Arms & Armour Press, 1999).

Sorley, Lewis. *A Better War* (New York: Harcourt Brace, 1999).

_____. *Vietnam Chronicles: The Abrams Tapes 1968–1972* (Lubbock, TX: Texas Tech University Press, 2004).

Spector, Ronald. *After Tet* (New York: Free Press, 1993).

Staaveren, Jacob Van. *Interdiction in Southern Laos* (Washington, D.C.: Center for Air Force History, 1993).

Stanton, Shelby. *Green Berets At War* (Novato, CA: Presidio Press, 1985).

_____. *The Rise & Fall of an American Army* (Novato, CA: Presidio Press, 1985).

_____. *Vietnam Order of Battle* (Washington, D.C.: U.S. News Books, 1981).

Summers, Harry. *Historical Atlas of the Vietnam War* (New York: Houghton Mifflin, 1995).

_____. *On Strategy* (Novato, CA: Presidio Press, 1995).

_____. *Vietnam War Almanac* (New York: Facts On File, 1985).

Sutherland, Ian. *Special Forces of the United States Army: 1952/1982* (San Jose, CA: R. James Bender Publishing, 1990).

Swift, Earl. *Where They Lay* (Boston, MA: Houghton Mifflin, 2003).

Taylor, Chris. *Special Forces Camps in Vietnam 1961–1970* (Oxford, UK: Osprey, 2005).

Telfer, Gary, *et al. U.S. Marines In Vietnam: Fighting The North Vietnamese, 1967* (Washington, D.C.: History and Museums Division, Headquarters, U.S. Marine Corps, 1984).

That Thien Ton. The Foreign Policies of the Communist Party of Vietnam (New York: Crane Russak, 1989).

Thomson, Leroy. *US Elite Forces—Vietnam* (Carrollton, TX: squadron/signal publications, 1985).

Tilford, Earl. *Setup* (Maxwell Air Force Base, AL: Air University Press, 1991).

Tolson, John and Bowers, Verne. *Airmobility 1961–1971* (Washington, D.C.: Government Reprint Press, 2001).

Truong-Chinh. *The Resistance Will Win* (Honolulu, HI: University Press of the Pacific, 2001).

Truong Nhu Tang. *A Viet Cong Memoir* (New York: Harcourt Brace Jovanovich, 1985).

Tucker, Spencer. *The Encyclopedia of the Vietnam War* (New York: Oxford University Press, 2001).

Turner, Robert F. *Vietnamese Communism* (Stanford, CA: Hoover Institution Press, 1975).

Veith, George J. *Code Name Bright Light* (New York: The Free Press, 1998).

Voral, Gregory. *Ashau*, unpublished novel by a former SF/SOG one-zero (recon team leader).

Walton, Dale. *The Myth of Inevitable U.S. Defeat In Vietnam* (Portland, OR: Frank Cass, 2002).

Warner, Wayne. *One Trip Too Many* ([n.p.]: Independent Publisher, 2011).

Westmoreland, William C. *A Soldier Reports* (New York: Doubleday, 1976).

Wiest, Andrew (ed.). *Rolling Thunder in a Gentle Land* (Oxford, UK: Osprey, 2006).

Wilkins, Warren. *Grab Their Belts To Fight Them* (Annapolis, MD: Naval Institute Press, 2011).

Willbanks, James H. *The Tet Offensive* (New York: Columbia University Press, 2007).

Windrow, Martin. *The Last Valley* (Cambridge, MA: Da Capo Press, 2004).

Winters, Harold *et al*. *Battling the Elements* (Baltimore, MD: Johns Hopkins University, 1998).

Woodruff, Mark W. *Unheralded Victory* (Arlington, VA: Vandamere Press, 1999).

Yarborough, Tom. *Danang Diary* (rev. ed.) (New York: St Martin's Press, 2000).

Zabecki, David (ed.). *Vietnam, A Reader* (New York: ibooks, 2002).

Zaffiri, Samuel. *Westmoreland* (New York: William Morrow, 1994).

Zumwalt, James. *Bare Feet, Iron Will* (Jacksonville, FL: Fortis Publishing, 2010).

ARTICLES

"Airlift at Kham Duc", http://members.aol.com._ht_a/blindbat/khamduc.html

Andrade, Dale. "Westmoreland was right: learning the wrong lessons from the Vietnam War" in *Small Wars & Insurgencies*, Vol. 19, No. 2 (June 2008), pp. 145–81.

Anonymous. "GI Helo Downed, Toll High" in Stars and Stripes (August 28, 1970).

Anonymous. "Jolly Greens, A-Hs Pull Daring Rescue" in *Seventh Air Force News* (June 12, 1968).

Anonymous. "The Glorious Month of May" in Quan Doi Nhan Dan (editorial) (June 4, 1968). Barnett, A.C. "Kham Duc Airstrip Retaken" in *Southern Cross*, Vol. 3, No. 33.

Anonymous. *Time* magazine, "The High Cost of Maintaining Appearances" (May 24, 1968).

Anonymous. *Time* magazine, "Vietnam, Lessons From A Lost War" (April 15, 1985).

Belshaw, Jim. "Looking for Old Friends" in *Vietnam Veterans of America Magazine* (June 1999).

Brownlow, Cecil. "Coordinated Effort Saves Force" in *Aviation Week and Space Technology*, 89, pp. 92–98.

Bogue, Hardy Z. "The Fall of Ngok Tavak" in *Vietnam* magazine (August 1992), pp. 21–25.

Chen Jian. "China's Involvement in the Vietnam War, 1964–69" in *The China Quarterly* (1995), pp. 356–87.

Cutts, Bob. "On a Wing and a Prayer" in *Pacific Stars and Stripes* (11 August, 1968), pp. A-3, A-6.

DuPre, Flint. "Rescue at a place called Kham Duc" in *Air Force and Space Digest*, Vol. 52, No. 3, pp. 98–100.

Elegant, Robert. "How to Lose a War: The Press and Viet Nam" in *Encounter* magazine (London), Vol. LVII, No. 2 (August 1981), pp. 73–90.

Evans, Earl and Busbee, Larry. "Story of Kham Duc as Told to Earl Evans", www. theboxcar.org.

Frisbee, John L. "Deliverance at Kham Duc" in *Air Force Magazine* (November 1985).

Gowan, Annie. "At Long Last, Honors for 12 Fallen Men" in *Washington Post* (October 8, 2005).

Griffen, Ronald. "Sapper Attack At Kham Duc" in *Vietnam* magazine, vol. 22, no. 1 (June 2009), pp. 33–37.

Lundie, James. "Kham Duc, South Vietnam, 12 May 1968" in *Combat Controllers Newsletter* (undated).

McGowan, Sam. "American airlift crews proved their skill and persistence one afternoon at Kham Duc" in *Vietnam* magazine (Summer 1988), pp. 10, 64–66.

_____. "Operation Golden Valley: Airlifters' Finest Hour" in *Vietnam* magazine (April 1998), pp. 18–24.

Muluck, Roger. "Get everybody Out" in *Vietnam* magazine (June 2018).

Newsweek. "In Dubious Battle" (May 27, 1968).

Percoskie, Tony. "Reflections of Kham Duc" in *Vietnam Combat* (September 20, 1989).

Pribbenow, Merle L. "North Vietnam's Master Plan" in *Vietnam* magazine (August 1999).

Spector, Ronald. "The Evacuation of Kham Duc" in *MHQ: The Quarterly Journal of Military History*, Vol. 5, No. 3 (Spring 1993), p. 40.

Sturm, Ted R. "Flight Check to Glory" in *Airman*, Vol. XIII, No. 9, pp. 52–54.

_____. "The Lucky Duc" in *Airman*, Vol. XIV, No. 9, pp. 26–29.

Taylor, Donald. "The Huey", projetdelta.net, pp. 1–8.

Waldo, Daniel. "Soil Cement for Pavement Patching" in *The Military Engineer* Vol. 62, No. 405 (Jan–Feb, 1970).

White, J. E. D. "Venison and Valour" in *Australian Infantry* (Jan–Feb 1971), pp.10–15.

wikimedia.org/wiki/Category:Battle_of_Kham_Duc.

Index

A Shau Valley 52, 61
Abrams, Creighton 100, 103, 104, 194, 212
Adams, Robert 72
Aerospace Rescue and Recovery Squadron 169
Air Force Cross 139, 141, 153
aircraft 113, 123, 127
  A-1E Skyraider 60
  AC-47 "Spooky" 71–72, 75, 111–12
  B-52 "Arc Light" bombers 98, 124, 125
  C-7 Caribou 77
  C-123 153
  C-130 control aircraft (Hillsboro) 119
  C-130 transport planes 41, 93, 119, 128, 129
    evacuation operations 138–39, 141– 42, 146, 148, 150–51, 152
  Cessna 01 FAC 43, 98
  F-4 Phantom 117, 118
  F-105 fighter bombers 126
  RC-135 29
  SR-71 Blackbird 29
  destructive powers of 123, 149
  fixed-wing aircraft 119, 121
  losses of 167
  photo reconnaissance planes 149
  sorties 149–50
  tactical aircraft 149
  see also helicopters
Aiken, Clay 62

Alphin, Talmadge 40, 51
Arlington National Cemetery 177, 179
artillery fire bases 65, 90
August 1945 Strategy 6
Australian forces 61–62
  dispute over orders 81
Aycock, Robert 40, 131

"bait", Kham Duc battle as, xii, 30, 44, 46, 110, 163, 194
  US escapees used as 171–75
Bank, Aaron 203
Bao Dai, Emperor of Vietnam 199
Benway, Kenneth 62
Bernhardt, Eugene 39, 68, 69
Black, Reese 97, 143, 145
Bledsoe, William 115, 140
Blohm, Ron 122
Blomgren, David 62, 72, 76
bombs and bombing 124, 125
  see also cluster bombs; high explosive bombs; napalm
booby traps 102, 116
Bowers, Richard 103, 111, 177
Boyd, William 141
Bradford, Leon 133–34
Brady, Patrick 77–78, 136–37
Brown, Tim 177, 178, 179
Buchner, Bernard 138, 141
Buchwald, Donald 92–93, 96, 97–98, 111, 115, 116, 127, 130, 136, 146
  factual AAR account of battle 164

Buddhism 19
bunkers 101
Busbee, Larry 162

Cambodia 5, 195, 196
    Ho Chi Minh Trail 44
Cameron, Don 62, 76, 81
Camp Conroy 38, 42, 91
Campbell, Jesse 153
Campbell, Richard 77, 138, 152
Carlyle, Larry 139
Carson, Ray 120, 133
Carter, Johnny 102, 103, 110–11, 177
Central Highlands, 4, 34, 206
    climate 35–36
    wildlife 34–35
Central Identification Laboratory 177,
        178, 180
Central Intelligence Agency (CIA) 203,
        205
    memoranda predicting attacks by
        NVA, 11
Central Office for South Vietnam
        (COSV), 3
Chandler, Harris 112, 116, 135
Chevane, Laos 59
China 194
    influence in First Indo-China War 2
    invasion of by Japan 198
Churchill, Winston 202
Cihak, Bill 78
Civilian Irregular Defense Group
        (CIDG) 10, 37, 39, 66, 68,
        100, 112, 201, 138, 205–7
    alleged platoon at Ngok Tavak
        65–66, 67–68, 69–70, 72
    communication with LLDB 39
    deserters 127, 131–32, 138
    trainees at SF camp 38
    VC infiltrators 206
civilians: evacuation from KD 127–29,
        130, 138
Clausewitz, Carl von 184, 186
    nine principles of war 186–90

cluster bombs (CBU) 121, 124, 143
Coburn 122
Coen, Harry 102, 114–15, 116, 137
Cold War 192, 203–4
Cole, Darryl 127, 128, 134, 141
Colonna, John 103, 111, 153–54,
        167–70
"combat friction" 184
communications 108–9
CONEX containers 40, 95
Confucianism 18–19, 199
Conklin, Richard 74
Connolly, John 111
Corps Tactical Zones (CTZ) 207
counterinsurgency 204
coup de main strategy 5–6
Cowburn, Fred 135, 138
Craven, Andrew 112, 114, 116, 135
cross-border missions and reconnaissance
        44, 45, 200, 212
Cuban crisis (1962) 211
Cushman, Robert 87, 89, 100,
        103, 194
Cutler, Gary 130
Cyrus, Ray 122

Dak Se River 69, 79
Dak To 12, 27, 43, 185
Danang 61, 64
    controversial decisions at 64–66
Decoux, Jean 198
Deleshaw, Jack 77
Delmore, John 141–2
Democratic Republic of Vietnam
        (DRV)
    commemorative dates 10
    effects on economy of US bombing
        campaign 5
    government co-operation in search
        for missing troops 178
    strategy to conquer RVN 1–2
    totalitarianism 19, 20
    use of propaganda xvi, 12, 13, 20,
        103

see also Central Office for South
    Vietnam (COSV); Politburo;
    Subcommittee for Military
    Affairs (SMA), 1–2
deserters 127, 131–32, 138
Dien Bien Phu xv, xvi, 6, 7, 9, 12, 96,
    189, 191, 192
"Dien Bien Phu gambit" 11, 12
Dineen, Don 145
Distinguished Service Cross 140, 214
Dodge, Melvin 40
Donohue, Joe 141–42
Donovan, William 203
Duncan, James 39, 71

economy of force: principle of war
    187, 213
ELINT (electronic intercepts) 29
Eoff, Bill 120
Ezell, Edward 122

Farrar, Walter 127, 128
Fitzsimmons, Edward 122
Flater, Rhett 80
"fog of war" 108
Foreman, Wilbert 103, 111, 153–54,
    167–70
Forward Operating Base 4 (FOB) 43,
    45–6, 212, 214
foxholes 101
France
    presence in SE Asia 198, 202
    surrender to Germany (1940) 198
    withdrawal from Indochina xv
Freedman, Morton 93, 128, 134, 152
French Foreign Legion 201–2
Fuentes, David 75
Fuller, Elbert 46–47

Gallagher, John 93, 128
Gannon, Vicky (sister of Danny Widner)
    178, 179
Garlitz, James 73

Garwood, Robert 172
Gatewood, Medley 119, 133, 149
General Offensive/General Insurrection
    ("Tet" Offensive) 5, 6, 7–8,
    9, 11, 44
"Mini' Tet" 11, 103, 165, 185
Geneva Conference (1954) 2
Gilkey, Gerald 140
Gill, Richard 39, 97
Glick, Jacob 163–64
Goodpaster, Andrew 109
graves registration team 176–77
Green Berets *see* Special Forces (SF)
Greenwood, Kenneth 49, 151
Guzman, Antonio 102, 115–16, 177

Hatchet Force, 49, 148, 213
helicopters, 42, 45, 43, 54
    AF HH-3 60
    CH-34 Sikorsky 43, 47
    CH-46 80
    CH-47 66, 75, 96, 120–21,
        139–40, 152
    CH-53 65, 66
    UH-1 "Muskets" 112, 135–36
    UH-1H medical evacuation ("Dust
        Off") 77, 136–37
    crew not awarded honors 164
    evacuation operations 77–78, 89,
        133, 139–40
Henderson, Robert III 39, 59, 91–92,
    99, 128, 131, 132, 146, 152
    call for emergency rescue 60
high explosive bombs 124, 125
Hill, Richard 112, 116, 135
Hillsboro 119–20, 123, 126, 131,
    150–51
Ho Chi Minh 1, 6, 12, 196–97
Ho Chi Minh Trail 3, 41, 44, 59, 200,
    208–11
    Cambodia 44
    Laos 41, 44
Hoa Lo prison ("Hanoi Hilton") 174

Hoffman, Dovie (sister of Danny Widner) 178, 179
Hostler, Donald 121

Ia Drang Valley, battle of 4
indigenous troops 49, 61, 119
   losses of 167, 213
Indo-China War
   1st (1946-54) 2, 196, 201, 207
   2nd (1957–75) 1, 197
insurgents 204
intelligence gathering
   NVA 45
   US 29–30
interception of NVA communications by US 29–30

Jackson, Joe 153
Jackson, William 201
Japan
   extension of control in SE Asia 198
   invasion of China 198
Jeanotte, Alfred 152–53
Johnson, Lyndon Baines xvi, 11–12, 110, 191, 192, 194–95, 196
Johnson, Willard 114, 118, 128, 169
Johnson, William 88
Joint Personnel Recovery Center 175
Joint Task Force 177
Joint POW/MIA Command (JPAC) 177
Jones, L.B. 40, 51
Jones, Omar 98

Kemp, Larry 139, 140
Kennedy, John 204, 211
Kham Duc xi–xiii, xiv, xv, 34, 36, 41
   After Action Reports (AAR) 164–65
   aftermath 163, 176
   airstrip 37, 41, 42, 121–22, 198–99
   analysis of battle 184, 194
   casualties xiii, 136–37, 163–64
   change of command structure 130

   destruction of weapons and equipment before evacuation 129–30
   evacuation from 131, 133, 136
   finding of missing troops 176–77
   failure of NVA tactics xiv–xv
   filming of the battle 140–41
   function of xv, 89
   Grand Slam Emergency 123
   guilt of survivors 177
   inner fortifications 37–38
   internal defense of 48–49
   lack of leadership 166
   losses 166–67
   NVA film of 189, 191, 192
   obstacles to attack from east 50–51
   official version of battle 163–64
   photographic analysis of battle 175
   recovery of equipment and supplies 176
   rescue operations 77–80, 127–29
   road and airstrip building by France 198–99
   suspension of evacuation from 128–29
   tactical synergistic serendipity 186
   vulnerable to tank attack 67
Kham Duc Victory (film) 167
Khe San xvi, 6–7, 9, 12, 41, 96, 142, 185, 191
Khrushchev, Nikita 204
King, Gerald 74, 76
Koster, Samuel 47, 87, 89, 90, 92, 100, 103, 127, 132
Kusher, Floyd 173

Ladd, Jonathan 87–88, 103, 104
Lang Vei camp 66, 89
Lanier, James 121
Lao Dong (Workers Party) 1, 19
Laos 5, 44, 195, 196, 200
   Ho Chi Minh Trail 41, 44
Laotian Panhandle 40, 41

Le Duan 1, 5–6, 8
leeches 24, 35, 168, 171
Lenin, Vladimir Ilyich: *coup de main*
    strategy 5–6
Lloyd, Randall 103, 111, 177
Long, Julius 102, 114–5, 115–6, 137,
    154, 178
    capture and imprisonment of 171–5
Long, Wayne 199–200
Long Range Reconnaissance Patrols
    (LRRP) 100–1
Long Thanh training camp 43
Luc-Luong Dac-Biet (LLDB) 204, 206
Lucas, Frank 62, 76, 81
Lumpkin, John 39
Lundie, James 93, 128, 134, 152
Lyles, Ronald 177

McLaughlin, Burl 128, 141, 152
    anger at CCT men 134
McLeroy, James 40, 48, 71, 98–99, 147,
    148, 149, 150, 151,
    165–66, 178
    launch of napalm bomb 144–46
    maintained distance from SOG
      troops 52
    officer in charge of SOG 49–50
McWilliam, Bob 136
Makinowski, Eugene 76–77, 79, 81, 152
Mao Tse-tung 2, 5, 195
Matheney, Jack, 77
Medal of Honor 153, 214
mercenaries 199–200
Military Assistance Command, Vietnam
    (MACV), 29, 30, 212
    official statement on KD battle 165
Miller, Glenn 62, 75
Mills, Billy 148
Momyer, William 110, 123, 132,
    140–41, 165, 184
monsoons 35–6, 52, 154, 192
Montagnards 61, 100, 148, 202,
    205, 206

Montgomery, Franklin 146
Moore, Maurice 103, 111
morale of troops 44, 71, 118–19
Morris, Lance 91

napalm bombs and bombing 118, 124,
    145–46
National Security Agency (NSA) 29, 30
Navy Cross 74, 75
Nelson, Robert 90, 93, 96, 98, 100,
    111, 128, 148
    After Action Reports (AAR) 94
    challenge to authority of 94, 99
    changes numbers of OPs 99
    false statements by 164
    incompetence of 101, 126–27
    mistakes by 98, 99
New York Times 9
Newsweek 165
Ngo Dinh Diem 3, 199
Ngo Dinh Nhu 199
Ngok Tavak 12, 59, 60–61, 63, 65, 69,
    201–2
    alleged CIDG platoon at 65–66,
      67–8, 69–70, 72
    base for training patrols 200
    casualties xiii–xiv, 74–76, 78–79, 81
    controversial decisions at 66
    escape column of US troops 79–80
    evacuation from 77–81
    fortification of 65, 67, 70–71
    identification of remains 178–79
    losses 81, 166–67
    Marines at 65, 73–76
    memorial ceremony 178
    Nung troops 73, 76
    patrol by Mike Force 63
    unburied troops left behind 79
Nixon, Richard 192
North Vietnam, Army *see* People's Army
    of North Vietnam
Nung troops 40, 61, 62, 67, 118, 142,
    148, 207–8

Hatchet Force 49
  at Ngok Tavak 73, 76
  weaponry 62

observation posts (OPs) 38–39, 99,
      101–2
  OP 1 (SF 3) 101, 103, 110,
      112–15, 135
    escape from 135, 137
  OP 2 (SF 1) 102, 110, 110–12,
      126, 142
  OP 3 (SF 5) 103, 115
  excavation of 178
  finding of missing troops 176–77
  numbering of 38, 99
Office of Strategic Services (OSS)
      203, 212
Operation *Delaware* 52, 61
Operation *El Paso* 41
Operation *Elk Canyon* 176
Operation *Golden Valley* 46–47
Operation *York* 41
Opheim, Glen 136
Orr, Warren 138
Overby, Lauren 48, 88, 131, 147,
      148–49
Owens, Garland 89, 90, 91–92, 97, 99,
      126–27

Paris Peace Talks 11, 12, 109, 191
Parrett, Dean 74
patrol bases 65
Pelkey, Chris 130
Pentagon *see* United States Pentagon
People's Army of North
      Vietnam (NVA) 18
  2nd Division (PAVN) 10, 26, 27–29
  59th Transportation Division 3, 209
  assault tactics 190
  casualties xiii–xiv
  discipline 20
  failure of DRV strategy 9
  film of battle 189, 191, 192
  film crew 109, 167

human wave assaults 25, 143, 143–46
  infiltration of RVN 205–6
  intelligence gathering by 45
  losses 4
  medical conditions and hospitals
      22–24
  offensive tactics 25
  officers 25
  photographic reconnaissance 30,
      140–41, 175
  political indoctrination 20
  preparations for attack on KD 27–29
  reconnaissance scouts 21–22
  resumption of road works after battle
      175–76
  road building 60, 61, 67
  sources of "combat friction" 184–85
  strategic advantages of 195–96
  structure and organisation of 21
  tactical objectives of 13
  "three-man cell" structure 21
  training of recruits 21–22
  uniforms and equipment 24
  use of propaganda xvi, 12, 13,
      103, 109
  use of US weapons 126
  vulnerable to attack by patrols 200–1
Perry, Thomas 77, 79–80
Pham Xuan An, 8
Phan Thanh Du 10
Pierce, Edward 115
"Platinum Gardens" (prison) 174
Politburo (DRV), 1, 3–4, 192
  long-term total war strategy 194,
      195, 196
Portinho, Paul 38, 71
Pound, Larry 77
Powell, John 121
"principles of war" (Clausewitz)
      186–89
prisoners of war, American: treatment
      by NVA 172–75, 176
Project Delta 61, 175
Purdy, Lee 49, 51, 118, 142

Purple Heart 213
Pyrrhic victory 194

QL 14 (road) 10, 59, 60, 67, 69, 101,
        198, 199, 201, 202
Quang Tin Province 41

radio communication 100, 101, 108–9,
        112, 118, 128, 132, 133
    discrepancies in 109
    OP 1 115
Ranger techniques and training 204
Ransbottom, Fred 102–3, 111–12
Ransbottom, Laverne (mother of Fred)
        178, 179, 180
Reed, Jack 136
refugees 138
Republic of Vietnam 9
    infiltration by NVA 1, 3–4, 205–6
    US forces in 196
Republic of Vietnam Army (ARVN)
        200, 207
Ripping, Terry 136, 137
Roosevelt, F. D. R. 203
Rostow, Dr. Walt xvi, 110
Route 165 59
Saigon, US journalists and reporters in
        8, 165
Sanders, Walter 46–7
Sands, Richard 139
Santa Barbara Project 41
Sassenberger, Edward 103, 111, 153–54,
        167–70
"saving face" 19
Scarborough, Griffen 98
Schrope, Bill 91
Schultz, George 133–34
Schungel, Daniel 61, 66–7, 78, 88, 131,
        147, 148, 149, 152
    After Action Report by 167
    dispute over orders 81, 164
    false statements by 64–65
Schunk, Henry 72, 74–75

security: principle of war 188–89
serendipity 186
Sewell, Don 136
Sharp, U.S.G. 109
Sheeler, Sidney 40, 131
Shelton, Ray 131–32
SIGINT (signal intercepts) 29
Silva, Christopher 39, 70, 71, 74, 92
Silver Star 153, 164
Simpson, Joe 101, 114, 115, 117, 136,
        137, 154, 171
Singlaub, John 88, 89
Single Manager for Air system 165
Sisk, Harry 116, 177
Skivington, Bill (father of William) 178
Skivington, William 103, 111
small-unit combat leadership 75
Smith, Bob 112
Smith, William 78, 91, 92
Smotherman, Phillip 132
South Vietnam see Republic of Vietnam
South Vietnamese civilians: alienation of
        by VC 7
South Vietnamese "regroupees": move
        to North Vietnam 2
Special Forces (SF) 37, 87 95, 202–4
    5th Group 88, 175
    A-Team 39, 118
        capture of prisoner 68–69
    arrival at KD 199–200
    CIDG trainees 38
    defense of camps 37–38, 46, 49
    estimate of size of NVA threat 89,
        92–93, 186
    evacuation from camp 37, 147–50
    failed NVA attack on 71–72, 73–81
    indigenous troops 49
    NVA assault on 142–43
    recruitment of Nung troops 207
    relations with local civilians 39
    separation between Army and SF 92
    trainees 204
    training of mercenaries 200

Special Operations Executive (SOE)
202–3
Special Operations Group (SOG) 40,
42, 43, 48, 71–72, 118–9,
164–65
attack on trench 143–44
Presidential Unit Citation 214
losses 213–24
operational problems 45
reconnaissance commando teams 212
reconnaissance missions 35, 43,
44, 45
Spier, Wilbert 113–14, 154
Standard Operating Procedures 45
Stanley, Charles 139
Stephenson, William 203
Stilwell, Richard 87, 92
Studies and Observation Group (SOG)
88, 212
Operation 35 88, 212–13, 214
Stuller, John 103, 110–11
Sturdevant, Joe 113, 120
Subcommittee for Military Affairs
(DRV) 1–2, 4, 7
surprise: principle of war 189
surveillance troops 100–1
Swain, James 121–22, 141
Swenarski, Paul 74
Swicegood, Willie 62
Sykes, Ken 98
synergism 186

Tactical Air Control Center
(TACC) 119
Tactical Area of Responsibility
(TAOR), 40
Tactical Operations Center (TOC) 37,
95–96, 118
tactical synergistic serendipity 186
"Tet" Offensive see General
Offensive/General
Insurrection
Thomasson, John 138

Thompson, Bobby 90, 92, 135,
138, 140
"three-plane" cells 124
"three-stage total war" strategy (Mao
Tse-tung) 2, 3–4
Time magazine 165
Todd, John 133
Truong Son Mountains 30, 34, 35, 36,
205, 206
Truong Son Strategic Supply Route see
Ho Chi Minh Trail

unconventional warfare 202–3, 204
United States
anti-war movement 10–11
effects of bombing campaign on
economy of DRV 5
lack of centralised command 186
reporting by press 7–9, 165, 191
tv news reporting 9, 96, 191
United States Air Force
1 Corps Direct Air Support Center
(IDASC) 113, 128, 132
Assault Support Helicopter Company
(ASHC) 113
Combat Control Team (CCT)
93, 134
Forward Air Controllers (FAC)
113, 119, 131
Ground Control Approach (GCA)
42, 47
Medical Evacuation Company 136
spy planes 29–30
Tactical Air Control and Navigation
(TACAN) 42, 47, 119
troop morale 44
United States Army
198th Light Infantry Brigade 46, 89
E-Company 99, 101
American Division 13, 46, 87,
89, 132
inquiry into evacuation
operation 166

lack of intelligence 89
Operation Elk Canyon 176
reinforcement plan 163, 185
A-Company engineers 41–42
differences in military cultures 99
Mobile Strike Force (Mike) 38, 47,
 61, 63, 100, 207, 208
trainees 77
separation between US Army and
 SF 92
sources of "combat friction" 185
troop morale 44
United States Marine Corps 89
Marine Amphibious Force III (MAF)
 46, 64, 87, 88
press conference 163
United States Navy 204
United States Pentagon 179, 211–12
Special Warfare Division 203
"unity of command" 87, 188

Van Cleeff, Jay 134, 152
Van Tien Dung 6
Vasquez, Orlando 102, 110, 114,
 115–16, 135
Viet Cong (VC) 4–5, 6, 7, 9, 44,
 205, 206
desertions 4
Viet Minh 3, 199, 202, 207
Vietnam Veterans of America 177–78
Vietnamese ethnic lowland peoples 205,
 206
visibility see weather
Vo Nguyen Giap xv, 6

Waldo, Daniel 91, 97, 100, 121
Wallace, James 150
weapons and artillery 64–65, 130
AK-47 assault rifles 72, 73
MI-carbines 66, 72

M-60 machine guns 74
claymore mines 67, 102, 114
concertina wire 67–68, 102, 114, 116
fougasse 67
howitzers 64
magnesium flares 111
mortars 60–61, 66
of Nung troops 62
red tracers 76, 112
trip flares 67
white phosphorous grenades 145
white phosphorous rockets 114
see also bombs and bombing
weather 41, 42, 43–44, 52–53, 111 112,
 184–85
Weatherman, Earl 172
Westmoreland, William xii-xiii, xvi, 29,
 53, 64, 87, 88, 100, 103,
 109, 110, 165, 212,
access to intelligence 29
approves evacuation order 104, 194
award of honors 164
strategy and tactics of xiii, 4, 30, 41,
 110, 185, 194
"what if" theories 190
Wheeler, Earl G. xvi, 109, 110
White, John 61–62, 63, 65, 67, 69, 70,
 72, 76, 78, 79, 80, 81
Widdison, Imlay 103, 110–1
Widner, Danny 103, 111, 178, 179
Wietting, Wayne 103, 115
Williams, Bud 49, 51, 118
Williams, Roy 103, 110–1
Windley, M. C. 40, 50, 51, 52, 71, 94,
 119, 143–44
Woodard, Houston (Mac), 40, 60, 68,
 118, 128, 132
Wright, Bill 101, 112–13, 135, 178

Young, George 90